ANTHROPOLOGICAL PERSPECTIVES ON KINSHIP

Anthropology, Culture and Society

Series Editors:
Dr Richard A. Wilson, University of Sussex
Professor Thomas Hylland Eriksen, University of Oslo

ANTHROPOLOGICAL PERSPECTIVES ON KINSHIP

Ladislav Holy

Pluto Press

LONDON • ANN ARBOR, MI

First published 1996 by Pluto Press
345 Archway Road, London N6 5AA
and 839 Greene Street, Ann Arbor,
MI 48106, USA

British Library Cataloguing in Publication Data
A catalogue record for this book is available from
the British Library

ISBN 0 7453 0918 6 hbk

Library of Congress Cataloging in Publication Data
Holy, Ladislav,
    Anthropological perspectives on kinship/Ladislav Holy,
        p.   cm. — (Anthropology, culture and society)
    ISBN 0-7453–0918–6 (hbk)
    1. Kinship. I. Title. II. Series.
GN480.H625   1996
306.83—dc20   96–8271
                                                          CIP

10   9   8   7   6   5

Designed and produced for Pluto Press by
Chase Publishing Services, Fortescue, Sidmouth, EX10 9QG
Typeset from disk by Stanford DTP Services, Northampton
Printed in the European Union by
Antony Rowe Ltd, Chippenham and Eastbourne, England

CONTENTS

ACKNOWLEDGEMENTS

This book has grown of my courses on kinship, marriage and alliance which I gave over the last few years at the University of St Andrews. I wrote it when I was a Visiting Professor in the Institute of Social Anthropology at the University of Oslo in the academic year 1994–95. I am grateful to Signe Howell for having invited me to become a temporary member of the Institute and to all her colleagues in Oslo for their friendship, help and interest and for collectively creating an environment in which it was a real joy to work.

Over the years, many colleagues and students have helped to shape my views. It is not possible to express gratitude individually to all of them but I feel especially obliged to the students in Oslo who attended my course on kinship in 1995. The numerous points which they raised in discussion helped me to clarify a number of issues which I address. I am grateful to Richard Wilson who was kind enough to read an earlier draft of the book and provided helpful comments on numerous specific points, and to Olaf Smedal who read carefully and critically the final manuscript and whose incisive questioning of a wide range of issues helped to formulate better a number of arguments. Needless to say, although I have been helped on my way by students and colleagues, all the omissions and mistakes are solely my own.

INTRODUCTION

In 1967, Fox could justifiably say that 'kinship is to anthropology what logic is to philosophy or nude is to art; it is the basic discipline of the subject' (1967: 10). At the time, kinship was undoubtedly the aspect of social life to which anthropologists paid most attention. Between the time when the precursors of modern kinship studies like Maine (1861), McLennan (1865) and Morgan (1871) published their works and Fox expressed his views on the centrality of kinship to anthropology, a huge body of literature on kinship and marriage had accumulated, which by the middle of this century accounted for probably more than half of the total literature of anthropology. In the first half of this century, anthropological theories on kinship and marriage definitely outnumbered theories which anthropologists formulated on other aspects of social life and there was then hardly an anthropologist of some import who did not contribute to the ongoing theoretical discussion of kinship. If there was a subject which anthropologists could have rightly claimed to be their own, it was kinship. In all other aspects of social life which anthropologists also study, they share their interest with specialists from other disciplines and they often seek their theoretical inspiration from them. In the field of kinship studies, anthropologists have traditionally been the leading theoreticians. Given their agreement on a few basic assumptions about kinship, particularly the assumption that kinship everywhere is based on attributing social significance to the natural facts of procreation, much of their theorising has often resembled exercises in formal logic rather than being concerned with solving particular problems arising from empirical observation. Much of it has been concerned with refining conceptual distinctions and with coining new latinisms for more and more elaborate classifications. The ensuing jargon put off many students on the one hand, and on the other hand created the impression of the

1

study of kinship as a 'very mature and complex' subject with a 'highly developed technical vocabulary' (Fox 1967: 50).

The traditional anthropological preoccupation with kinship was not an haphazard result of peculiar interests and hobbies of several generations of anthropologists. It was logically related to the way in which anthropology came to be constituted as a specialised subject in its own right, in the early twentieth century, when the term 'social anthropology' came to refer to the study of the social organisation of what were at that time conceived of as primitive societies. When it came to conceptualising this form of social organisation, kinship played a distinct analytical role:

At least as far as men were concerned, no one thought it was just to do with households, marriage and the family. Rather in the creation of ties through reproduction and succession, British social anthropologists saw in many of the societies that were their subject of study *models of social life*. Kinship, in short, played the role for the members of these societies that social theory played for the anthropologists, at once a model of and explanation for the dynamics of relationships. (Strathern 1994: 270; reference omitted, original emphasis)

At least since the time of Malinowski, the anthropologist's task was seen as the understanding of the studied society 'from the natives' point of view'. In the effort to gain that kind of understanding, actors' models of kinship relations, which were seen as their insights into the workings of their society, gained logically methodological prominence. Kinship came to be seen as indispensable for the proper understanding of how any small-scale society considered as 'primitive' was organised and how it worked. The result was a particular conceptualisation of this type of society which was based on a few basic assumptions about 'primitive' social organisation. The most important of them was that in 'primitive' societies, kinship is 'one of the irreducible principles on which ... organized social life depends' (Fortes 1949a: 340). Kinship organisation of most 'primitive' societies was seen as based on descent groups which were exogamous and were mutually related through a series of marriage exchanges. Kinship terminology was a linguistic expression of this type of social organisation (Kuper 1985: 758). This state of affairs was in marked contrast to Western societies in which other institutions, particularly the workplace and the state, perform the wide-ranging functions which are performed by kinship groups in 'primitive' societies (Collier and Yanagisako 1987: 3).

great change ↓

Since its establishment as a specialised branch of scholarship in the first half of this century, the study of kinship has undergone noticeable changes in its theoretical orientation. They reflect the general theoretical and epistemological shift in anthropology which parallels the paradigm shift which is observable in science generally and which may be seen to follow a few basic trends. The most important of them is the shift from structure to process, from the objective science to epistemic science, and from the part to the whole (Capra, Steindl-Rast and Matus 1991).

The shift from the preoccupation with the structure of kin groups (for example, Fortes 1953) to an interest in the process of the reproduction of observable structural forms was heralded in the late 1950s and 1960s by the notion of the developmental cycle in domestic groups (Goody 1958), which enabled a whole new understanding of the dynamic aspects of families and households, and by Lévi-Strauss's view that kinship exists in self-perpetuation achieved through specific forms of marriage (1963).

The shift from the objective to epistemic science is a shift from the concern with facts as they have been established through empirical research to the concern with the claims to knowledge about these 'facts'. In the field of kinship studies it manifests itself in the move from conceptualising kinship as a way in which people everywhere cope culturally with the universal natural processes of procreation to the concern with specific cultural conceptualisations of what in different cultures constitutes relationships which people in the West call kinship. The resulting new approach, epitomised most significantly in Schneider's critique of the study of kinship (1984), had its predecessors in a number of attempts to rethink the core concepts of kinship and the methods of its study in the 1960s and 1970s (Leach 1961a, Schneider 1964, 1972, Needham 1971). It is an approach specifically concerned with the epistemological problems surrounding kinship as a distinct domain of analysis which can be separated from other well-established analytical domains, such as economics, politics and religion. Such separation, which requires a clear conceptualisation or definition of kinship relations, is coming increasingly under scrutiny.

The shift from the part to the whole manifests itself in the 'dissolution' of particular analytical categories which parallels Lévi-Strauss's dissolution of totemism as a specific category. An example is Goody's (1971) view (endorsed by Barnard and Good 1984: 92–3) that 'incest' should be seen within the context of the entire, structured field of heterosexual offences which includes not only incest but also fornication, adultery and what Goody calls incestuous adultery (1971: 74). Another case in point is Rivière's suggestion that 'marriage' should be seen not as an isolable relationship but as one aspect of the totality of the roles of male and female and as a particular consequence of the relationship between these two categories in any given society (1971). The shift from the part to the whole is most clearly apparent in the growing realisation of how difficult it is to conceptualise as separate not only particular analytical categories, like incest or marriage, but the whole domain of kinship as such. During the past three decades, the realisation that kinship, after all, may not be a separate analytical domain has manifested itself in a change from the interest in kinship as an autonomous system of relations into the interest in kinship as an aspect of more inclusive social and cultural domains. This shift was already precipitated in the early 1960s by Leach. In his study of Pul Eliya village in Sri Lanka, he specifically criticised the prevailing view that kinship could be studied as an analytically separable domain of social reality and argued that 'kinship systems have no "reality" at all except in relation to land and property' (Leach 1961b: 305; but see Strathern 1985). The studies by Terray (1972), Friedman (1974) and Meillassoux (1981) concentrated on kinship as an aspect of political economy, and anthropologists primarily interested in gender relations saw kinship as an aspect of a broader system of inequality in which gender is a key element (Collier and Rosaldo 1981, Ortner and Whitehead 1981). Yanagisako (1979), in her study of the variation in domestic organisation, questioned the validity of the analytical distinction between the domestic and politico-jural domains which was formulated by Fortes (1969) and which informed much of the traditional concern with kinship *per se*. Schneider, in his cultural analysis of American kinship, argued that in fact the 'domain of kinship' itself may not be distinctly different from some other cultural domains, in particular 'nationality' and 'religion' (1969, 1980) and he repeatedly made the point that 'the arbitrary segregation of a rubric like "kinship" taken out of context of the whole culture, is not a very good way to understand how a culture is structured' (1984: 8). Recently many more anthropologists have been pointing out the interrelationship between kinship and such other cultural domains as ethnicity, social class, commensality, gender and the concept of 'person' (Schneider and Smith 1973, Chock 1974, Schieffelin 1976, Alexander 1978, Yanagisako 1978, 1985, Strathern 1981, Howell and Melhuus

1993). Kinship as an autonomous domain of analysis has been particularly strongly questioned by students of gender. They call into question the traditional analytical boundary between gender and kinship and argue that these two analytical domains are mutually constructed (Yeatman 1983, Collier and Yanagisako 1987).

The traditional anthropological preoccupation with kinship was not only underpinned by the conceptualisation of anthropology as a branch of scholarship specialising in the study of society conceived of as 'primitive', but also by its theoretical interest in the description and analysis of the social structure of particular 'primitive' societies. With the subsequent shift of interest from the structure of social relations to the process of social life, the study of kinship inevitably lost its central position in anthropological scholarship. While at one time anthropologists were interested in, for example, the role which the family plays in reproduction, contemporary interest focuses on the process of reproduction and on investigating which social institutions, including the family and other kinship groups, are involved in this process and how they are shaped by it (Robertson 1991). Similarly, while at one time anthropologists were interested in the role which kinship and descent groups play in the economy, their interest now focuses on the study of the processes of production and exchange, and on investigating which social institutions, including kinship and descent groups, are involved in these processes and how they are shaped by them. The anthropological interest in kinship has thus not vanished but has changed its focus. Instead of starting from the description of the kinship system of any particular society, anthropologists now pay attention to kinship relations inasmuch as these are of relevance in the processes on which their study focuses. In consequence, rather than occupying a central place in the theoretical debate of the discipline, kinship has become one of a number of specialised fields of anthropological inquiry. In many departments of anthropology it is no longer taught as a separate course, but various aspects of kinship and marriage are discussed alongside the issues of gender, the problems of inequality, or as part of the wider problems of the social construction of self, personhood and identity.

The declining importance of the study of kinship in anthropology can be seen as the result of the shift in contextualisation. Traditionally, kinship was the focus of analytical attention and economy, politics or ritual were analysed in the context of the attention paid to kinship relations. Nowadays, analytical attention focuses on the processes of reproduction, construction of gender and sexuality or of self and personhood, and kinship is discussed in the context of these processes. New insights into kinship have been gained, as new insights are always gained, through this shift in contextualisation. Goody's theory of the evolution of domestic groups established that the processes of production and the transmission of property shape the evolution and form of families and households (1973a, 1976). Bourdieu's research demonstrated how particular marriage strategies are embedded in the existing relations of production while reproducing the existing system of social inequality (1977).

What differentiates the contemporary debate about kinship and its study from the debate in the middle of this century is the fact that it is not so much the various technical problems of kinship analysis which are called into question, but the very basic assumptions about what kinship is all about and whether, in fact, there is a domain of kinship which is universally recognised as such in all human societies. The most severe criticism of the traditional assumptions which have informed the study of kinship since the time when Maine, McLennan and Morgan founded it as a specialised branch of scholarship, has come from those who see kinship more as a cultural system of symbols and meanings than as a system of social roles and relationships, and from anthropologists inspired by feminist scholarship. There is a distinct overlap between anthropologists interested in cultural understanding and those inspired by feminism and they often draw their inspiration from each other.

The questioning of basic assumptions and first principles which characterises the debate about kinship today has shown that our various assumptions about kinship and many aspects of the received kinship theory are no longer tenable. But in itself, this questioning has not led to the formulation of a consensus on how to proceed with the study of kinship in future. A lot of our present-day critical attitude to the work of our predecessors is undoubtedly justified, but most of it is negative rather than positive. There are numerous calls for new analytical emphasis and various programmatic pronouncements abound. But the many critical voices have not generated the analytical confidence and certainty which characterised the discipline until the middle of this century. The new insights into kinship, however important, have so far been partial and fragmented, and they have certainly not resulted in a clear and concise formulation of a new theory. Considering that the critical attitude to established kinship theory has been concerned primarily with deconstructing the traditional anthropological conceptualisation of kinship, no single new monolithic theory of kinship is probably attainable. But if we lose the once existing analytical certainty to gain a better insight into how different peoples conceptualise relationships which we call kinship, the result can surely not be mourned as a loss.

The redefinition of what are nowadays seen as the main problems in kinship studies, which need to be tackled in novel ways, is part and parcel of the reorientation and redefinition of the discipline of social anthropology as a whole. To write on kinship in this fluid situation is a daunting task. It is certainly not helped by the fact that it goes, as it were, against the grain of current anthropological practice. As in the heyday of structural-functionalism, this essay starts with kinship rather than coming to it via gender, reproduction, personhood, ethnicity or whatever else is the topic of current anthropological interest. However much I try to pay attention to the new insights into kinship which have been generated by the shifting interest in anthropological scholarship, I cannot do more than to sketch what the contemporary debates about kinship are all about and what the present controversies and problems are. These controversies and problems have, of course, not emerged out of the blue. They are reactions to previous debates and controversies, most of which have been abandoned rather than satisfactorily resolved when new questions have been posed. They form, nevertheless, a background against which the problems and controversies which animate us today make sense, and for this reason I pay attention to them in the following text. To know whence the present-day problems sprang and to what precisely they are a critical reaction is, in my view, a necessary precondition for their critical evaluation. Hopefully, when seen in the context of their historical genesis, they may inspire a new positive approach to the study of kinship as an important aspect of social and cultural reality. Even if kinship has probably lost forever its centrality in ethnographic description and in the theoretical debate about the organisation of human society, it remains, nevertheless, a significant aspect of life in either so-called simple societies or in modern industrial ones. For this reason, it certainly will not altogether disappear from the future anthropological research agenda.

This book is not meant to provide an exhaustive survey of the history of kinship studies and to pass critical comments on the technical problems of various aspects of kinship, descent and marriage which were discussed at length in the past. Other textbooks on kinship have done this and the present one should be seen as a complement to them rather than an attempt to replace them. When paying attention to past debates and controversies as a background to understanding present-day problems in the study of kinship, I concentrate only on those which I consider to be the most important. Needless to say, the selection of problems on which I concentrate reflects my own theoretical and epistemological bias.

1 FIRST PRINCIPLES

The received wisdom in anthropology is that kinship represents the very essence of being human and that in all societies, 'networks that connect individuals as relatives are apparently universally recognized and universally accorded social importance' (Keesing 1975: 14). This is an unobjectionable position as long as it is taken to mean that in all human societies some people consider themselves to be more closely related to each other than they are to other people, and that this mutual relatedness is the basis of numerous and varied interactions in which they are involved or provides legitimisation or rationalisation for them. The difference between those who see themselves as related to one another and those who are not so related underlies differentially distributed rights, duties, roles and statuses. In this sense, it is recognised as a difference that makes a difference. However, the received wisdom starts to look problematic when we consider the culturally specific reasons why people see themselves as related and the various ways in which they draw the line between those to whom they see themselves related and those to whom they do not.

PROCREATION AND NURTURE

People's own explanations as to why some of them are mutually more closely related than others differ from society to society but they are generally based on a notion of consubstantiality (Pitt-Rivers 1973: 92): people see themselves as mutually related to each other because they share a common substance and they see themselves as unrelated to those with whom they do not. In different societies, people consider themselves related because they share the same blood, bone or semen. But they may consider themselves related because they have suckled the same milk or eaten the same food. Some societies thus emphasise procreation as a defining characteristic of relatedness and see some people

9

as mutually related because they share blood, bone, semen or some other substance transmitted in the process of procreation; alternatively they assume that some of the child's substance, for example bones, was created by the child's father, and some, for example flesh, by the child's mother. Watson (1983) designates this notion of mutual relatedness as 'nature kinship'. Other societies emphasise nurturance and see some people as related because they are of the same substance created through suckling the same milk or eating the same food. Watson calls this notion of relatedness 'nurture kinship'.

One of the problems to which many anthropologists working in New Guinea have paid particular attention is the problem of the rapid and full incorporation of immigrants into groups, usually described as 'clans', whose members see themselves mutually related through the ties of kinship and consider themselves to be 'brothers' or 'sons of one father'. When considering the process through which the Bena Bena grant the status of full group members to immigrants, Langness noted that 'the sheer fact of residence in a ... group can and does determine kinship. People do not necessarily reside where they do because they are kinsmen; rather they become kinsmen because they reside there' (1964: 174; emphasis deleted). Andrew Strathern subsequently argued that food is a mediator between locality and kinship and that eating food grown on clan land creates substance which the immigrants share with other clan members:

clansmen share substance in some way through their descent from an ancestor. Another way in which they share substance is through consumption of food grown on clan land. Food builds their bodies and gives them substance just as their father's semen and mother's blood and milk give them substance in the womb and as small children. Hence it is through food that the identification of the sons of immigrants with their host group is strengthened. Food creates substance, just as procreation does, and forms an excellent symbol both for the creation of identity out of residence and for the values of nurturance, growth, comfort and solidarity which are associated primarily with parenthood. (Strathern 1973: 29)

As long as one is describing the notions about what makes people related to each other – or what constitutes kinship – in a particular society, one can resort to native or emic views of this matter. But for comparative purposes, an analytical or etic notion of kinship is needed which is valid not only for this or that culture or society, but cross-culturally. This notion was established at the very beginning of the modern scholarly study of kinship by the founding father of this branch of scholarship, Henry Lewis Morgan, who stated that kinship was based on the folk knowledge of biological consanguinity. By most modern students of kinship this idea is expressed in the definition of kinship as a system of social ties based on the acknowledgement of genealogical relations, that is, relations deriving from engendering and bearing children. But how do societies whose members stress the nurturing aspect of kinship and believe that people are kin because they suckled the same milk or were fed the same food fit into this definition? Cucchiari, who points out that kinship systems emphasise either nurturing or procreative notions of consubstantiality, maintains that kinship categories everywhere have procreative referents and that kinship systems can universally be expressed in some cultural model of procreation rather than nurturing:

> That is, even where parents are defined more as the people who protect, feed and raise the child, the relationship is still expressed in genealogical idiom. Note, for example, that although the Navajo idea of motherhood is *either* the woman who bore or the one who raised the child, a mother can only be a woman – a person at least theoretically capable of bearing the child. One would expect that a completely nurturing model of the mother–child relation would be capable of including both men and women. (Cucchiari 1981: 35; reference omitted)

So even if nurturance can in some systems lead to the notion of shared substance created, for example, through food, the procreative notion of consubstantiality seems indispensable if the kinship system is to achieve a differentiation between those who are and who are not of the same substance, and a differentiation between those who share substance according to the amount they share. Translating all the cultural notions about shared substance into analytical terms then leads to the view of kinship as a system of genealogical relations.

Cucchiari spells out quite clearly why a kinship system *must be* built on some cultural acknowledgement of genealogical relations deriving from procreation:

> In primitive societies characterised by a pervasive general reciprocity, a kinship system based *exclusively* on the nurturing idea would fail clearly to mark off categories even within the nuclear unit – parents from older siblings, for example. If the defining characteristic of the category 'parent' is the one who feeds and cares for the child, even the generational distinction would be weakened as parent and grandparent cooperated in child rearing. Indeed all categories – parent, child, sibling, and spouse – would tend to be semantic

domains with variable boundaries and include no fixed catalogue of relationships. It is for this reason that procreative models are essential to kinship systems in providing the discrete genealogical points that connect broad social categories – a kind of social map. (Cucchiari 1981: 37; original emphasis)

Cucchiari insists on procreative models as essential to kinship systems because such models are logically necessary if we want to isolate kinship analytically from other social relations. Without this logical precondition we would simply not be able to postulate kinship as a separate domain of social relations. I quoted Cucchiari at length for he makes explicit what most kinship theorists implicitly accept, namely that the logical requirement for postulating a separate domain of kinship is to define this domain as a system of social ties deriving from the recognition of genealogical relations. Even anthropologists who noted that creating substance through food plays an important role in the way kinship is conceptualised in some cultures, saw the creation of substance through feeding as analogous to adoption – a legal fiction through which people not related biogenetically become related in social sense. For example, Schieffelin writes of the Kaluli of the Southern Highlands of New Guinea:

A person's mother is thought less as the person who brought him into the world and more as a person who gave him food. Thus, a woman who feeds a child comes to be thought of as his mother after a time, and her children as his siblings. This becomes particularly apparent when the child gets married. Claims for a piece of the bridewealth are in part based on the contribution the person made to 'giving the child food'. After marriage, an avoidance relation is observed between a man and his wife's mother. If for some reason the girl was brought up principally by some woman other than her mother, it will be that woman to whom the avoidance is extended, even if the *real mother* is alive and present in the same longhouse community. In cases like this *'feeding'* amounts approximately to adoption. (1976: 64; emphasis added)

This quote makes it clear that a woman who feeds the child is thought of and is treated as the child's mother. But she is not its 'real mother' just as in the Western conceptualisation an adoptive mother of the child may be thought of as its mother and treated as such but the child's 'real' mother is, nevertheless, a different woman. According to Schieffelin, among the Kaluli, as in the West, a distinction is maintained between ties created through procreation and those created by social convention. In his critique of the study of kinship, Schneider (1984) called the notion of kinship as a system of social ties deriving from the recognition of genealogical relations the 'Doctrine of the Genealogical Unity of Mankind'. This doctrine is not the generalisation of the observable facts. It is a prerequisite for the conceptualisation of kinship and, moreover, a prerequisite which is not built on some culture-free or cross-culturally applicable logic but which is deeply rooted in Western cultural assumptions. I shall return to this point again in the last chapter.

Kinship as an analytically separate domain of social relations is much more than merely an aspect of social reality which can be conveniently isolated from other aspects of social reality and analysed independently of them. It has been a time-honoured adage in anthropology that to understand the kinship system of any simple society is a necessary basis for studying all social activities in that society. Kinship ties which people acknowledge and distinguish determine whom to marry, where to live, how to raise children, which ancestors to worship, how to solve disputes, which land to cultivate, which property to inherit, to whom to turn for help in pursuing common interests and many things besides. But why should this personal system of relations, typical of many simple societies which anthropologists traditionally studied, be built out of kinship relations? Why exactly should kinship, of all relations, be so tremendously important? Beattie answers this question in the following way:

[In] all human communities, even the most technologically simple ones, the categories of biological relations are available as means of identifying and ordering social relations. This is so even though some of these categories may be differently defined in different cultures. Everywhere man is begotten by men and borne by women, and in most societies the bond of parenthood and the bonds of mutual dependency and support that it implies are acknowledged. This leads to the recognition of other links, such as those between siblings and between grandparents and their grandchildren. So even in the simplest societies kinship provides some ready-to-hand categories for distinguishing the people one is born among and so for ordering one's relations with them. Apart from sex and age, which are also of prime importance, there is no other way of classifying people which is so 'built in' to the human condition. (Beattie 1964a: 94)

The generally accepted definition of kinship derives from this assumed universal utilisation of biological relations among people as the basis for ordering their social relations. Morgan, the founder of modern kinship studies, speculated in his *Ancient Society* (1877) about the earliest stage in the evolution of human social organisation in which no notion of an incest taboo existed. With the gradual introduction of the ban on marriages between parents and children, a 'consanguine family' emerged from this original stage of 'primitive promiscuity'. It was a group based on the intermarriage between brothers and sisters. In this type of marriage it could not have been known who was the actual biological father of a child and a kinship terminology, which Morgan considered to be a survival of this extinct form of human mating, reflected this fact. Morgan found such terminology in Hawaii, where all relatives of the parents' generation were called by a single term and the terminology differentiated only between males and females. This means that the same term was applied to one's father, to all his brothers and other collateral male relatives of the father's generation (like the sons of the father's parents' siblings or grandsons of his grandparents' siblings) as well as to mother's brothers and her other male collateral relatives. Similarly, not only one's own mother but also all her sisters and other collateral female relatives as well as all father's sisters and other collateral female relatives on the father's side were called by the same term. To Morgan, this suggested that if the mother's brothers were called by the same term as the father, they must have all been previously the child's fathers and that was possible only if brothers were married to their sisters and had sexual access to them. Mother's sisters were called by the same term as one's mother because they were all wives of one's fathers. The other kinship terms in the Hawaiian system supported this speculation. In Hawaii, a man called not only his own children sons and daughters but also all his nephews and nieces. This was again because, according to Morgan, all the man's sisters were his wives and they were simultaneously wives of all his brothers. If they were his wives, then logically all their children were equally his children. And according to the same logic, in one's own generation the same term as to one's own brothers and sisters applied to all one's cousins.

Van Gennep (1906) was the first to criticise the notion of the ignorance of biological paternity which, according to Morgan, must have existed in his hypothetical 'consanguine family' and he pointed out the basic difference between *parenté sociale* and *parenté physique*. In his early study of the family among the Australian aborigines, who were reported to be ignorant of physiological paternity, Malinowski clearly drew the difference between biological kinship and its social or cultural conceptualisation. He emphasised that consanguinity as a sociological concept is 'not the physical bond of common blood, it is the social acknowledgement and interpretation of it' (Malinowski 1913: 182). He made it clear that consanguinity 'is the set of relations involved by the collective ideas under which facts of procreation are viewed in a given society' (1913: 179). Schneider sees this shift of emphasis from the social recognition of biological bonds arising out of procreation to the sociocultural aspects of the real or putative biological relationships as the major modification in kinship studies since Morgan (Schneider 1984: 54). Since this shift, anthropologists have been at pains to emphasise that the genealogical relations of interest to students of kinship are not biological but social relations. As Wagner expressed it, 'the essence of kinship is *interpretation* of genealogy, rather than genealogy itself' (1972: 611; original emphasis). Or in the words of Lévi-Strauss, '[a] kinship system does not exist in the objective ties of descent or consanguinity between individuals. It exists only in human consciousness; it is an arbitrary system of representations, not the spontaneous development of a real situation' (1963: 50).

As recently as in the late 1950s and 1960s, the question of to what extent kinship relations can be seen as based on actual genetic relationships between individuals re-emerged in the debate about the 'nature of kinship' triggered off by Gellner's consideration of the philosophical problem of the ideal, that is, fully unambiguous language. Gellner suggested that kinship terminology might provide a suitable avenue for investigation and he argued that physical and social kinship are logically distinct but, nevertheless, inextricably linked in practice (Gellner 1957: 235–6). His view provoked a response from a number of kinship theorists (Needham 1960b, Barnes 1961, 1964, Schneider 1964, 1965, Beattie 1964b, Buchler 1966) who, looking at the problem of what kinship is all about from different angles and viewpoints, all agreed that Gellner's insistence upon the biological nature of kinship was entirely misplaced (for the review of the debate see Harris 1990: 27–39). [who was wrong]

Kinship theorists are agreed that genealogical relations are not relations of biological or genetic connection. They define them as relations deriving from the engendering and bearing of children as this process of human reproduction is known or understood in any given society and not as it may be known by biologists or geneticists. As Scheffler has expressed it, 'the foundation of any kinship system consists in a folk-cultural theory designed to account for the fact that women give birth to children, i.e. a theory of human reproduction' (1973: 749). All societies have their own theories about how women become pregnant. As these theories may ascribe widely different roles to men and women in procreation, the notions concerning the relation between the child and its father and the child and its mother may differ considerably from society to society.

THE FATHER–CHILD RELATIONSHIP

Since Malinowski's study of *The Family among the Australian Aborigines* (1913), anthropologists have made a distinction between two kinds of 'fathers' designated by terms borrowed from Roman law as *genitor* and *pater*. Genitor is not the genetic father, that is, a man who 'supplies the spermatozoon that impregnates the ovum that eventually becomes the child' (Barnes 1961: 297) but a man who is believed by members of his community to have impregnated the child's mother or to contribute in some other way to the being of the child. In all societies, including the Western ones in which the genitor is ideally held to be the genetic father of the child, the role of a genitor is assigned on the basis of cultural rules even if modern medicine can through DNA testing confirm or eliminate genetic fatherhood in particular cases. The role of cultural rules in determining fatherhood was made abundantly clear in a recent lawsuit in Norway which was widely reported in the press and subject of a special documentary in Norwegian television. It concerned a man who conceived a child in an adulterous union with a married woman and who wanted to assume his parental responsibility towards the child and claim his parental rights. To prove that he was indeed the child's father he wanted to subject himself to a DNA test but was prevented from doing so by a court order which invoked the family law of 1981 according to which the father of a child born to a married woman is the man who is legally married to her. Barnes (1964), who stressed the importance of distinguishing between the genitor and the genetic father pointed to various legal conventions which modern societies use to assign paternity as examples of the fact that in all societies, including those equipped with the knowledge of the laws of genetics, the role of the genitor is assigned on the basis of indigenous theories of procreation and on the basis of people's knowledge and opinions about the sexual conduct of the putative parents.

Unlike the genitor, the pater is a socially recognised father, through whom the child may claim kinship with other people. The principle of the Roman law according to which the child's pater is a man who can prove that he married the child's mother, or the principle of proverbs such as 'children belong to the man to whom the bed belongs', is the basis for assigning legal fatherhood in many societies. The Nuer of the southern Sudan not only followed this principle but developed it up to the limits of its logical possibilities. They legalised marriage by transfer of bridewealth cattle and the pater was always the person in whose name the cattle had been transferred to the woman's kin. Every Nuer man should have married and had sons through whom his name would have been remembered. But often a man died before he was married, some married men had only daughters, or their sons died before their marriage arrangements had been completed. In these cases it was a duty of one of the man's kinsmen, usually his younger brother, to marry a wife in his name. If this obligation of kinship was neglected, the dead man's ghost might haunt his kin. In this type of marriage, the legal husband and pater of the children born to the woman was not the man who married her on behalf of his deceased kinsman, and who cohabited with her, but the 'ghost' of his deceased kinsman. As brothers married in order of seniority, the man who married on behalf of the ghost would himself die without heirs and another kinsman would have to make a 'ghost marriage' for him. Evans-Pritchard estimated that there must have been as many ghost marriages as ordinary marriages among the Nuer (1951: 109–11).

Among the Nuer, it was also possible for a barren woman to provide bridewealth cattle and to marry another woman. The woman-husband then asked one of her male kinsmen, friends or neighbours to beget children by her wife. The woman-husband had the same legal rights as any other husband and she could claim damages if her wife had relations with men without her consent. She was the pater of all the children borne by her wife and they addressed her as their 'father' (Evans-Pritchard 1951: 108–9).

Sometimes the assignment of legal fatherhood is dependent on the performance of specific rituals. For example, among the Toda of southern India, it was customary for a woman to be married to several husbands, who were ideally brothers. The socially recognised father of the children was that one of them who, before the birth of her first child, performed the ritual of 'presenting the bow'. Until another of her husbands performed the ritual, he was the pater of all the subsequent children, even if he died before their conception (Rivers 1906).

Among the Nayar castes of Kerala in southern India, a girl was regarded as having attained the status of a mature woman, ready to bear children, after she had undergone a ceremony in which her ritual bridegroom tied a gold ornament (*tāli*) round her neck. After this ceremony, she might have sexual relations with any number of men of her own or an appropriate higher caste. When she became pregnant, one or more men of appropriate caste had to acknowledge paternity by making gifts to her and to the midwife immediately after the birth. Any man who had visited the woman in the appropriate time period was required to make these gifts and if no man would consent to make the delivery payments, the child was deemed to be illegitimate and the woman and her child were expelled from the caste and funeral rituals were performed for her (Gough 1961a: 358–61).

As the result of the speculations of Victorian scholars about the ignorance of physiological paternity in the early stages of the evolution of human society (Bachofen 1861, Engels 1884, McLennan 1865, Morgan 1870, 1877), anthropologists have been intrigued by the possibility that the role of sexual intercourse in reproduction and hence the contribution of the man to the birth of a child are not recognised in some societies. In his celebrated essay on virgin birth, which triggered off extensive debate in the pages of *Man* in 1968 and 1969 (see Barnard and Good 1984: 170–4), Leach argued that natives' statements denying the role of men in procreation should not be treated as instances of their ignorance or as objective statements about factual knowledge. They should instead be interpreted as social dogmas or ideology. They do not suggest that natives are necessarily ignorant of the facts of physical paternity, but that they regard it as irrelevant. The ideological denial of the relevance of physical paternity can be expressed in ideological doctrines of virgin birth or in beliefs of conception by clan spirits (Leach 1966). The best examples of societies which held precisely such beliefs were some Australian Aborigines and the Trobriand Islanders of Melanesia. The Trobrianders alleged that the birth of a child was caused by the spirit (*baloma*) which entered the woman's body through her head, or through her vagina when she was wading in a lagoon. The 'spirit child' was always the reincarnation of one of her ancestors, whose spirits had departed after their deaths to the Island of the Dead and eventually had returned to earth floating on water. During pregnancy, the woman ceased to menstruate because the blood nourished the child in her womb. Although the *baloma* spirit was the real cause of conception, a woman could conceive only after the way had been 'opened' for the entry of the spirit child. This was normally accomplished by intercourse but the Trobrianders saw it merely as a mechanical process which could be accomplished in other ways (Malinowski 1929: 179–86).

According to this theory of procreation, the mother and child shared the same substance – blood – because the mother made the child out of her blood while the father did not contribute anything to the child's substance. This led Malinowski to conclude that the Trobriand father was not the child's kinsman but merely the child's mother's husband, that is, a person related to the child only affinally through a marriage link. This was the reason why the Trobrianders referred to the father as *tomakava*, which means 'stranger' or 'outsider' (1929: 50–7).

The Trobriand Islanders traced descent in the matrilineal line, which meant that mother and child belonged to the same subclan while father and child were members of different subclans. Examining the symbolic aspects of paternity and affinity in the Trobriand Islands, Sider argued that the paternal relation was one of affinity only when it involved the relationship between father and child as representatives of their respective subclans but not when it involved their relationship as private individuals (Sider 1967). The Trobrianders maintained that a child never resembled its mother, brothers and sisters, or any of its maternal kinsmen but that children always resembled their fathers (Malinowski 1929: 204). The paternal resemblance derived on the one hand from the father nursing the baby in his arms or holding it on his knees and 'because his hands have been soiled with the child's excrement and urine' (1929: 20–1). On the other hand, it derived from the personal relation between husband and wife. The Trobrianders explained it in the following way: 'Put some soft mash on [the palm of the hand] and it will mould like the hand. In the same manner, the husband remains with the woman and the child is moulded' (1929: 207). Although the Trobrianders did not posit any physical connection between father and child in the sense that they did not suppose that father and child shared any physical substance, they supposed that copulation functioned to form or shape the foetus so that children resembled their fathers in some aspect of their appearance. Sider (1967) argued that, as a symbol of relationship, shared appearance resembled blood in that it too was a characteristic which was involuntary, unalterable and permanent; it was transmitted from individual to individual and did not disappear upon the death of the father or the divorce of parents. After his death, the dead man's kinsmen and friends came to visit his children so that they could 'see his face in theirs' (Malinowski 1929: 207). While blood and appearance shared common characteristics as a symbol of relationship, they differed from the symbolic aspects of affinity which was a relationship established voluntarily and one which was not permanent and unalterable but could be terminated either by death or divorce. Although the Trobrianders' notions about the father's role in reproduction might have been completely different from the notions current in modern Western societies and from the notions of biological science, it would be wrong to assume that the Trobrianders had no notion whatsoever about the genealogical connection between the child and its father.

THE MOTHER–CHILD RELATIONSHIP

While the Trobrianders' theory of procreation does not credit a man with contributing anything to the physical substance of the child, according to other folk theories it is the women who do not contribute anything to the physical or spiritual substance of the children. Such theories have been reported from some Australian Aborigines (Montagu 1937), from Ancient Egypt (Barnes 1973: 68) and from some Melanesian societies. For example, among the Baruya in New Guinea, a mother is not seen as contributing anything to the child's substance. The substance of the child, whether a boy or a girl, is created solely from the semen. The mother's milk is also seen as male substance in female form, for when copulating with his wife, her husband makes her milk from his semen. When the woman nurses the child with her milk and makes it grow, she therefore again nurses it with the substance created in her by her husband. The mother's body acts solely as a mediating vessel for passing on the male substance both before the delivery, when the foetus in her body is created from the male substance, and after the birth when the child is made to grow by being again nourished by the male substance (Godelier 1986). Other Melanesian peoples, for example Madak (Clay 1977) or Gimi (Gillison 1980) maintain that a child's body is made solely of the father's substance. The Gimi liken the mother's womb to an empty bamboo vessel in which the child is merely 'housed' for the period of gestation (Gillison 1980: 163). Similar views have not been absent from the West. An example of them is the Turkish villagers' theory of procreation according to which the man plants the seed and the woman is seen to be like a field. The nurture that women provide during pregnancy in the form of blood in the womb and after parturition in the form of milk affects the growth of the child but not its identity, which comes exclusively from the father (Delaney 1986: 496–7). This was clearly stated by a Turkish villager:

If you plant wheat, you get wheat. If you plant barley, you get barley. It is the seed which determines the kind of plant which will grow, while the field nourishes the plant but does not determine the kind. The man gives the seed, and the woman is like the field. (Meeker quoted in Delaney 1986: 497)

However, the two opposed cultural views, which allege respectively that either the man or the woman does not contribute physically to the child, are not simple mirror images of each other. What makes them different is the fact that women give birth to children after the period of gestation of the foetus in the womb. This fact, which has been experienced and repeatedly observed by people everywhere, makes all the difference in the way in which the roles of mother and father are socially assigned. While the role of genitor is always ambiguous and can be assigned only on the basis of specific cultural rules and beliefs, its female equivalent – the role of genetrix – is always unambiguous because it is determined by the natural fact of parturition and not established on the basis of culturally specific theories and beliefs. This asymmetrical construction of motherhood and fatherhood has been part of anthropological kinship theory from its very inception (Weismantel 1995: 691). Morgan's view that matriarchy preceded patriarchy in the evolution of human society followed logically from the assumption that under the conditions of original primitive promiscuity and the 'group marriage' which evolved from it, only the mother and not the father of the child could have been known and therefore descent could only be traced in the female line. Whilst motherhood has always been taken as a 'natural' fact, the father can only be identified through his relationship to the mother of the child. And as Strathern notes, 'we should not be confused here with the issues of legality. The so-called "natural" father has to demonstrate a "social" relationship to the mother as much as the jural father whose paternity is established through marriage' (1992b: 149). The Norwegian case which I mentioned before bears this out. It triggered a debate about the change in legislation and the Norwegian Department of Justice is considering whether a man who claims to be a child's father should be permitted to have his case tried and the child's genetic material compared with his own even if the child's mother is married to or lives with another man.

Because the father could only be presumed, that is defined on the basis of his relationship to the mother of the child, the father could be split into the genitor, who is presumed to be genetically linked to the child, and pater, who is linked socially to the child through his relationship to the mother. As the relationship of the mother to the child was constituted in nature and hence observable, the splitting of mother into the genetrix and mater did not seem necessary. Whereas fatherhood was socially constructed, motherhood was part of nature and not the result of social construction. As Barnes (1973: 59–61) put it, physical maternity is empirically self-evident through the biological facts of pregnancy, parturition and lactation in a way that physical paternity is not.

This view may well correspond with the Western view of procreation but as Strathern argues (1988, 1992a), Western notions about procreation and nurture which postulate maternity and paternity as irreducible facts, cannot be assumed to apply everywhere. Although undoubtedly everywhere physiological maternity is more visible than paternity, the Western view of maternity as certain and obvious and paternity as always only presumed or socially constructed would not make sense to societies whose theories of procreation are different from those held in the West. According to theories of procreation and nurture reported from various parts of Melanesia, paternity may be as self-evident as maternity and maternity may not simply be imagined as a 'natural fact'. For example, among the Baruya (Godelier 1986), relations between mothers and children, which appear to the Westerners as natural, are consistently denied. On the other hand, paternity is far from as inferential as the nineteenth-century theorists presumed when they postulated matriarchy as a stage which preceded patriarchy in the evolution of human society. If anything, while paternity may be seen by the Baruya as certain, maternity is 'patently secondary' (Jolly 1991: 55).

The same can be said of the Nuer. Although they made a distinction between genitor and pater and although they recognised the relationship between genitor and his offspring, they were remarkably unconcerned with physiological paternity, did not attach any great value to it and paid little regard to the manner of begetting. What mattered to them was that each child should have a legal father or pater (Evans-Pritchard 1951: 120). His identity was not established on the basis of his sexual relationship with the woman who bore the child but through the transfer of cattle to the woman's family. In the way the Nuer talked about children, it is as if they imagined that cattle and not men begot children: 'our children' are 'children of our cattle' – *gat ghokien*, they used to say (1951: 22, 78). Paternity established through the transfer of cattle was neither inferred nor ever in doubt. As maternity was visible in the actual birth of the child, paternity was visible in the distribution of cattle because, as the Nuer used to say, 'the cattle and the child must not meet in one place' (1951: 120). When the boys grew up in a domestic union with their mother and a man who was their genitor, in every practical sense they regarded their genitor as their father. However, this situation changed when they reached adulthood:

A youth with close kin who possess herds does not care to live in the home of his genitor after his initiation, for he is always regarded there as to some extent an outsider, whereas in the home of his pater he is there by right of birth: 'He will visit his mother and the man who begat him now and again, sometimes for a month or two, but his home is the home of his dead father.' (Evans-Pritchard 1951: 149)

In a very real sense, the Nuer saw their paters as their 'real' fathers. In that respect, their ideas about paternity differed from those prevalent in the West. In the West, adopted children see their biological fathers as their 'real' fathers. Although a Nuer boy may have grown up with his genitor whom he treated as his father, he was eventually pulled towards those to whom he was related through 'real' paternity which was as self-evident as maternity.

Even in the West we have recently become aware that the asymmetry in the conceptualisation of motherhood and fatherhood does not derive from the 'nature' of these two relationships but from the way we conceptualise them. They are both social constructions (Scheffler

1991: 372). This was made obvious by the consequences of new reproductive technologies. Whereas before assisted reproduction became available the facts of nature had been, as it were, indivisible in the sense that fertilisation, gestation and parturition could not be separated, the new reproductive technology has separated conception from birth (Rivière 1985: 5). The availability of new reproductive technologies has brought into question not only who the child's 'real' father is but also who its 'real' mother is (Warnock 1985: 37), that is, who is going to count as the child's genetrix. In case of the surrogate mother, it is possible to split apart ovulation and gestation, which in nature are contained in the body (Strathern 1992a: 39), and if the ovum belongs to one woman and the womb to another, the question then poses itself of who is the genetrix. This question was one of those which arose in the debate on assisted reproduction which went on in Britain in the 1980s and which was, among other things, specifically concerned with the problem whether the woman whose ovum was fertilised outside her body should count as the child's 'real' mother or genetrix, or whether the genetrix is the woman in whose womb the fertilised ovum was implanted and who subsequently gave birth to the child (Strathern 1992a: 53). Ultimately, who is to count as the child's genetrix has to be defined by law. Genetrix : genitor is thus not nature : culture (Barnes 1973). Both genitor and genetrix are cultural constructs which invoke the facts of nature.

The new reproductive technologies have opened the possibility of realising even more complex departures from the previously existing indivisibility of fertilisation, gestation and parturition:

Take the case of an infertile husband with a wife who is fertile but cannot, for some reason, give birth. Her flushed-out ovum could be combined with sperm from a donor and implanted in a surrogate. Here we would have four people involved: a genetic mother married to a prospectively social father plus a genetic father (probably unknown) and an actual genetrix, or birth mother. One can run around the possibilities, with the most bizarre being sperm and eggs from unknown donors being externally fertilized and then implanted in a surrogate who surrenders the eventual child for adoption to two other (possibly infertile) social parents: five people, none of whom had sex with any others. In the case of frozen sperm, a child could be that of a dead man; and with frozen embryos a child could be born to long-dead parents. With frozen sperm and ova from dead parents combined, children could technically be orphans at the moment of conception. (Fox 1993: 120; emphasis omitted)

The Western conceptualisation of kinship is that of shared biogenetic substance and it is the science of biology which tells us not only what this substance is but which also ultimately decides who shares it and who does not. Schneider points out that whatever scientists may find out about biogenetic relationships in the future would constitute knowledge about kinship (1980: 23). According to Marilyn Strathern, 'his prophecy seems to have come true with respect of the reproductive model'. However, she also adds a sceptical note: 'Except that I wonder if the result will be kinship' (Strathern 1992b: 177). Without venturing into speculation about their future development and its social consequences, the new reproductive technologies and their discussion among specialists and general public have significant consequences for the anthropological study of kinship. The reason is that they bring clearly into relief the culturally specific Western assumptions about kinship which inform its conceptualisation and which have guided research into kinship from its very beginning.

If the perceived asymmetry in the conceptualisation of fatherhood and motherhood is no longer tenable, what about the role of mater, the female equivalent of pater, that is, the socially recognised mother through whom the child claims kinship links with other people? Fortes mentions the biblical story in which the barren Rachel sends her maidservant Bilhah to her husband Jacob and the child born to Bilhah is counted as Rachel's child (Fortes 1969: 256). In the Cayman Islands in the West Indies, a girl who stays on in her parents' house becomes a 'sister' to her own children who then refer to her own mother as their 'mother' (Buchler 1966). Although the facts of birth make it possible to identify the genetrix as a result of a natural process which cannot be culturally manipulated, there are situations in which it may become problematic to ascertain who the child's genetrix actually is. The stories about changelings and about children being mixed up in maternity hospitals point to this uncertainty. Special efforts may be made to eliminate such uncertainty in situations where the mother's status is of particular social significance: a high court official had to witness every royal birth in England until quite recently (Bock 1969: 88). These cases and stories indicate that the difference between the role of a mater and that of a genetrix is culturally recognised. Surprisingly enough, although anthropologists have elaborated at length on the roles of paters and genitors in the societies they studied, they have hardly ever commented on the equivalent roles of maters and genetrices and the difference between these two roles has hardly ever become the object of elaboration by kinship theorists or even attracted their attention. In spite of the denial by many peoples of the shared substance between a mother and her child and in spite of the fact that the social significance of the mother–child relationship is highly variable across cultures, anthropologists never presumed the existence of peoples 'ignorant of maternity', not even of physical, biological or physiological maternity (Scheffler 1991: 372) in the same way in which they presumed the 'ignorance of paternity'. Kinship theorists have generally assumed that the mother–child (or more precisely genetrix–offspring) relationship is a 'cultural universal' and 'the foundation of any kinship system consists in the folk-cultural theory designed to account for the fact that women give birth to children' (Scheffler 1973: 749). Van Baal expressed the same view by boldly stating that 'motherhood is the basis of all kinship' (1975: 79). This is because the mother–child bond arises from common elements of human biology and is the biological heritage which humans share as the result of evolution. Research into the social organisation of contemporary primates has shown that, in spite of all its existing variation, the stable grouping within their bands is the association of the mother and her young offspring. This led Freeman to argue that 'kinship is an extension and a sort of reenactment of the primary bond so central in the emotional life of each of us' and that 'kinship systems build on the close biopsychological bonding between an infant and the adult, normally mother, who provides closest nurturance in the first year of life' (Freeman 1974). Freeman here aptly summarises the views of a number of kinship theorists who saw the universal experience of 'mothering' as necessary for the biological survival of helpless infants (Fox 1967, Fortes 1969, Goodenough 1970, Keesing 1975). This view has been most succinctly formulated by Barnes:

the mother–child relation in nature is plain to see and necessary for individual survival. An infant may be free to form attachments to mother-surrogates, but most societies would agree that a woman's response to an infant after she has given birth to it is at least in some degree innate or genetically determined. Hence a relation of physical as well as social motherhood is always recognized culturally and institutionalized socially. (1973: 73)

Because a real world which we call nature exists independently of the way in which we socially construct it, 'cultural motherhood is a necessary interpretation in moral terms of a natural relation' and 'our concept of motherhood is more closely constrained [than our concept of fatherhood] by our lives in the womb and as young children while we are still largely creatures of nature' (Barnes 1973: 73).

Fox has recently summarised the results of scientific research into the bond between mother and child, that is their intense emotional attachment which results from their psycho-physical interactions. The reciprocal mother–child bond starts during pregnancy and continues to develop after parturition (Fox 1993: 68–89). Acknowledging the findings of physiological and psychological research, Fox has the following to say:

I would agree, for example, with those who say that the nuclear family is not a sacrosanct 'natural' entity but simply one kind of institutional possibility. I have been saying so for thirty years or more. But as a student of mammalian behavior, I would have to disagree that 'motherhood' is a similar construct depending on context for its meaning. As a first approximation I would say that no matter the provenance of the genes, a hard look at the mammals tells us that the genetrix does indeed bond with child in the womb and at parturition, and hence has a 'natural' claim to it. (1993: 121–2)

This may well be so. But humans are mammals who differ from other mammals in their possession of culture and there are ample examples which can be adduced to show that culture interferes strongly with, and often effectively overrides, what is ostensibly in our 'nature' as the result of '128 million years of mammalian evolution, 72 million years of primate, and 5 million years of hominid evolution' (Fox 1993: 73–4; see also Fox 1967, 1973). Not only are humans the only mammals who, for centuries, have been able to control procreation in one way or another and who have the ability to terminate unwanted pregnancies. They also practice infanticide and adoption not only when the mother has died or is incapable of nursing the child. They could not do all these various things if their behaviour was determined solely by their biology. However biologically determined the bond between a mother and her child may be, humans have consistently showed through their various social practices that this bond is not unbreakable. — *adoption, abortion*

The positing of the mother–child bond as a 'natural fact' is rooted in assumptions about the natural characteristics of women and their natural role in sexual reproduction. These assumptions are now coming under attack from feminist writing, a great deal of which is aimed at establishing that biology is not destiny (Sacks 1976, 1979, Schlegel 1977,

Leacock 1978, Caulfield 1981). Feminist writers argue that what we have been used to seeing as a natural relation may not be the result of our unbiased understanding of the natural world but a function of our cultural assumption of universal sexual asymmetry:

> [t]here are no 'facts', biological and material, that have social consequences and cultural meanings in and of themselves. Sexual intercourse, pregnancy and parturition are cultural facts, whose form, consequences and meanings are socially constructed in any society, as are mothering, fathering, judging, ruling, and talking with gods. (Yanagisako and Collier 1987: 39)

The assumption of the naturally constituted affective tie between mother and child has been criticised for taking for granted what it should explain, namely how the process of human reproduction comes to be cast as the cause of the creation of difference among people that is seen as making a difference in all societies. This line of criticism emerged as the result of the whole development of feminist anthropology. From its original concern with understanding the position of women in society, it gradually moved to the study of variation in women's roles and experiences, and eventually to its present-day concern with understanding the construction of gender in specific societies. According to some writers, its 'next contribution to the study of gender and kinship should be to question the difference betwen women and men', or 'to question the assumption that "male" and "female" are the natural categories of human beings whose relations are everywhere structured by their biological difference' (Collier and Yanagisako 1987: 7). What is posited as problematic in this approach is

> whether the particular biological difference in reproductive functions that our culture defines as the basic differences betwen males and females, and so treats as the basis of their relationship, is used by other societies to constitute the cultural categories of male and female. (Yanagisako and Collier 1987: 48)

This type of criticism does not deny the biological differences between men and women. It argues, however, that to acknowledge them does not mean to accept at the same time that they are the basis for the cultural construction of the categories 'male' and 'female' in every society. What is called into question is the assumption that all the observable cultural variations in gender categories are nothing more than different elaborations of the same natural fact. Once we realise that the categories 'male' and 'female' are variously defined in different societies, the assumption that the difference between men and women is grounded in nature becomes open to question. The assumed naturalness of the mother–child bond is grounded in the assumption that nurturance by the mother is necessary for the biological survival of the helpless infant and that, consequently, people everywhere ascribe cultural significance to this fact (Yanagisako 1979: 197). But this very assumption is called into question by the increasing evidence that the variation in conceptualisation of gender and women's experiences can be linked to different forms of economic, political and cultural organisation. Research into gender ideologies suggests that 'motherhood' is not universally construed in the same way and that different gender ideologies place different emphasis on it (Rosaldo and Atkinson 1975, Rosaldo and Collier 1981). The cases of nannies, wet nurses and surrogate mothers (Boon 1974, Drummond 1978) make the assumption about the mother–child bond as inherent in nature look rather dubious. They suggest that this bond can, after all, be culturally constructed as natural and hence commonsensically experienced as such. If that is indeed the case, the assumption of much kinship theorising that mother–child bonding is rooted in humans' primate nature and hence is something immutable to which any culture can only adapt itself but cannot change, will need to be reconsidered.

BASIC UNIT OF KINSHIP

[handwritten marginal note: Some cultures don't acknowledge poppy dads & moms]

It is easy to state in general terms that kinship is a system of social ties based on acknowledging genealogical relations but the fact that some societies hold that all the child's substance comes only from its mother, some allege that it comes only from its father and yet others that both parents contribute to it, raises the theoretical problem of *which* specific genealogical relations are universally to be seen as lying at the core of all existing kinship systems.

Kinship theorists have adopted two positions with regard to this problem. Starting from the recognition that no society denies the natural fact that women give birth to children, whatever the native theories of procreation may be, Fortes sees 'the mother and child couple' to be 'the unique and irreducible source of all human existence' (1978: 21) and argues that 'in primitive societies the domain of domestic relations is commonly organized around a nucleus consisting of a mother and her children' (1958: 8), although he attributes at the same

time 'the central position in the kinship system ... to the constellation
of the relations of mother and child and the child's begetter' (1978:
21). Adams (1960), Bohannan (1963: 73) and Goodenough (1970: 18)
consider the woman and her dependent children the 'nuclear' or
'elementary' familial group in all human societies. This position has
been most clearly formulated by Fox who takes 'the mother–child tie
as inevitable and given' (1967: 40) and considers the 'basic unit' of all
kinship systems to be 'the mother and her child, however the mother
came to be impregnated' (1967: 39). The attachment of the child's
genitor to this basic unit is highly variable. When he is attached to it
in the role of the woman's husband and her children's father, the result
is a nuclear, elementary, individual or conjugal family, as it has been
variously called. However, in some societies there is no such attachment
at all. Among the Nayar, a woman who went through the *tāli* ritual
continued to live in her natal household which consisted of her
siblings, her mother and her siblings, the children of her mother's sisters,
and possibly her maternal grandmother, her siblings and the children
of her sisters and her sisters' daughters. The woman's brothers acted
as providers and guardians of her children. Her ritual 'husband', that
is, the man who tied the *tāli* ornament round her neck, and who
remained secluded with her for three days and nights in a room of the
ancestral house as part of the *tāli* ritual, had no further obligations towards
her once the ritual was over. He was not obliged to visit her, and if
he did so, he had no prior claims on her against other men who were
her regular visitors and who would come to her after eating supper
in their natal home and leave before breakfast. When a man came to
visit, he placed his weapons outside the woman's door as a sign to others
that he was in the house. If two men came on the same night, the
one who came last might sleep outside on the veranda. A woman's
regular lovers usually knew one another and informally agreed the order
of their visits among themselves. Women could reject particular men
and both women and men could terminate their liaisons without any
formality. The woman received all her food, shelter and clothing
from her natal household and her lovers and her ritual 'husband' had
no economic obligations of any kind towards her. On her part, she
had no obligations towards them other than granting sexual privileges.
Her only obligation towards her ritual 'husband' was that, after his
death, she and all her children had to observe fifteen days of ritual
pollution (Gough 1961a: 358–61).

A similarly fleeting and tenuous relationship between a man and a woman and her children is characteristic of 'matrifocal families' in the Caribbean in which women and their children form the core of many households. A man may be attached to the woman only temporarily, usually as her lover but not necessarily as a 'father' to her children. Whatever his particular attachment, he occupies only a marginal role in comparison with the close bonds between mothers, children and daughters' children (Smith, R.T. 1956).

A different view of genealogical relations that are basic to all kinship systems also starts from the recognition of a natural fact, namely that it takes a man and a woman to produce a child. Parenthood is thus an inevitable result of the biological process of human reproduction irrespective of how the role of the man who begot the child and of the woman who bore it may be conceptualised in different cultures, and irrespective of which social significance may be attributed to their relationship with the child. Fortes formulated this position very clearly:

The fact of parenthood – that is, the complex of activities which includes the begetting, bearing and rearing of children by specified parental kin – are empirically identifiable in all societies, even if parents and children are not permanently co-resident. At any rate, ethnographers have not failed to find the mother and child couple, and to get evidence of the recognition of genitors and fathers, even in societies where the ostensibly husbandless 'matrifocal family' is the common form, or where physiological paternity is ignored or not understood, as classically among the Trobrianders and the Australian aborigines. (1969: 255; reference omitted)

The cultural recognition of filiation, that is, of the 'fact of being a child of a specified parent' (Fortes 1959: 206) implies the recognition of four sets of relationships: those between the woman and the man who engendered the child, between the child and its mother, the child and its father, and between siblings, that is, children of the same parents. Expressed differently, it implies the recognition of eight 'primary kin types': father (F), mother (M), husband (H), wife (W), son (S), daughter (D), brother (B) and sister (Z). A group which is based on these four sets of relationships and which hence includes the eight primary kin types, is a group which has variously been called the nuclear, elementary, individual or conjugal family. As it is a group which has been considered to be an inevitable result of the biology of human reproduction and seen as necessary for human survival, modern sociologists and anthropologists did not see it as a late product of the evolution of human society as their Victorian predecessors did, but as the basic unit of human society (Bell and Vogel 1960: 2, Goode 1964) and as the basic building block of all kinship systems. This view has been most clearly expressed by Radcliffe-Brown:

> The unit of structure from which a kinship is built up is the group which I call 'elementary family', consisting of a man and his wife and their child or children .... The existence of the elementary family creates three special kinds of social relationship, that between parent and child, that between children of the same parents (siblings), and that between husband and wife as parents of the same child or children .... The three relationships that exist within the elementary family constitute what I call the first order. (1941: 2)

Murdock (1949: 94) called the eight kin types connected through this 'first order of relationships' (that is, F, M, H, W, S, D, B, Z) the 'primary relatives'.

According to Radcliffe-Brown, the genealogical connections between parent and child are extended to connect each individual to the parents of his or her parents and to the children of his or her children; connections between siblings are extended to connect each individual with his or her siblings' children; and connections between spouses are extended to connect each individual with his or her spouse's parents and siblings. These connections constitute what he called 'relationships of the second order'. They result from 'the connection of two elementary families through a common member, such as father's father, mother's brother, wife's sister and so on' (Radcliffe-Brown 1941: 2). Thirty-three different kin types of this order, or thirty-three different types of 'secondary relatives', as Murdock called them, can be theoretically distinguished. Beyond the range of the secondary kin, genealogical relations are extended to the primary kin of the secondary kin who represent the tertiary kin in relation to *ego* (the point of reference). Theoretically, everybody can distinguish altogether 151 tertiary kin types, as for example, FZH, WZD, all first cousins, etc. People have not only their primary, secondary and tertiary kin but also more distant kinsmen – the primary, secondary and tertiary kinsmen of their own tertiary kinsmen. As Radcliffe-Brown says, 'we can trace, if we have genealogical information, relationships of the fourth, fifth or *n*th order' (1941: 2). All individuals who see themselves as genealogically connected to some other individual are conceptualised as belonging to a specific category and the verbal label for this category is appropriately glossed as 'kin' (Scheffler 1973: 751).

According to Murdock, the nuclear family was a 'distinct and strongly functional group in every known society'. It was universally present in all societies either as such or as a basic building block of more complex family forms (1949: 2). New ethnography which has come forward since the publication of Murdock's book has shown that this view was misleading. I have already mentioned the Nayar and the societies of the Caribbean which obviously lack a social group of this kind. Kinship theorists now generally acknowledge that the nuclear family is neither universal nor inevitable (Fallers and Levy 1959, Fox 1967, Buchler and Selby 1968, Clignet 1970, Goodenough 1970, Keesing 1975, Yanagisako 1979) and they point out numerous problems which arise from treating it as a building block of all kinship systems.

One such problem is the assumption that kinship is a system of social ties based on the acknowledgement of genealogical relations following from a jurally recognised marriage union and from the procreation of descendants within it. In other words, only 'legitimate' genealogical connections (that is, those established in wedlock) are acknowledged or recognised for social purposes as Malinowski (1962: 65) and Radcliffe-Brown (1950: 4) seemed to suggest. This is palpably not true. To give just one example: among the Nuer, when a woman married another woman, she counted as pater of all the children borne by the woman she had married, irrespective of who the children's genitor or genitors were, and in a ghost-marriage, the pater of the children was the deceased man in whose name the marriage had been contracted. But it was not only these 'legitimate' connections which were recognised by the Nuer for social purposes. The known genitor also had certain rights and duties with respect to his offspring. When the daughter whom he begot married, he might claim 'the cow of the begetting' or 'the cow of the loins' as his part of her bridewealth (Evans-Pritchard 1951: 121–2) and the prohibition on marriage among close kin applied irrespective of whether their relationship was traced through a pater or a genitor (1951: 31). Children were said to be bound to their genitor by a mystical tie, even if he had little to do with them, and if he was ill-disposed towards them they might suffer injury. A natural son treated all the near kin of his genitor as his own kin and they recognised him as their kinsman. A genitor helped with the marriage of his natural son, if he could. A son sacrificed a bull not only in honour of his pater but also in honour of his genitor and if his genitor did not beget his own legal descendants, he might have married a wife in his name (1951: 150).

Cases like this lead Scheffler (1973) to emphasise that the various rights, duties, privileges and obligations which are normally associated with fatherhood in Western society, may be allocated to different men in many non-Western societies. A man assumes some of these rights because he is the presumed genitor, others because he nurtures the child and cares for it, and yet others because he is the child's mother's husband. As a note in parenthesis it could perhaps be mentioned that the existing male bias in the study of kinship is indicated by the fact that anthropologists have not paid any attention to the possibility that various rights and duties, which are normally associated with motherhood in Western society, may also be separated and assigned to different people. The neglect of this problem stems of course from accepting the mother–child bond as naturally constituted and biologically determined.

Scheffler argues that all societies posit the existence or necessity of genitors, albeit often in culturally specific ways which differ from Western notions about the relationship of the child to its presumed genitor. Trobrianders' views of fatherhood, which I have mentioned before, are the case in point. As Scheffler sees the relationship between a genetrix and her offspring and the genitor and his offspring as complementary cultural universals, he concludes that: '[t]he elementary relations of any kinship system are best defined as those of genitor–offspring and genetrix–offspring per se' (Scheffler 1973: 755).

Scheffler is undoubtedly right to point out that it is unwarranted to assume that only 'legitimate' genealogical relations are recognised for social purposes and to emphasise that social relations based on 'illegitimate' genealogical connections are equally part of the kinship system of the societies in which they occur. However, his conceptualisation of the genitor–offspring and genetrix–offspring relations as the elementary relations of any kinship system may be as restrictive as the conceptualisation of kinship as based only on the recognition and acknowledgement of 'legitimate' genealogical connections. Noting the fact that people unrelated genealogically may become related in a social sense, as happens, for example, in cases of adoption, or when social fatherhood is assigned to a man who is not the child's genitor, many anthropologists argued that a cross-culturally valid definition of kinship cannot be exclusively based only on the notion of genealogical connection but must take account of social as well as genealogical relationships (Malinowski 1913, 1962, Radcliffe-Brown 1950: 4, Beattie 1964b, Schneider 1969). In the words of Lowie, '[b]iological relations merely serve as a starting point for the development of sociological conceptions of kinship' (1950: 57), and in the words of Keesing, kinship is 'the network of relationships created by genealogical connections, and by social ties (e.g. those based on adoption) *modelled* on the "natural" relations of genealogical parenthood' (1975: 13; emphasis added).

To assume that each person is immediately genealogically connected to two others (his or her father or genitor and his or her mother or genetrix) and that this relationship of filiation engenders the set of eight primary kin types through whom each individual is related to many others, does not mean that one has to assume that the unit from which kinship is built is the nuclear family. Scheffler explicitly rejects this assumption (1973: 754) and Buchler and Selby, who do likewise (1968: 23–5), maintain that in every society there is a relational set of primary kin types which arises from the cultural recognition of the relationships of descent, affinity and consanguinity together with the recognition of sexual differences. Descent refers to the relation between parent and child (a relation which Fortes considers not to be that of descent but of filiation), affinity refers to the relation between spouses and consanguinity refers to the relation between siblings (1968: 22, 36).

These terms were defined in this way by Lévi-Strauss (1963), who advanced a powerful argument both against the treatment of the nuclear family as the basic unit of all kinship systems and against seeing the relations created through the engendering of offspring, whether in the context of a nuclear family or in its absence, as primary. As he points out, kinship is not a static phenomenon but exists only in self-perpetuation. A unit consisting of parents and their children cannot perpetuate itself because of the universality of the incest taboo which prevents mating between the members of a nuclear family or between the 'primary kin'. His point is that the nuclear family, because of the incest taboo, is left without a beginning because the woman who bears the children cannot be her husband's sister, as she would have to be if the nuclear family were a self-perpetuating group. For a kinship system to exist, a man must obtain a woman from another man who gives him his daughter or sister. The most elementary form of kinship, or the basic unit of kinship, is thus not the nuclear family but the *avunculate*, that is, a structure which consists of a brother, his sister, sister's husband and sister's son, or, in other words, a man, his wife, their son and the wife's brother who gave the man his sister in marriage. This elementary structure expanded through the integration of new elements is the building block of more complex systems. It is a structure in which the relation of consanguinity, the relation of affinity and the relation of descent are present. The irreducible character of this basic unit of kinship is the result of the universality of an incest taboo in human society, and it is the incest taboo which explains the inclusion of the maternal uncle (the wife's brother) and which accounts for the fact that the relationship between 'brothers-in-law' (that is, the man and his wife's brother) is the necessary axis around which the basic unit of kinship is built. As the group which gives a woman in marriage to another group must be compensated in following generations by receiving a woman in exchange for the one which it gave away, the basic unit has to contain a man who, in the next generation, will give his own sister either directly or indirectly to the group which gave his mother to his group in the first place.

It is theoretically possible to imagine a basic unit of kinship in which the sexes would be reversed and which would involve a sister, her brother, brother's wife and brother's daughter. But in practice such a unit cannot exist for, as Lévi-Strauss argues, it is always the men who exchange the women and not the women who exchange men (1963: 47). This view has been criticised by many anthropologists (Rubin 1975, Weiner 1976, 1992, Raheja 1988) mainly because it reduces women to objects and denies them any active role in the institution of marriage. This is simply not borne out by ethnographic facts. Goody points out that in Asian societies 'women are never simply the pawns of others but themselves players in the game, especially as heiresses' (1990: 68). He argues that the Lévi-Straussian model of the exchange of women hinders our understanding of the role of marriage in creating social relations for it implies women's complete incorporation into the kin groups of their husbands and the severing of their relations with their natal kin. Not only is this only rarely the case but there are societies like the Ata Tana'Ai on Flores, where it is men, rather than women, who are in this position (Lewis 1988: 208). On the basis of Malaysian ethnography, it appears that to conceptualise marriage as an exchange of women by groups of men is at least a dubious generalisation. Peletz suggests that among the Malays of Negeri Sembilan men, and not women are exchanged in marriage and, moreover, they are exchanged by groups of women rather than by other men (1994: 142–3). Anthropologists who have paid particular attention to native conceptualisations of what is actually being exchanged in marriages point out that it is too simplistic to view marriage as an exchange of whole persons, whether female or male. Writing of the Etoro, among whom both the groom and bride subscribe to arrangements made on their behalf by senior males, Kelly points out that

it is misleading to describe this as an 'exchange of women' without adding a number of qualifications. It would be more accurate to say that senior males exchange the reproductive capacities of both male and female persons. The implicit distinction between 'exchangers' and 'exchanged' that is contained in the phrase is appropriate in the Etoro case, but the 'exchanged' are not whole persons and are of both genders. (1993: 470)

Even if the Lévi-Straussian model of marriage as an exchange of women between groups of men cannot be maintained, his more general view that kinship perpetuates itself only through specific forms of marriage is incisive. Its logical consequence is that the relationships which Radcliffe-Brown called 'relationships of the first order' depend on and are derived from relationships which he considered secondary (Lévi-Strauss 1963: 46–51).

According to Lévi-Strauss, 'the primitive and irreducible character of the basic unit of kinship' (1963: 46) as he has defined it, is a direct result of the universality of an incest taboo. For him, the incest taboo is the first truly cultural act and the essential criterion of cultural life. It marks the transition from 'nature' – the life of other animals who have no cultural tradition to transmit to the new generation and to increase it with every generation – to 'culture' – the mode of life peculiar to humans (Lévi-Strauss 1969: 12). The problem of the incest taboo and its origin has been hotly debated by anthropologists. Attempts to solve these problems in a universally valid way have produced mutually contradictory explanations of the origin and persistence of incest prohibitions (see Fox 1967: 54–76). Given the fact that the range of persons with whom sex is forbidden varies tremendously from society to society, Needham expressed doubts as to whether incest prohibitions constitute a class of phenomena which can be cross-culturally defined as such. In consequence, there cannot be a general theory which applies to all of them for '[a]ll that is common to incest prohibitions is the feature of prohibition itself' (1971: 29).

Recently, Fox (1993) has argued that incest prohibition is not 'culture itself' as Lévi-Strauss would have it (1969: 12). It is not

the appropriate cultural starting point since avoidance of close inbreeding is common to most sexually reproducing organisms. Taboo certainly is unique to man since it involves language for interdictions, but avoidance is not unique. (Fox 1993: 192)

Certainly the primatologists now appear to be in agreement that mating in primate groups is neither random nor incestuous. The avunculate – a special relationship between mother's brother and sister's son – is thus not the result of the incest taboo and the benefits of exchange. According to Fox, it is built into the dynamics of the mother–child bond – 'the only universal mammalian relationship'. Starting with that relationship, mating can be seen as consisting of the courtship phase, which brings the male and female together, and the parental phase, which keeps them together at least until the offspring reach viability. An alternative to uniting the genitor and his mate in a 'pair bond' is to use for parental purposes the siblings who are united by a common bond with the mother but have an asexual relationship because of the natural avoidance of incest. The latter alternative is a particularly viable option in any situation where, for whatever reason, the mating bond is weak but males still need to be attached to the mother–child unit to protect it or to assist with the nurturance of the infant. As humans can and do separate the courtship bond from the parental bond, this seems to be the step which they have taken 'beyond the primate baseline'. It was thus the combination of the mother–child unit with relatively permanent mating that gave rise to human kinship into which was built a primitive avunculate – 'the first true cultural incursion into nature' (1993: 193).

Although it may seem strange to Westerners on the basis of their own cultural experience, avunculate plays a central role in theories of what it means to be human:

Animals don't do it, even if they may occasionally, as with the primates, end up in a 'special relationship' with the maternal uncle. It seems to be a peculiarly human thing to allow the asexual brother–sister tie to take over certain aspects of the parental role from the husband–wife tie. This gives rise to avuncular responsibilities that may flower into full-blown matrilineal succession and inheritance, or to the classical indulgences of the patrilineal avunculate, or to the sacred duties towards mothers' brothers in bilateral systems, or even to the 'love triangle' conflicts with them where the power of the maternal uncle threatens to rob the young males of their breeding preferences (Fox 1993: 227).

Certainly, in Fox's view, it is the avunculate and not the incest taboo that is the defining principle of humanity and culture. The mother's brother is in some sense a primitive given in the basic unit of kinship, irrespective of whether we want to regard his special status as the result of the incest taboo and the benefits of exchange, as Lévi-Strauss argued, or as built into the mother–son–daughter triad, as Fox argues.

mother's brother = basic unit of kinship
– comes from incest taboo or
benefit of exchange – nobody
can decide.

2 KINSHIP, DESCENT AND MARRIAGE

Most anthropologists have taken kinship to be the network of genealogical relationships and social ties modelled on the relations of genealogical parenthood (Keesing 1975: 13). Every individual is at the centre of such a network which is potentially boundless. If people are assumed to be directly related to their parents through a genealogical tie, they are also assumed to be less directly related to those individuals who are connected to their parents and children through a direct genealogical link and beyond them to many more individuals to whom they are connected through their parents' siblings and other collateral relatives, that is siblings of lineal forebears (parents, grandparents) and their descendants (Scheffler 1973: 751, Keesing 1975: 13). Obviously, people cannot expect the same help and support from all those to whom they can trace a genealogical connection and they obviously cannot have the same obligations towards them. To make genealogical relations meaningful and practically operational, people everywhere somehow have to limit the range of those who are seen as being genealogically related and to whom an individual can turn for help and support and who can expect similar help and support from him or her. Individuals who are presumed to be genealogically related to each other are usually conceptualised as forming a distinct category – the category of kin.

CATEGORIES OF KIN

If we had the necessary information available about all past genealogical connections, we would be able to put all the members of any given society on a huge genealogical chart. In practice, we cannot do that because we lack the necessary information. So lapses of memory are responsible for the fact that we do not categorise all people we know

40

or know about as our kinsmen but only some of them. In British or American society, people whom anthropologists call kinsmen are usually called 'relatives' or 'family'. Americans state explicitly that relatives are persons related by blood or marriage but when a decision is to be made about who is and who is not a relative, or who is to count as a close or as a distant relative, the actual genealogical distance may be just one of the factors taken into consideration. A physical distance or what might be called a socio-emotional distance are also taken into consideration when a decision is made about whether a particular person is a relative or not (Schneider 1968: 62–75). The British draw the boundary around the category of people whom they consider their kin in pretty much the same way (Firth, Hubert and Forge 1969: 92, Robertson 1991: 7). The lack of any formal or clear-cut way of delineating the category of kinsmen is a characteristic feature of the kinship system of modern Western society. In many other societies, categorisation of some people as kinsmen and of others as non-kinsmen is not left solely to the failures of individual memories or to individual idiosyncrasies and preferences. There are other means for categorising only some people as kinsmen, which are established as culturally appropriate, or other culturally appropriate means for drawing a boundary around the category of people considered to be kin. There are basically two ways in which this can be done.

The first is by tracing a genealogical connection to some living person, that is, to define egocentrically the category of people considered to be kin. A focal point of this category is a particular living individual and all members of the category are related to him or her but are not necessarily related to one another because they do not share a common ancestor. There is a considerable confusion in anthropological writing about the analytical term by which to describe such a category in societies in which it exists as a culturally meaningful one. Firth, Hubert and Forge (1969) use the terms 'kin unit', 'kin set', 'kin group' or 'kin network' when talking about it, but the most widely used term is 'kindred' (Freeman 1961, Mitchell 1963, Scheffler 1973: 751).

Kindred is an ego-centred kinship category. It may be visualised as a series of concentric circles with ego in the middle, surrounded by members of her or his nuclear family and beyond them by circles of more distant kinsmen, the knowledge of whom becomes less and less intimate the further removed they are from ego, and the relationship with whom is seen as being progressively less determined by the mutuality of kinship. Because kindred is an ego-centred category, kindreds necessarily overlap: every individual is potentially a member of many categories of kindred and only full siblings share the same kindred.

The overlapping nature of kindred and the fact that any individual may be a member of a number of kindreds, make it difficult for a kindred to crystallise as a group. One kindred cannot be, for example, in feud with another when both share members who would have to decide which side to join and support. Similarly, because the boundaries of kindred are defined only from the point of view of a particular individual, kindred cannot corporately own land or any other property.

Kindreds act as groups only occasionally and the groups recruited on the basis of kindred membership have typically a character of action groups or task groups. They consist of individuals who assemble in some organised fashion to perform jointly a specific task. They have only a limited existence in time and they dissolve once the task for which they organised themselves has been completed. Groups whose members belong to the same kindred crystallise in action especially for the performance of life cycle rituals like births, initiations, marriages or funerals or, particularly in Western society, for periodic reunions at special birthdays or 'family' holidays like Christmas. The distinction between kindred as a culturally recognised category and an action group whose members are recruited because of their membership of the category, is phrased by Firth, Hubert and Forge in terms of a difference between 'kin *units* of more regular nature' and '*assemblies* of kin for specific social occasions' (1969: 266; original emphasis).

When action groups get formed for specific social occasions, it is the membership of the kindred that makes any person eligible for becoming a member of the group. But genealogical relationship is often not the only principle of recruitment into the group assembled for a specific social or ceremonial occasion. Actual attendance at these occasions is determined as much by proximity in space and socio-emotional distance as by closeness of genealogical relationship. The vague boundaries of kindred become an inconvenience mainly at celebrations such as weddings where the number of guests must be restricted and those who have not been invited might feel offended.

Functionalist anthropologists tended to see kindreds as kinship categories typical of Western industrial societies in which kinship is not an important structuring principle. In pre-industrial, non-Western societies, which were seen as 'kinship based', genealogical connections linking the members of kindred could not serve as a means of basic social differentiation as kindred do not form distinct segments of society. As Radcliffe-Brown pointed out, only groups formed on the basis of unilineal descent do not overlap, are clearly bounded and can therefore constitute such segments (1950: 14). Probably as a result of his theoretical influence, most anthropological research into kinship conducted by anthropologists of structural-functional persuasion has concentrated on the study of unilineal forms of organisation which were seen as essential for the continuity of social structure in simple pre-industrial societies in which political and economic relations are expressed in a kinship idiom.

However, even research conducted within the structural-functional paradigm has shown that not only Western societies, but social systems of many simple societies can work efficiently without any form of large corporate kin groups. Such forms of social organisation exist not only among hunter-gatherers or nomadic peoples, like, for example, the Lapps (Pehrson 1954, 1957), but also among sedentary agriculturalists. The Subanun shifting horticulturalists of Mindanao (Frake 1960) and the Iban rice-cultivating farmers of western Borneo (Freeman 1955, 1958, 1960) are the best-known ethnographic examples of societies in which nuclear or extended families constitute the main kinship groups and larger groups are mobilised, when needed, from among the kindred. Writing against the tide of seeing the continuity of social structure as based on the existence of clearly bounded and permanent descent groups which form distinct segments of society, Frake has characterised in the following way the continuity of Subanun social structure:

Despite [the] network of formal and informal social ties among families, there have emerged no large, stable discrete socio-political units .... The Subanun family [is]... largely a 'sovereign nation'. But ... [its] corporate unity endures only as long as does the marriage tie of its founders. The continuity of Subanun society must be sought in the continuous process of corporate group formation and dissolution rather than in the permanency of the groups themselves. (1960: 63)

While the first way of delineating categories of kin consists of defining them ego-centrically by tracing a genealogical connection to some living person, the second way is to define categories of kin socio-centrically. People are members of such categories not because they have a kinsman in common but because they have a common ancestor, that is 'any common genealogical predecessor of the grandparental or earlier generation' (Fortes 1959: 207, 1969: 281). Since they are comprised of someone's descendants, such categories are called descent categories.

A descent category includes only those individuals who are descended from an ancestor in a particular way and various descent rules define a particular kind of descent sequence that specifies who is a member of the category. Only three such rules may be distinguished. The first one is the rule of patrilineal or agnatic descent which stipulates that only individuals who trace their descent from an ancestor through an unbroken chain of male links are members of the descent category. Expressed differently, it means that members of the category trace their descent from a particular ancestor through their father, their father's father, their paternal great-grandfather, and so on. The second rule is that of matrilineal or uterine descent which stipulates that descent is traced from an ancestor or ancestress down through an unbroken series of female links, that is, through the ancestor's daughter, daughter's daughter, daughter's grand-daughter, and so on. The third descent rule is the rule of cognatic descent which applies when descent is traced from an ancestor or ancestress down through a series of links that can be male or female, or any combination of the two. In other words, when cognatic descent rule determines the membership of a category, the sex of any genealogical link that connects the category members to their common ancestor is irrelevant. The rules of patrilineal and matrilineal descent, since each traces an unbroken chain of genealogical links through only one sex, are classed together as rules of unilineal descent and they jointly contrast with cognatic descent, which traces an unbroken chain of links through either sex.

KINSHIP AND DESCENT

Underlying the notion of descent as a 'relationship by genealogical tie to an ancestor' (Scheffler 1966: 542) is the analytical differentiation between kinship and descent drawn by Fortes. In Fortes's conceptualisation, descent is a relation mediated by a parent between ego and an ancestor and it has to be distinguished from filiation – a relation deriving from the fact of being a child of one's parent. Filiation and its corollary, siblingship, are for him primarily phenomena of the domestic domain and form the basis of domestic relationships of kinship. Descent, on the other hand, is a phenomenon of the public or politico-jural domain (Fortes 1953, 1959, 1969). Fortes himself considered the analytical separation of the politico-jural domain from the domestic or familial domain to be 'the major advance in kinship theory since Radcliffe-Brown' (Fortes 1969: 72). According to him, 'human social organization everywhere emerges as some kind of balance, stable or not, between the political order – Aristotle's polis – and the familial or domestic order – the oikos – a balance between polity and kinship' (Fortes 1978: 14). Fortes considered the distinction between the two domains to be

a methodological and analytical distinction. The actualities of kinship relations and kinship behaviour are compounded of elements from both domains and deployed in words and acts, beliefs and practices, objects and appurtenances that pertain to both of these and to other domains of social life as well. (Fortes 1969: 251)

But that more than 'a methodological and analytical distinction' was involved in the separation of the two domains is indicated by the fact that in Fortes's conceptualisation, the distinction between the two domains parallels the distinction between kinship, the ego-centred system of bilateral relations arising from procreative activities taking place in the domestic domain, and descent, the sociocentric system of genealogical relations defining first of all the political affiliations of individuals in 'kinship-based social systems' (1969: 72). Because of the different character of relations pertaining to the domestic and the politico-jural domain, the activities and behaviour pertaining to each domain are regulated by different norms. The domestic domain is governed by 'private', 'affective' and 'moral' norms which underpin the prescribed altruism or 'amity' among kinsmen (1969: 250–1). The 'affective and moral components' of interpersonal kinship relations are generated by the 'reproductive nucleus' of the mother–child unit:

The nodal bond of mother and child implies self-sacrificing love and support on the one side and life-long trust and devotion on the other. The values mirrored in this relation have their roots in the parental care bestowed on children, not in jural imperatives. Their observance is dictated by conscience, not legality. (1969: 191).

The politico-jural domain, on the other hand, is governed by jural norms upheld by 'external' or 'public' sanctions. As Scheffler pointed out, Fortes tended 'to treat social relations ascribed by reference to relations of common descent as though they were necessarily "politico-jural relations"' (Scheffler 1970b: 1465).

Scheffler, who takes the distinction drawn by Fortes between kinship and descent further than any other anthropologist, describes the ego-centric systems of social identities and statuses as kinship systems and the ancestor-oriented systems as descent systems (1973: 756). As he says: 'To all appearances, all societies have kinship systems (as defined above), and a great many have descent systems as well' (1973: 758). This means that a society which orders social relations among its members by reference to their genealogical connections in terms of common descent, orders them also ego-centrically. Descent rules therefore do not imply only the recognition of certain genealogical ties and the exclusion of others. A society in which descent is traced in a matrilineal line does not deny the genealogical tie between a person and his or her patrilateral kin (kin on the father's side). The same situation obtains with regard to matrilateral kinsmen (kin on the mother's side) in societies in which descent is traced patrilineally. The rule of descent is only a social rule which identifies individuals with a selected category of their kin for specific purposes. People have also certain rights towards the kin of the parent with whom they do not share membership of the same descent category.

This fact led Fortes to develop his concept of 'complementary filiation' (1959). By this term he describes the relation of an individual to the people with whom he is related to that one of his parents through whom he does not trace descent. Thus in a patrilineal society, a man is bound to his father by descent, his relationship to his mother is that of complementary filiation. It is the other way around in a matrilineal society where descent is traced from and through one's mother and the relation to one's father is that of complementary filiation. According to Fortes, complementary filiation has very important social consequences in the situation where unilineal descent groups form the main segments of society. If only ties which bind together members of a descent group were acknowledged, each descent group would remain isolated from all others and it would not be bound together with them into one society. This is one of the reasons why, in patrilineally organised societies, people have certain rights and duties not only to members of their own descent group but also to the members of their mother's group, and why great importance is often attached to the relationship between a man and his mother's brother. This relationship is an important tie which binds the sister's son to the descent group of which he is himself not a member but whose members are, nevertheless, closely related to him. The tie of complementary filiation constitutes, as Fortes metaphorically expressed it, 'a break into the fence of agnatic kinship' which surrounds each individual in a patrilineally organised society.

What Fortes is basically talking about is the functional difference between kinship and descent and the complementary role which they play within the total social system. However, the notion of complementary filiation implies that it is the descent system which is structurally primary and that the kinship system is secondary and that it is merely derivative of the descent system. This is a line of criticism which was raised by Dumont (1971: 76–7). Keesing is critical of the concept of complementary filiation on the grounds that it may in fact confound the principle of bilateral kinship and that of cognatic descent which should analytically be kept separate (1975: 47). The notion of complementary filiation also implies that the ties of marriage which link the members of two descent groups are purely personal and therefore structurally unimportant. This is a line of criticism which was raised by Leach who finds particularly wanting Fortes's assumption that 'any Ego is related to the kinsmen of his two parents because he is the descendant of both parents and not because his parents were married'. In Leach's view, Fortes 'while recognizing that ties of affinity have comparable importance to ties of descent, disguises the former under his expression "complementary filiation"' (1961a: 122).

MARRIAGE

It has been a received wisdom in anthropology that although categories of people who trace descent from a common ancestor are not everywhere culturally recognised, people everywhere recognise relations of genealogical connection and use them as criteria for the allocation of rights and duties. In other words, although not all peoples have a concept of descent, they all recognise culturally a domain which we call kinship. The relations of kinship and descent are conceptualised as those established in the process of reproduction, that is, as those deriving from genealogical parenthood and the birth of children. Since incest prohibitions almost universally rule out mating among close kin, parenthood presupposes the relationship of affinity, that is a relationship by marriage. The study of the way in which people see themselves as mutually related is thus concerned with three kinds of relations which can be analytically separated: those of kinship, descent and affinity. It is a study of groups and categories which are formed on the basis of these relations, the activities which they perform and the role which they play in social life.

Having already dealt with the difference between kinship and descent, a few words need to be said about marriage. The issue of a cross-culturally valid definition of marriage was debated in anthropology in the 1950s particularly in relation to the interpretation of the *tāli*-tying ritual of the Nayar which I mentioned in the preceding chapter. As an analytical term, the term 'marriage' is taken from the ordinary English language, as indeed are most other analytical terms and concepts employed in sociology and anthropology: concepts like family, kindred, lineage, descent, religion, myth, politics and many others can serve as examples. The difficulty is that in ordinary English usage such words are usually polysemic, that is, have several different meanings. As Leach pointed out, in ordinary English usage, the word 'marriage' is employed in at least four distinguishable but overlapping senses. It is used to refer to the rights and duties of the spouses vis-à-vis each other and to the rights and duties between the wife's husband and her children whom the marriage provides with a legitimate status in society; to the arrangements by which the couple and their children form a domestic group; to the wedding ceremony; and to the relationship of alliance which links the families of both spouses (1982: 182–3). The meaning of the word 'marriage' in ordinary English is therefore too loose to be used without further definition in ethnographic description and cross-cultural comparison. It has habitually been used by anthropologists in the first of its above mentioned meanings to refer to a 'union between a man and a woman such that children born to the woman are the recognized legitimate offspring of both partners' (*Notes and Queries in Anthropology* 1951: 110). Gough interpreted the *tāli*-tying ritual of the Nayar, and the subsequent relations between the woman who has undergone it and the men with whom she cohabited, as marriage, because they limited and regulated sexual relationships and because they served to legitimise children. She emphasised that sexual relations between a woman and her husband were not promiscuous. They were forbidden within the lineage, within a certain range of affines, and, most categorically, with men of lower caste. It was therefore necessary to have some procedure for legitimising children and for showing that they have been fathered by men of appropriate status. The legally obligatory payments by husbands at the time of birth accomplished this and if no man could be found to make the payments, the woman and her child were expelled from the caste (Gough 1959: 23–4, 1961a: 362–3).

To Gough, the 'creation of legitimacy' (Leach 1982: 203) is the defining feature of any institution labelled 'marriage'. To be able to accommodate not only the Nayar case in a general definition of marriage but also the Nuer woman-to-woman and ghost marriages, she proposed that:

marriage is a relationship between a woman and one or more other persons which provides that a child born to the woman, under circumstances not prohibited by the rule of the relationship, shall be accorded full birth-status rights in his society or social stratum. (1959: 23–4)

Serious objections have been raised against defining marriage as an institution whose main function is to legitimate the offspring. Rivière pointed out that all such definitions are purely circular in the sense that the marital institution and its function are being used to define each other: if the function of marriage is the legitimation of children, the legitimacy of children clearly depends on marriage (1971: 60–2). According to Leach, definitions which seize on the notion of the legitimation of offspring do not hold even within the ordinary English usage: marriages without issue do not cease to be marriages and adopted children are certainly not considered to be illegitimate simply because they have not been born to their adoptive mother. The point which Leach emphasises is that legitimacy is a social concept which 'is not tied in with the issue of who is the biological parent of the child' (1982: 185–8). The Nuer linked legitimacy to the transfer of cattle through which any valid marriage was established and Nayar legitimacy was established by the child's mother having undergone the *tali* rite and the child's presumed genitor not being of lower caste than its mother (1982: 203). Furthermore, among the patrilineal Brahmans, with whom it was appropriate for the Nayar women to cohabit, only the eldest son was allowed to marry with full Vedic rites and to produce legitimate offspring. To prevent the fragmentation of the patrimonial estate, this privilege was denied the younger sons who took women of the matrilineal Nayar castes as their consorts. The Brahmans considered these women to be concubines whose children affiliated with their mothers' and not their fathers' caste. From the point of view of the matrilineal Nayar, the children belonged to their mother's caste in any case and the unions of Nayar women with Brahman men were seen as highly prestigious (1982: 190–1). Here, then, we have a case where the children were treated as legitimate offspring by their mother and her people but not by their father and his people.

As a result of all this, Leach refused as feasible any definition of marriage as an institution whose main function is the legitimation of children and argued that no definition could be found which would apply to all the institutions which ethnographers commonly refer to as marriage. He suggested that we ought to feel free to call 'marriage' any institution which gives rise to the establishing of legal parenthood, monopoly in the spouse's sexuality, rights in the spouse's labour services and property, socially significant 'relationship of affinity', and possibly many more similar rights (Leach 1961a: 107–8). Leach's position has been endorsed by Needham (1971: 6) and more recently reiterated by Barnard and Good (1984: 89–91).

3 KINSHIP AND THE DOMESTIC DOMAIN

Kinship studies conducted by British anthropologists in the first half and in the middle of the twentieth century were concerned mainly with investigating the nature and significance of unilineal descent groups. As a result of the work of Radcliffe-Brown (1935), Evans-Pritchard (1940) and Fortes (1953), most of the important debates and theoretical controversies about kinship have been concerned with what could be seen as the politico-jural aspect of kinship in Fortes's terms. Fox's (1967) and Keesing's (1975) discussion of kinship are good examples of this tendency. They focus mainly on the problems in the conceptualisation of descent groups and on marriage systems as they relate to the structure and interweaving of descent groups, and they pay only marginal attention to family and domestic groups. Like Fox and Keesing, most modern kinship theorists have seen the extra-domestic or 'public' domain of kinship as the main location for the theoretical debate. The result of this concentration of interest was the theoretical clarification and the increasingly precise definition of the basic concepts employed in the analysis of the public domain of genealogically constituted relations which was not paralleled by a similar clarification of concepts employed in the analysis of the domestic domain. Well into the 1960s and 1970s, a discussion went on among anthropologists about how the particular units of the domestic domain should be conceptualised and defined in ways that would be applicable cross-culturally. Henrietta Moore pointed out this conceptual vagueness when she observed that

the major difficulty in talking about the 'domestic' is that we automatically find ourselves having to consider a range of amorphous concepts and entities like 'the family', 'the household', 'the domestic sphere' and 'the sexual division of labour', which overlap and interact in complex ways to produce a sense of the domestic sphere. The family and household are two terms which are particularly difficult to separate clearly. (Moore 1988: 54)

Although many anthropologists still often use the terms 'family' and 'household' interchangeably, most of them conceptualise family as a kinship group and household as a local group, or as an aggregate of people who reside together and in virtue of their spatial proximity carry out domestic activities, however these may be defined in particular societies (Fortes 1958, Keesing 1958, Bohannan 1963, Bender 1967, Buchler and Selby 1968, Hammel and Laslett 1974, Cohen 1976).

When we conceptualise family as a unit, the referent of which is kinship, and household as a unit, the referent of which is spatial propinquity or common residence, it is possible to draw a distinction between them even in societies where the personnel of these two groups overlaps fully. What is much more problematic is not the separation of the family from household, but its separation from other kinds of groups, the referent of which is also kinship. In most anthropological and sociological writing, the term 'family' is still used without any definition and it is left to the readers to fill in what is meant by the term on the basis of their own cultural experience. After all, we all have a 'family' and we understand each other when we use this term in our discourse. In this usage, the term 'family' is employed as a blanket term for a set of relationships and activities which are 'domestic' rather than 'public' and which imply intimacy, emotional closeness and a host of other unanalysed concepts. Because family is a group recognised in Western society, and most anthropologists until recently have been Westerners, the study of family organisation in non-Western societies has been affected by particularly Western cultural assumptions much more than the study of all other groups formed on the basis of kinship and descent of which the Westerners have no personal experience.

If the term 'family' is to retain any analytical usefulness in the study of kinship and marriage in general and domestic organisation in particular, it has to be analytically differentiated from all other groups and categories formed on the basis of kinship and descent. As it is generally recognised that a new family is brought into being with marriage, it follows that it is a group which contains affines as well as kinsmen and hence a group which can be differentiated from other kinship groups by the fact that it contains both affinal and consanguineal relationships (Bohannan 1963: 72–4, Bender 1971: 223). Whenever such a group is recognised by the members of the society themselves as a culturally meaningful unit, it is appropriate to gloss it as 'family'. The obverse of this fact is that any culturally meaningful unit which does not comprise both affines and consanguineals, should not be glossed as 'family'. By this criterion, the 'matrifocal family' is not a family, as indeed the 'one-parent family' of contemporary Western society cannot be analytically seen as family. It may be the residue of what at one time (before the divorce of the parents or the death of one of them) might have been a family, or it may be the result of an unmarried woman giving birth to a child. But in strictly analytical terms, it is not a family, which fact we commonsensically acknowledge by often talking about the 'fragment of a family'.

My suspicion is that talking about 'matrifocal families' instead of 'matrifocal households' (although this term also often appears), is again influenced by the Western notions of family and home, of the notion of 'home' as a 'family living in a household' (Bohannan 1963: 86, Schneider 1980: 34–5, 45–6) and of the culturally specific conceptualisation of family in terms of co-residence of its members and their mutual affective bonds. This culturally specific way of talking about families and households in terms of each other engenders also the concept of 'one-parent family'.

The distinction between the family as a group whose members are bound together by specific ties of kinship and affinity and household as a residential unit was prompted by the recognition of the inadequacy of Malinowski's conceptualisation of the family, which had a long-lasting effect in anthropology. In his early study of the family among Australian Aborigines (1913), he asserted that the family was universally present in all societies because everywhere it fulfilled a universal human need for the nurturance and upbringing of children. In his view, the family was a bounded social unit distinguishable from other similar units and its characteristic features were the existence of a set of emotional bonds among its members and their co-residence in a particular physical location where the activities associated with the nurturance and care of children were performed. Since the time of Malinowski's early writing, it has been customary among anthropologists to conceptualise the family not merely as a unit whose members are bound together by specific relations of kinship and affinity, like those between husband and wife, between parents and children and between siblings, but also to ascribe to it functions which it universally performs in all human societies. For example, Murdock opened his discussion of social structure by stating:

The family is a social group characterised by common residence, economic cooperation and reproduction. It includes adults of both sexes, at least two of whom maintain a socially approved sexual relationship, and one or more children, own or adopted, of the sexually cohabiting adults. (1949: 1)

It may be a cultural ideal of Western society that a group which consists of sexually cohabiting adults of both sexes and their children should constitute a residential unit, but even there it is an ideal which is often not followed. Grandparents, parents' siblings, children's spouses and even people who are not relatives at all, like friends, lodgers or servants, form part of many European and American households in addition to their nuclear family core. In other societies, not only people who are not members of the family can live with it in one household, but husbands and wives can inhabit altogether separate households. Such a situation existed, for example, among the Ashanti of Ghana. A typical Ashanti household consisted of a woman, her brothers, daughters and sons, and her daughters' children. The woman's husband lived in his own household together with his sister and possibly a brother, his sister's sons and daughters and his sister's daughter's children. Obviously the husband's and wife's households had to be close to one another to enable the spouses to maintain sexual and other relationships. In consequence, about 80 per cent of all marriages were concluded within the same village. The husband visited his wife regularly and he spent nights together with her in her household. To a certain extent, the married couple and their children constituted an economic unit. The wife cooked for her husband and little girls who at sunset carried dishes with food from the households of their mothers to the households of their fathers were a familiar sight in an Ashanti village. The husband was obliged to supply his wife and children with food and clothes and, should he refuse to do so, his wife would insist on divorce. In his turn, the husband would demand divorce if his wife refused to cook for him or if she refused him sex. But a much stronger economic unit than the family was the household. A man, for example, could not request help in cultivating the fields or in paying off a debt from his sons. If he needed similar help, he might request it from his sister's sons with whom he lived in the same household and with whom he cooperated in various economic activities by virtue of their intimate day-to-day contact within the same household (Fortes 1949b).

Instead of following Malinowski's definition of the family, the distinction made between the family and household in terms of the contrast between kinship and propinquity stems from Radcliffe-Brown's definition of the 'elementary family' as 'consisting of a man and his wife and their child or children, *whether or not they are living together*' (Radcliffe-Brown 1952: 51; emphasis added). Implicit in this definition is the distinction between the family as a kinship group and a co-residential group whose personnel may or may not be congruent with the personnel of the family. It is a similar distinction which Fortes made implicitly in his study of the Tallensi (1949a) and explicitly in his account of the Ashanti (1949b).

However, the attempts to differentiate between the family as a kinship unit and household as a residential unit have still been plagued by an attempt to ascribe specific functions to the family and household as Malinowski and Murdock did. Thus Fortes, although he states that it is useful to distinguish between the domestic group and the family in the strict sense, still regards the nuclear family as

the reproductive nucleus of the domestic domain. It consists of two, and only two, successive generations bound together by the primary dependence of the child on its parents for nurture and love and of the parents on the child as the link between them and the reproductive fulfilment. The domestic group, on the other hand, often includes three successive generations as well as members collaterally, or otherwise, linked with the nucleus of the group. In this domain, kinship, descent and other jural and affectional bonds (e.g. of adoption or slavery) enter into the constitution of the group, whereas the nucleus is formed purely by the direct bonds of marriage, filiation and siblingship. The domestic group is essentially a householding and housekeeping unit organized to provide material and cultural resources needed to maintain and bring up its members .... The actual composition of the nuclear family and the domestic group may be identical, as it generally is in our own society; but the strictly reproductive functions ... are distinguishable from the activities concerned with the production of food and shelter and the non-material means of ensuring continuity with society at large. (Fortes 1958: 8–9)

According to Goody, who follows basically the same distinction between the family and the domestic group, the main contexts in which family and domestic group emerge are the two basic processes of production and reproduction. The nuclear family differentiates itself in the process of reproduction, while the persons constituting the domestic group act together in the four main phases of food production:

production, distribution, preparation and consumption (Goody 1958: 56). The main point of Fortes's and Goody's distinction between the domestic group and the family is the contrast between the productive group and the reproductive group. In other words, they distinguish between a group of individuals whose cooperative endeavour produces the material conditions necessary for safeguarding the physical existence of its members, and a group of individuals ostensibly concerned with the biological reproduction of human beings.

Bohannan draws the division between the family and household differently. According to him, the two functions of the family are regulation of sex and provision of new members of the community (1963: 83–4). How far the functions of controlling sexual activity – which has to be controlled and in one way or another is controlled in every society – can be ascribed primarily to the family is, of course, highly questionable. Although the individual family provides institutionalised means for sexual gratification, in many societies premarital or extramarital sexual license is allowed and the satisfaction of sexual needs is certainly not restricted to marital relations (Pasternak 1976: 85). Provision of new members of the community is a different matter. Mating is a biological fact and humans would certainly not die out as a biological species in the absence of families. Only the mother–child relationship is needed for successful biological reproduction of the species once the woman has been successfully fertilised (Adams 1960: 41). But obviously the reproduction of individuals cápable of full social life involves more than that. Many anthropologists have stressed that in almost every society, for a person to become a fully fledged member of the community he or she has to have both a recognised mother and a recognised father. Thus almost everywhere the family is the means by which the necessity for the replacement of the mortal members of the social group is met. But there are exceptions. In many societies which trace descent in the female line, the status of a person born to an unmarried woman is not affected. For example, on Truk in Melanesia, a woman can have sexual relations and bear children when she has passed menarche and any children she bears thereafter are legitimate members of society. They may be handicapped by having no paternal kinsmen but they are certainly not stigmatised in any way (Goodenough 1970: 10). In many other societies where individuals acquire their social position and their rights and privileges on the basis of their descent from their mothers, the role of the father often becomes irrelevant to a considerable degree and consequently the family is not necessarily the only permissible means by which the necessity for replacement of the members of the social group has to be met. According to Bohannan, food getting, provision of shelter and bodily comfort are functions usually performed by the household, and the household has yet another important function: almost everywhere it is the unit responsible for bringing up the children and teaching them the culture by which they must live (1963: 98).

I have mentioned only three authors to show that anthropologists hold considerably different views on the functions of the family and household. Other anthropologists would draw the line between the functions of these two units differently again, depending on their particular field experiences. This has led to increasing doubt about the possibility of ascribing to the family functions or activities which this group invariably performs. Objections to defining the family in terms of its functions were summarised by Bender (1967: 499–504) who has clearly demonstrated that it is impossible to ascribe to the family any functions which it would invariably perform in all human societies. Many of the functions that have been variously ascribed to it are often performed by groups that we would not commonsensically describe as families or even households and there appears no single function that is invariably performed by a set of genealogically related individuals. However, this does not mean that the family cannot be defined in purely formal terms. The formal aspects of the nuclear family are usually described as a system of eight kinship roles (H, W, F, M, S, D, B, Z) bound together by eight relationships (H–W, F–S, F–D, M–S, M–D, B–B, Z–Z, B–Z) (Bohannan 1963: 73), as a system of specific kinship statuses (father/husband, mother/wife, brother/son, sister/daughter), or as a combination of conjugal or sexual dyad and maternal dyad whose linking together generates the paternal dyad and the sibling dyad (Adams 1960: 39).

As far as the ascription of specific functions to the household is concerned, anthropologists differ as much as they differ in the ascription of functions to the family. It is, however, much more difficult to define household in purely formal terms than it is to define the nuclear family. All the distinctions between family and household draw on residential propinquity as the defining criterion of the household. It would be possible to define household in terms of this criterion, if the boundaries of households could be specified in a way which would

be universally applicable cross-culturally. But this is by no means the
case. As Yanagisako points out, concentrating on residential propinquity
as the defining criterion of the household does not solve the problem of

how to treat residential groupings that move through a seasonal cycle of dispersal
and concentration, how to handle the movement of personnel between
dwelling units, particularly in societies where there is great mobility between
these units, whether to define as a single household the huts or houses that
share a common yard, which may or may not be enclosed from other yards,
and whether to include servants, apprentices, boarders, and lodgers as members
of the household. Certainly there are discrepancies in our usage of the term
household if its sole referent is residential propinquity. Why then do we regard
solitaries (individuals living alone) as constituting households, while we
exclude institutions like orphanages, boarding schools, men's houses and army
barracks? (1979: 164)

Goody has emphasised that domestic organisation does not focus
exclusively on 'one multi-functional unit which emerges in all domestic
situations. There are a number of such units which appear in different
situations' and which he calls 'domestic groups'. One of them is the
'dwelling group' which forms the 'inclusive setting' for the other groups
which emerge in 'the two basic processes of production and
reproduction' (1958: 56). In a similar attempt to avoid the association
of the term 'household' with specific domestic functions, Bender
considers it useful 'to distinguish between co-residential groups and
domestic functions. Co-residential groups have as their referent
propinquity, domestic functions have as their referent social functions'
(1967: 495) and 'are concerned with day-to-day necessities of living,
including the provision and preparation of food and the care of
children' (1967: 499). These two approaches thus distinguish three social
phenomena which may vary independently: families, co-residential
groups and domestic activities or functions. They obviate the difficulty
of distinguishing households from other co-residential groups and of
deciding on what should be treated as the basic co-residential group
in any particular society. For example, Bender is able to identify two
kinds of co-residential groups among the Mundurucu. One is formed
by adult males who live in men's houses and the other consists of a
woman and her children. Once we stop searching for a 'household'
in Mundurucu society, we also stop making any unwarranted assumption
that either of these co-residential groups is the most important group
charged with the performance of domestic functions. As the domestic

activities are mostly performed in a way which involves adult males as a group and adult females as a group, 'the whole village forms the domestic unit, the sexual division of labor in domestic activities being at the village level' (1967: 495).

However, even after analytically distinguishing families, co-residential groups and domestic activities or functions as independent variables, the problem of defining what precisely are 'domestic' activities or functions remains. All the various definitions which have been proffered so far in anthropology concentrate on activities pertaining to food production and consumption and on those pertaining to social reproduction including nurturance and rearing of children (Fortes 1958, 1978, Goody 1958, 1972, Bender 1967, Smith 1973, Hammel and Laslett 1974, Yanagisako 1979, Moore 1988). There is no doubt that these definitions are influenced by the culture-specific Western conceptualisation of the 'domestic' and 'public' or the specifically Western differentiation between 'home' and 'work'. Such differentiation is, to a great extent, the product of nineteenth-century social theory and the late nineteenth- and early twentieth-century ideology which accorded different rights to men and women within the 'domestic' and the 'public' spheres. That ideology asserted that men were to govern the public sphere of politics, work and business, and women the home (Coward 1983: 56).

Notwithstanding the difficulties in defining 'domestic' activities or functions in a way which would be cross-culturally applicable, the analytical distinction between families, co-residential groups and particular activities which they perform, enables us to describe, in the societies studied, the functions of the groups which we normally call families and households, rather than to ascribe to them such functions on the basis of our own cultural assumptions.

VARIATION IN DOMESTIC GROUPS

Defining the 'nuclear family', not by ascribing to it specific functions or activities but in purely formal terms, has an apparent drawback in that it tends to postulate the family as a distinct, static and durable social unit which can be distinguished and separated from other units of the same kind. It engenders a view of society as a static structure of discrete units which can be enumerated and whose interrelationships can be analysed and eventually compared with the units and their inter-relationships distinguishable in other societies. But the network of relationships which we call society is far from static. It is in a constant flux and change resulting from the fact that human beings, whose mutual relationships constitute society, are born, mature, procreate and age before they eventually die. In different stages of their life cycle, they are involved in different patterns of social relationships. We can appreciate this ever-changing pattern of relationships by looking at families not as the building blocks of social structure but as units which people create in the process of their social life. If we retain the notion of the family as a group whose members occupy specific kinship statuses or are bound by specific kinship relationships, it follows that these statuses or relationships change during the span of one's life. A woman who has the status of a daughter or a sister in one set of relationships which constitute her family, later assumes the status of a mother or wife in a different set of such relationships. This recognition lies at the root of the distinction between the 'family of orientation' and the 'family of procreation' (Parsons and Bales 1955), or the distinction between the 'natal' and 'conjugal' family (Bohannan 1963: 100). The natal family is the family in which a person was born and reared and which includes his or her parents and siblings, and the conjugal family is the family which people have founded through their marriages and which includes their spouses and children. Although the distinction between the natal and the conjugal family still ultimately reduces the perpetual process of the creation, development and demise of families to static family types (Robertson 1991: 195–6, n. 15), it nevertheless makes it clear that families are not unambiguously bounded units. A married woman in Western society may think of herself as having left her previous family and having started a family of her own after she married. Although in most cases she lives on her own with her husband and children, who are her family, she is still bound through ties of filiation and siblingship to members of her natal family which remains significant in a whole range of activities in which she is involved. In specific contexts she may thus think of herself as a member of two families. Her Hopi counterpart would not think of herself as having two families because even after her marriage she would remain a member of the same family as before. Her husband and children would just simply be added to her family which typically consists of her parents, her sisters with their husbands and their married daughters and unmarried sons, and may include even her mother's sisters and their married daughters. If such a variation exists in the composition of families in different societies, how do we draw the boundary around these units without falling back onto the criterion of co-residence of their members and thus blurring once again the distinction between the family and the co-residential group?

If we are to retain the distinction between the family as a kinship group and household as a co-residential group, the only possible solution is to see as family that kinship group which the members of any particular society themselves identify as the culturally meaningful kinship unit of their society. However, in many societies no semantic distinction is made between the units which we analytically distinguish as families and households. For example, the Berti of the Sudan have only one term by which they denote both these groups: *bēt* (lit. house). This is a polysemic term which in a certain context denotes a homestead, that is, a cluster of huts and other structures surrounded by a straw fence and physically bounded from other homesteads which together form a village. In another context it refers to the inhabitants of the homestead who constitute a household and in yet another context it denotes a group consisting of a married couple and their children who in many, but by no means all cases, inhabit their separate homestead and constitute a household. It would be wrong to deduce that the Berti do not make a conceptual distinction between the family and household and that family does not exist as a culturally meaningful unit in their society. Even if they do not make the distinction between the family and household semantically, they still conceptually differentiate them as different systems of rights and duties through their actions (Holy and Stuchlik 1983: 63). For example, irrespective of whether they live together in the same homestead or not, the members of a nuclear family always keep the livestock, which they own individually, in one common herd. Children who live in a homestead different from that in which other members of their family live, tend the herd belonging to the members of the family in whose homestead they live; they do that not because they are tied to them by particular relations of kinship, but because they are members of their household. They keep their own livestock together with that of their siblings and parents and their livestock may be tended by some members of their parental household who are not their familial kin. It is not just ties of kinship as opposed to the ties of propinquity which determine in which herd one keeps one's cattle. The fact that not *any* close kinsmen but only married couples and their children keep their animals in a common herd clearly indicates that a nuclear family is recognised by the Berti as a culturally meaningful kinship unit of their society in spite of the fact that they have no special word for it. The Berti are not unique in this respect. The Nuer term *gol* (Evans-Pritchard 1951: 3) is as polysemic as the Berti term *bet*, as indeed is the English term 'family' for that matter. Whether in everyday usage the English term 'family' is used to denote a nuclear family or a more inclusive circle of relatives can only be decided contextually.

The procedure of equating family with the group which the natives themselves identify as the culturally meaningful kinship group has one predictable outcome. It is most likely to result in discovering that there are many kinds of families but no universal family (Yanagisako 1979: 198). Marriage appears central to the creation of these different kinds of families.

Because the rule of monogamy, which stipulates that a man may be married to only one woman and a woman to only one man at a time, has been the prevalent norm in European and many Asian societies, we have a tendency to regard a marriage union which results from this rule as the 'natural' one. But in many societies marriage is not so narrowly restricted and plural marriage (polygamy) is not only allowed but often considered an ideal form of a marriage union. Polygamy has two forms: polygyny – a simultaneous marriage of one man to two or more women, and polyandry – a simultaneous marriage of one woman to two or more men.

Polyandry is practised only in a handful of societies and the best accounts of it come from the Himalayas and Tibet where marriages of one woman to two or more brothers (so-called fraternal polyandry) occur, especially among the rich taxpayers. The reason for the existence of a polyandrous family constituting itself as a householding unit is probably to restrict the number of heirs and to adjust the size of the labour force to the amount of agricultural land, which is in short supply in the harsh mountainous environment. As a woman can become pregnant about every two years or so irrespective of how many husbands she has, fraternal polyandry ensures the perpetuation of families while simultaneously avoiding their expansion in size. If brothers married independently and each established a separate household after his marriage, the tendency to divide the family land would be much greater than when they share the reproductive capacity of one woman whose sons will jointly inherit the land and through their own polyandrous marriage to one woman pass it in turn undivided to their own sons (Goldstein 1971, Berreman 1978, Levine 1987, 1988, Schuler 1987, Goody 1990: 137–53).

Polyandry cannot result in the creation of separate households of husbands and their children for a woman who is married to several husbands cannot have a child with each of them at once. A polyandrous family is thus always a co-residential group and forms a single household in which co-husbands pool their labour. While polyandry seems to arise in very particular circumstances, polygyny is much more widespread and Africa in particular is the continent in which many men see it as an ideal form of a marriage union. Boserup (1970) linked the prevalence of polygyny in Africa and monogamy in all the major societies of Europe and Asia with the differences in the availability of land and labour and with the differences in the sex of agricultural labour. Until recently, land has been abundant in Africa and labour to work it has been scarce whereas many areas of Europe and Asia have suffered an acute shortage of land. In Africa, where the hoe is the main agricultural implement, most agricultural work is done by women whereas in the plough agriculture of Europe and Asia, it is predominantly men who farm. Men's tendency to accumulate wives is thus an optimum strategy in the situation where the critical factor of the economy is not shortage of land but shortage of labour and where that labour is female rather than male. Goody (1973b) acknowledges a high correlation between societies in which women farm and those with high rates of polygyny but points out that the critical consideration may be not the labour of the woman herself but of her children and he suggests that since maximum fertility is the optimum strategy under these conditions, men may desire to accumulate wives for reproductive purposes.

Even in societies in which polygyny rates are quite high, the majority of people still form monogamous unions. There may be social factors responsible for this for, as Mair observed, polygyny is not only a means to wealth but also 'the privilege of wealth' (1971: 153) and in many societies only men with high social and economic status can afford to be married to more than one woman. But primarily demographic factors underlie the fact that monogamous unions prevail even where polygyny is preferred or considered ideal. Unless skewed by female infanticide or the killing of men in war, the number of women and men is roughly equal in any given population. This means that if one man is married to two women, another man has of necessity to remain a bachelor. Without causing some men to remain single, the existence of polygyny is made possible by two factors. First, the marriage age of women is usually lower, and often considerably lower, than that of men, which means that at any given time there are more marriageable women in the population than there are men. Second, the high frequency of divorce enables the majority of men to be married at least during some stage of their lives, and at the same time it enables a certain number of men to be married to two or more women simultaneously.

The usual practice of estimating the polygyny rate by counting the number of wives in extant marriages does not give a very accurate impression of the actual prevalence of polygyny. Among the Berti, 80 per cent of men had only one wife at the time of my census, and only 20 per cent were polygynously married. One might easily conclude from these figures that only one man in five can actually afford to have more than one wife and that the polygyny rate is not conspicuously high. But 28.7 per cent of men I questioned were polygynous at least during a certain time of their life and only 71.3 per cent had been monogamous throughout their whole life. The proportion of polygynous unions was greater among the older than among the younger men. This is understandable because, as they grew older, men found a greater number of women whom they could marry, like middle-aged divorcees and widows whom young men would not marry. Among the men with married children of their own, 58.5 per cent were monogamists and 41.5 per cent polygynists at the time of my census. Only 40.3 per cent of the older men in my sample had always been monogamous while 59.7 had at some time in their life had two or more wives. In other words, three out of five men were likely to experience polygyny throughout the course of their lives.

The polygynous family contains relationships which do not arise in a nuclear family: those betwen co-wives, those between half-siblings (that is, children of the same father and different mothers), and those between a woman and the children of her co-wives. In consequence, problems of interpersonal relations arise in a polygynous family which do not exist in a nuclear family and the frequency of witchcraft accusations in many African polygynous societies is their clear expression. The problems specific to polygynous families concern the co-wives' access to resources, their relative power, conflicting economic interest with regard to their children and, possibly, sexual jealousy. The half-siblings, too, may have different and conflicting interests with regard to their mutual rights and their relation to their common father and different mothers. A whole range of cultural solutions to these problems is common in all societies with polygynous families. Often one wife, usually the one whom the husband married first, has a higher status than her co-wives and allocates domestic duties and economic tasks to them. The relations between co-wives are more likely to be amicable if the husband cannot be seen as favouring any of them over the others. He is usually expected to spend equal time with each of them and to move from one to another after an agreed interval and in an agreed order.

Since one of the main reasons for polygyny is the creation of a joint workforce and pooling of the productive efforts of several women, it is ideal for the polygynous family to form a single household in which all the co-wives share the burden of the domestic work. But very often this is the case only when they are sisters and when it can be expected that they can manage to live in the same household as they did in their childhood. In most cases, co-wives do not share a single household and hearth. For example, among the Tallensi, each co-wife has her own courtyard, her own sleeping room and her own kitchen in her husband's homestead. Only her children and her husband have free access to her living quarters. She cooks separately in her kitchen for herself, her children and her husband, when it is her turn to feed him and to sleep with him. The household of each wife is thus a distinct economic unit in the sphere of preparation and consumption of food. The economic role of the polygynous family as a whole is epitomised by the single granary in each homestead, which is under the husband's control. The household of each of his wives receives its supplies from it and in turn it helps to fill it with the produce of its labour (Fortes 1949a). The separation of the co-wives' households can be marked even more strongly. Among the Berti, each wife has her own homestead in which she lives with her children and the husband periodically shifts his residence between them. To diminish the possibility of any conflict beween co-wives, their homesteads are usually in different villages. Each wife cultivates her own field and keeps the produce in her granary. She uses it to cook for herself, her children and her husband when he stays in her homestead. The husband works for an equal time in the fields of all his wives and carries out any other work in the household of that wife with whom he momentarily stays.

Anthropologists who considered the nuclear family to be the building block of all existing family forms, conceptualised the polygynous family as a group which comes into being by joining together two or more conjugal families of one man. The husband was seen as being simultaneously a member of two or more nuclear families. To avoid the underlying assumption that the nuclear family is a universal social group which exists in all societies either as such or as a building block of more complex family forms, some anthropologists saw the polygynous family as composed of two or more mother–child units attached to a common man (Bohannan 1963: 105–6, Bender 1971: 226). However, the principle underlying the formation of various family forms cannot be universally formulated in terms of joining together either nuclear families or mother–child units. Because there is only one matricentric family in the polyandrous situation, the polyandrous family cannot be seen as the result of joining together either several nuclear families or several mother–child units (Bohannan 1963: 110).

Social groups which are usually classified as 'extended families' or 'joint families' have also been seen as resulting from linking together two or more nuclear families. When the man's conjugal family does not separate itself from his natal family, the resulting group is variously described as a patrilocal extended family (because the woman lives after her marriage with her husband, that is, patrilocally), or as a patrilineal, agnatic, or patrilineally extended family (because the linking of the two nuclear families is through a male and the extension is thus through a relationship traced in the male line). Among the Tiv, people who live together in the same compound and who form together one productive group constitute such a family. It consists of a man, his wives and children, his unmarried daughters and his married sons with their wives and children. Each wife in the compound has a separate hut in which she cooks for herself, her children and husband. Although the nuclear families, which are linked together to form an extended family, constitute separate units of consumption, the whole extended family acts as a joint productive group. It is under the authority of the oldest man who acts as its head, supervises production, arbitrates disputes among its members and through ritual control of magical forces protects the well-being of all its members (Bohannan and Bohannan 1968).

When two nuclear families are joined through a woman who is a wife and mother in one of them and a daughter and sister in the other, the result is a group usually described as a matrilocal extended family (because the husband moves after his marriage to the home of his wife, that is, resides matrilocally) or a matrilineal, or matrilineally extended family (because the linking of the two nuclear families is through a female and the extension is thus through a relationship traced in the female line). Groups like this existed, for example, among the Hopi Indians. A man joined his wife's natal household after his marriage and became a member of an extended family which consisted of his mother-in-law and possibly her husband, if he was still alive, her daughters with their husbands and children, and her unmarried sons.

In some societies, both sons and daughters can remain living at home after their marriage and become connecting links between their conjugal families and their natal family. The result is the bilocal or bilateral extended family which combines the nuclear family of the parents with nuclear families of some, but not all, of their sons, some, but not all, of their daughters, and possibly some of their grandchildren. Bilocal extended families do not occur as frequently as patrilocal or matrilocal extended families and the *bilek* of the Iban of Borneo is probably their best-known example.

In much ethnographic description as well as theoretical discussion, 'extended' or 'joint family' is a very ambiguous term because it is not always clearly specified in precisely what sense the natal and conjugal families are not separated, or in what sense they remain joined together. The variation in the way in which they remain joined can be quite considerable. The two or more nuclear families can inhabit a single homestead and thus form a co-residential unit, or a 'houseful' as Goody calls it (1990: 88, 211–12), as is the case among the Tiv, Hopi or Iban. When the members of the extended family are a co-residential group, they may constitute one undivided unit of production and consumption and thus form one single household. In that case the personnel of an extended family is coterminous with an extended or joint household in which all belongings may be held in common and which may operate a common fund for living expenses and incomes. But even when the members of an extended family reside together, each nuclear family within it can have its own household, at least in the sense of being a unit which differentiates itself in the preparation and consumption of food. Like a nuclear family, an extended family can also exist as a culturally meaningful unit even when it does not constitute a co-residential group. For example, in many parts of India, particularly among the high castes, sons usually form separate households after marriage but not necessarily separate productive units and they continue to farm as one joint family. An extended family jointly controlling its common property can exist as a culturally meaningful unit even when its members are widely dispersed, like, for example, when one brother goes into trade outside India and sends money into the family fund to be invested back home (Goody 1990: 211–13).

The possible conceptual confusion between extended families, extended households and co-residential groups is typified by the 'stem family', best known from the research of Arensberg and Kimball in County Clare in Ireland (1968). To prevent the fragmentation of the family estate, only one of the sons lived on the farm with his parents after he had reached adulthood. Often he was able to marry only when he was well into his 40s for he could have done so only after his parents handed the management of the farm to him and retired to the 'west room' of the house where they were provided for by him and his wife. Upon the death of his father, the son was the sole inheritor of the farm. His brothers and sisters, who moved out of the farm, received financial compensation, often paid from the dowry with which the new bride was endowed. The brothers who left the family farm and were prevented from marrying, often joined the army or the church, or migrated overseas.

Although the responsibility for the maintenance of the parents in a stem family falls upon the son who has inherited the family farm, it does not follow that their respective conjugal families have to form a joint household, because the elderly couple may constitute a separate unit of consumption, or even a joint co-residential group, because they may live in a separate dwelling from that of the son. Like 'nuclear family', the terms 'extended', 'joint' or 'stem' family thus also cover a whole range of different residential and householding arrangements. When used as a blanket term in the classification of family forms, they may hide more than they reveal.

When employed in the taxonomy of family forms, the terms 'extended' or 'joint' family are problematic for yet another reason. Unlike nuclear or polygamous families, which consist of members of two generations only, extended families expand vertically to include more generations and they consist of members of at least three or more of them. If expanding continuously by incorporating additional nuclear families in each generation, the extended family would eventually reach a point when it would outgrow its resources. It would then come to its fission, as a rule triggered off by quarrels and disputes among its members. These usually follow the death of the most senior man who occupied the position of the family head and who may be the last of a group of brothers whose sons, grandchildren and great-grandchildren all lived together in a single patrilocal extended household. He will be succeeded in his position by one of his sons but his other sons may not be willing to recognise the successor's authority and would prefer to move out of the original household and to establish households of their own. The unit which remains in the original household as well as that which moves out to set up its independent household, may both consist of a man, his wife and their married son or sons and their conjugal families and thus themselves have a character of extended families right from the beginning. But one of these units may consist solely of a married couple with their small children and thus be a group which we would classify as a nuclear family. Eventually, when the sons marry, they may not separate their conjugal families from their natal ones, which as a result would thus again become extended. Hence a nuclear family may be only a temporary phase in the developmental cycle of an extended family. Once we take into consideration the cycle of development of domestic groups, that is, the process of their continuous establishment, expansion and fission, it becomes obvious that extended families cannot be seen as distinct types or forms of domestic groups but rather, as Fortes put it, 'variations of a single "form"' (1949b: 75). Although originally developed to account for the dynamics of domestic groups in simple, pre-industrial societies, the concept of the developmental cycle has been successfully applied to the study of families and households in Europe (Laslett and Wall 1972, Netting, Wilk and Arnould 1984) and to the study of the social organisation of reproduction in pre-industrial as well as capitalist societies (Robertson 1991).

The recognition of the ethnocentric assumptions underlying the distinction between the 'domestic' and 'public' has been the main reason why the dichotomy between the 'domestic domain' and the 'public domain' came to be critically scrutinised in feminist writing. A long time ago, Rosaldo pointed out that the division into domestic and political spheres is the product of Western ideology with its underlying gender bias (1980: 406n.) and La Fontaine argued that such division is by no means made in all societies. Even in those societies in which it is made, it is 'not a description of structural cleavages but a symbolic statement whose meaning we must interpret in each instance where we find it' (1981: 346). The usefulness of the distinction between the 'domestic' and the 'public' domain has been criticised by many more anthropologists inspired by feminist theory (Rogers 1978, Tilly and Scott 1978, Rapp 1979, Yanagisako 1979, Rosaldo 1980, Strathern 1984, Burton 1985, Yanagisako and Collier 1987, Moore 1988). There is hence a distinct irony in the fact that it is kinship relations within the 'domestic domain' that have recently been brought into analytical prominence through feminist-inspired research. The reason for this move stems of course from the fact that a large part of women's lives and work, on which this research concentrates, is directly affected by the system of relations within the domestic sphere. This feminist-inspired research has shown at the same time that this system of relations is far from autonomous and that it is always affected by the political and economic relations of the 'public' sphere (see, for example, LaFontaine 1990, Whatmore 1991).

4   DESCENT AND THE PUBLIC DOMAIN I: LINEAGE THEORY

The main question to which the functionalist anthropologists sought to provide an answer was the question of what integrates society. As 'primitive' societies which anthropologists studied were seen as kinship based, the particular integration of primitive society must have been based on some aspect of their kinship system. British anthropologists 'took the kin relationships to be the locus of "law" or "rules" in tribal societies' (Wagner 1974: 101). Concentrating attention on the 'law' or the jural aspect of kin relationships was made possible by drawing the distinction between the domestic domain and the public domain. While the domestic domain was seen as regulated by the moral norms of interpersonal kinship, the public domain was seen as a domain in which jural rules applied. It was these rules which were seen as regulating relations between groups and binding them together into a society. As groups were seen as segments of society, they had to be clearly bounded. This condition was satisfied if they were unilineal descent groups.

In the heyday of structural-functionalism, the study of unilineal descent groups occupied a prominent place especially in the work of British social anthropologists and the recognition of the importance of unilineal descent as a principle of social structure has often been hailed as one of the most fruitful ideas of social anthropology as it developed in Britain in the middle of this century (Fortes 1953, Mair 1965: 67). Many monographs written by anthropologists at that time were concerned with societies whose social structure rested on a system of unilineal descent groups, creating the impression that most societies were so organised.

Tracing the historical development of descent or lineage theory, as it came subsequently to be known, Kuper (1982) noted that although it was presented as the most important theoretical achievement of British

71

structural-functional anthropology, it was in fact a transformation of the theoretical problems postulated by the nineteenth-century precursors of kinship studies, particularly Maine and Morgan. These early theorists focused much of their attention on the investigation of the relations between kinship and territory and of the relations between the family as a group based on bilaterally traced kinship and 'clan' or 'gens' as a group based on unilaterally traced kinship. Investigation of these relations was part of the main problem which occupied them, namely the problem of the constitution of primitive polity and of the evolution of the political order of human society. According to Maine (1861), in the earliest stages of history, human society was based on extended ties of kinship which only later came to be replaced by ties of territoriality as the basis of the political organisation of society:

The history of political ideas begins, in fact, with the assumption that kinship in blood is the sole possible ground of community in political functions; nor is there any of those subversions of feeling, which we term emphatically revolutions, so startling and so complete as the change which is accomplished when some other principle – such as that, for instance, of *local contiguity* – establishes itself for the first time as the basis of common political action. (1861: 106)

Morgan similarly maintained that all forms of government are basically of two kinds which follow each other in an evolutionary sequence:

The first, in the order of time, is founded upon persons and upon relations purely personal, and may be distinguished as a society (societas). The gens is the unit of this organization .... The second is founded upon territory and upon property, and may be distinguished as a state (civitas). (1877: 6–7)

Unlike their Victorian predecessors, British anthropologists of the mid-twentieth century were no longer interested in the problems of the evolution of human society, which had by then been dismissed as 'conjectural history'. They asked themselves the question of how society is constituted and how its various institutions are mutually interrelated and thus keep it together. In their view, society came to be seen as representing a systemic order. It came to be conceptualised as a system of interrelated parts which, on analysis, should be revealed as possessing some kind of a structure. By then, ethnographic evidence was already available which showed that territorial and descent groups coexisted within the same society. Kinship and territorial bonds, on which Maine and Morgan focused their attention, were interrelated. To find out precisely how society was structured led to asking the question of precisely how they interacted.

Society manifests itself, of course, in what its members do and in consequence the social structure of society had to be formulated by anthropologists through various processes of abstraction from their observation of actions of actual individuals (Radcliffe-Brown 1952: 129). However it was not these actions which were seen as in need of explanation. What needed to be explained was how society is structured and how it works or functions. On explanation, the concrete behaviour of individuals was seen as determined by demands of the social structure. To be able to treat it as such, groups which constituted society needed to be associated with systems of activities. The result of this endeavour was a formulation of corporate groups normatively performing certain activities and a conception of certain activities as performed by members of a specific group. The structure of society was conceptualised as the 'relations between groups of persons within a system of groups' (Evans-Pritchard 1940: 262). The group was conceptualised 'as persons who regard themselves as a distinct unit in relation to other units, are so regarded by members of these other units, and who all have reciprocal obligations in virtue of their membership of it' (1940: 262–3).

In this model of social structure as the system of discrete groups each of which performs a certain set of activities, the factors which determined the behaviour of individuals were identical with the factors which formed social structure. To be able to ascribe activities to groups, the groups which formed the components of the structure had to be discrete, clearly bounded and not overlapping, and with unambiguous membership; they had to be segments. It is obvious from this conceptualisation of the social structure and the group that kinship relations could not have been envisaged as a structuring principle because kinship does not provide the basis for the formation of enduring groups which could act as units in relation to other units of the same kind or, in other words, form clearly bounded and mutually separated segments of the whole society. Only descent provides such a basis because those who are unilineally descended from a common ancestor form a distinct group which, unlike an ego-centrically defined kinship category, is clearly bounded and exclusive. One either is or is not a member of a specific unilineal descent group and, moreover, one is a member of only one such group and cannot be simultaneously a member of two or more. For these reasons Radcliffe-Brown ascribed the unilineal forms of organisation to 'certain basic social necessities', which are, for example, a need for an exact formulation of rights to prevent conflicts and a need for the continuity of social structure which defines such rights. To achieve its continuity, every society needs the organisation of corporations which transcend individual persons. In kinship-based societies, unilineal descent groups constitute such corporations since only unilineal groups unambiguously define group membership (Radcliffe-Brown 1935). Radcliffe-Brown went as far as to assert that 'there are few, if any societies, in which there is not some recognition of unilineal descent' (1950: 14).

The theoretical assumptions of the structural approach led not only to the ascription of primary importance to the concept of descent but also determined the way in which descent was defined. The definition of descent as employed by structural analysts goes back to the work of Rivers, who distinguished it analytically from inheritance and succession and defined it as the process regulating membership of a social group or class either through the father or through the mother (1915: 851, 1924: 85–8). Implied in his definition is the notion that the term 'descent' should be used only in reference to groups to which recruitment occurs automatically by virtue of birth, and which are exclusive in membership, clearly bounded and do not overlap. In this usage then, descent was defined as a principle of recruitment into unilineal descent groups (Leach 1962: 130).

The difficulty of drawing a sharp analytical distinction between kinship and descent was one of the problems involved in the anthropological analyses of descent systems. A lot of analytical confusion also resulted from a rather promiscuous use of the notions of 'group' and 'corporateness'. The concept of 'group' has featured prominently in anthropology and sociology because of these disciplines' focus on social relationships that are habitual, institutionalised and relatively enduring. Group has been used in many different ways, but it commonly refers to a plurality of individuals bounded by some principle of recruitment and by a set of membership rights and obligations. In this conceptualisation, everyone fulfilling the recruitment criteria is a member of the group and has a specific status in the group, and every group member automatically has the rights and discharges the obligations of membership. As descent rules are specific criteria of recruitment, the units to which people are recruited on the basis of these criteria have traditionally been conceptualised as groups. Groups, in turn, were seen as the main elements of social structure.

In the structural model, the descent group has the identity of a single individual when viewed from outside or in relation to the jural-political sphere; it has an estate consisting of joint rights in material or immaterial property or differential privileges, and the relations within it are relations of incorporation and sharing. Not only is the recruitment of individuals into groups structurally determined by their descent, but also by their unquestionable and enduring loyalty to the group. Individuals derive their main social identity from their membership of the group. The concept of the unilineal descent group refers to formal jural criteria; in consequence, the rules governing each individual's behaviour *qua* member of the group, as well as the intergroup relationships, are envisaged as having jural force (Fortes 1953, 1959). This approach to the conceptualisation of segments of the total social system arbitrarily seizes upon descent as one aspect of social life and gives it an inflated importance that may far outweigh its significance for ongoing social processes. LaFontaine, in her defence of the structural model, explicitly advocated this approach in the following way:

It is clear that the principle of descent ... is a means of allocating membership of segments of society. That is, an individual is placed within the society into which he is born by reference to his membership of a segment of it. It underlies the allocation of status, including political privileges and liabilities, and often legitimizes rights to various forms of property. (1973: 36)

In British usage, the unilineal descent groups are called lineages and clans, the distinction between the two being purely a formal one. A lineage is usually taken to be a group of people who trace descent unilineally from a common ancestor through a series of links which can be enumerated; clan is a group based on the same principle but its members only presume to be descended from a common ancestor, whom they usually consider to be so remote that they are not able to stipulate the precise genealogical links through which they are descended from him. Where clans are recognised, they usually consist of several lineages.

The personnel of a lineage of course changes over time as the members of the oldest generation gradually die out and the members of a new generation are born. But the death of the oldest generation does not mean the end of the lineage; the personnel of the lineage is perpetually replenished and the lineage thus becomes a permanent social unit, resembling in this respect other corporations. This led many anthropologists to ascribe 'corporateness' to unilineal descent groups, often without specifying precisely what this term implies or using the notion of corporateness in a very broad sense intended to apply to a wide range of diverse societies (Barnard and Good 1984: 76). This practice led Keesing to observe that 'the anthropological literature is full of confusion about "clans" and "lineages" and "kindreds" where [the] distinctions between groups and categories, corporations and action groups, have been blurred or overlooked' (1975: 11). As I shall discuss later, a rigorous application of such distinctions has much advanced our understanding of the principle of descent and particularly our understanding of the difference between cognatic descent and the presumably universal kinship traced bilaterally.

The process of the perpetual replenishment of lineage personnel over time has important consequences for the internal structure of a lineage. Any time a new generation of lineage members is added, the lineage grows numerically bigger and bigger. This expansion may reach the stage when the lineage becomes so numerous that it outgrows its resources or that it becomes no longer possible effectively to manage its affairs. The lineage then has to split up. The process whereby sublineages are formed is known as lineage segmentation. Segmentation generally takes place along the cleavages or lines of fission implicit in the lineage itself. For example, a patrilineal lineage is most likely to split into two parts in terms of descent from one or the other of its founder's sons.

Not only the original or main lineage splits in this way into two or several sublineages. The sub-lineages themselves segment into sub-sublineages when they grow too numerous and the sub-sub-lineages themselves segment in their own turn. In this way, the segmentation of a lineage becomes virtually an automatic process. The most usual metaphor to describe a segmented lineage is that of a tree and its branches. The tree is the main lineage, the branches are its sub-lineages and the twigs are the lineages into which the sublineage itself is divided. The twigs can themselves be further segmented into leaves. Various societies use different metaphors. The Tallensi, for example, describe a lineage of any order as the house (*yir*) of the founding ancestor and they designate any segment of a more inclusive lineage as a room (*dug*). The designation of a lineage as a house or room is relative. In one context, the whole lineage may be described as the house of its founding ancestor and be seen as internally divided into separate rooms. In another context, the sub-lineages may themselves be described as houses named after their founding ancestors and their segments may be referred to as rooms. Lineages may also be described as the children (*biis*) of the founding ancestor. Lineage segments of the same order are then described as 'brother' lineages and their rights and duties with respect to one another are modelled on the mutual relations of brothers. In a similar way, lineages may be seen as being related to one another as 'mother's brother' and 'sister's son'. Tallensi thus employ kinship terms to describe genealogical and social relations between lineages as such. The relations between the branches of a segmented Tallensi lineage are brought out best in ancestor worship. Thus lineage segments worship their respective founding ancestors and they combine to worship the common ancestor of the whole lineage. Thus ancestor worship provides what Fortes called the 'calculus of the lineage system' (1949a). This process of lineage segmentation is modelled on the relations existing within a nuclear family or, more precisely, on the relations between father and sons and between brothers.

Another system of segmentation of a patrilineal lineage is modelled on the relations within a polygynous family. Thus a lineage may be subdivided into two sub-lineages, where the members of one of the sub-lineages are considered to be the descendants of the sons of one of the wives of the lineage founder, whereas the members of the other sub-lineage are considered to be the descendants of the sons of the lineage founder's other wife. This is a pattern of segmentation which exists, for example, among the Nuer. It prompted Evans-Pritchard to say that among the patrilineal Nuer, the descent is paradoxically traced through a woman: whereas the whole lineage forms a unity because its members are all patrilineally descended from its founding ancestor, the sub-lineages form mutually distinct units with respect to one another because their members are descended from different wives of the lineage founder.

THE SEGMENTARY LINEAGE STRUCTURE AND ITS EXISTENTIAL STATUS

Although Radcliffe-Brown was the first to formulate the basic principles of lineage theory, Evans-Pritchard was the first to interpret his ethnographic material in its terms and portrayed the Nuer society (1940) as one governed by the lineage principle. The Nuer became the 'paradigmatic case', or a concrete ideal type, of a society with the segmentary lineage structure. The smallest segments, associated with particular villages, were minimal lineages – groups of agnatically related men who were all descendants in a patrilineal line from a common ancestor, from four to six generations in ascent from the present day. A minor lineage, associated with a particular tribal area which Evans-Pritchard called the tertiary section, consisted of a number of minimal lineages, again descended from a common ancestor. These minor lineages might join to form a major lineage, associated with a secondary tribal section, and major lineages formed in a similar way a maximal lineage, associated with the primary tribal section. Several maximal lineages together formed a clan, the largest descent group, and each clan was associated with a particular tribe, which was the largest territorial and political unit that the Nuer recognised. This lineage system provided an idiom in terms of which the territorial political relations were articulated. If a man from one village killed a man from another village belonging to the same tertiary section, the two villages were forced into confrontation, the opposition between them being defined in terms of the minimal lineages dominant in these two villages. If a man in either of these two villages was killed by a man from another tertiary section, all the villages of his tertiary section united against all the villages in the killer's tertiary section. Their fusion was again defined in terms of the opposition between the two minor lineages dominant in the two sections. This principle of 'fission and fusion' operated at all levels of segmentation so that eventually one Nuer tribe could be united as a whole in a conflict with another Nuer tribe.

The concept of the segmentary lineage has been developed as a model of empirically observable social processes. It

contains a theory of social cohesion.... The idea underlying the theory is that the functions of maintaining cohesion, social control, some degree of 'law and order', which normally depend largely on specialised agencies with sanctions at their disposal, can be performed with tolerable efficiency, simply by the 'balancing' and 'opposition' of constituent groups. (Gellner 1969: 42)

That the segmentary lineage structure is a representation of ongoing social processes is implied in those classifications which distinguish it as a specific type of a political system (Fortes and Evans-Pritchard 1940,

Middleton and Tait 1958). The view that the concept of the segmentary lineage structure has a substance in behavioural reality has been subscribed to, with qualifications, by Gellner (1969: 62–3) and particularly by Salzman (1978), who argues that even in societies where the dictates of the segmentary lineage structure are not always followed in action, the lineage ideology can, nevertheless, be seen as having some constraining effect on action. Fortes has gone even further and postulated a direct relationship between the segmentary lineage structure and the observable social processes. In reference to the Tallensi, he says that the

Tale society is built up round the lineage system .... It is the skeleton of their social structure, the bony framework which shapes their body politic; it guides their economic life and moulds their ritual ideas and values. (Fortes 1945: 30)

He says of the Nuer, the Tallensi and the Tiv that they

may be said to think agnatically about social relations, like the Romans and the Chinese .... The paradigm of patrilineal descent is not just a means of picturing their social structure; it is their fundamental guide to conduct and belief in all areas of their social life. (Fortes 1969: 290–1)

Sahlins's argument that the segmentary lineage system is an organisation of predatory expansion and a social means of intrusion and competition in an already occupied ecological niche, derives directly from the assumption that the segmentary lineage structure depicts the ongoing social processes. Sahlins explicitly maintains that segmentary sociability is a salient mechanism of the political process in segmentary lineage systems 'operating automatically to determine the level of collective political action' (Sahlins 1961: 332, see also Kelly 1985). Turton has subsequently argued that lineality is not a necessary feature of a system in which segments 'mass' for external opposition and that the observed expansion of one ethnic group at the expense of its neighbours does not necessarily have anything to do with military effectiveness which, according to Sahlins, segmentary lineage organisation produces. He suggests that the whole problem of territorial expansion might be misconstrued by ascribing an unreal temporal and spatial permanence to the ethnic groups considered (Turton 1979).

On closer inspection, it therefore appears that the assumption that the segmentary lineage structure is a representation of empirically observable social processes is not that well founded.

Most of the available case histories of hostilities between Nuer tribal sections and their political alliances (Evans-Pritchard 1940: 144–5, 229–30, Howell 1954: 19–20) indicate that the opposition between tribal sections was not as balanced as Evans-Pritchard's model suggested and that the realities of Nuer politics were much more complex than the simplistic concept of the segmentary lineage structure suggested (Holy 1979b). This fact was, to a certain extent, recognised by Evans-Pritchard himself in his admission that the hostilities and alliances between tribal sections were not always as regular and simple as they were explained to him and as he stated them to be (1940: 144) and in his admission that

political actualities are confused and conflicting. They are confused because they are not always, even in a political context, in accord with political values, though they tend to conform to them, and because social ties of a different kind operate in the same field, sometimes strengthening them and sometimes running counter to them. (Evans–Pritchard 1940: 138)

If the segmentary lineage structure is not a representation of ongoing social processes, what then is the set of ideas to which it refers? There seems to be almost a general consensus among anthropologists that the concept of the segmentary lineage structure is the actors' folk model. Peters emphatically presents it as such for the Bedouin of Cyrenaica (1967). Southall sees it as part of the natives' 'projective system' (1952: 32). Talking about the Nuer, the Tiv and the Bedouin, Lewis points out that their 'political-jural ideology is uncompromisingly one of descent' (1965: 97). He clarifies what this ideology is meant to be by a quotation from Middleton and Tait: 'co-ordinate segments which have come into existence as a result of segmentation are regarded as complementary and as formally equal' (Middleton and Tait 1958: 7). The fact that the descent or lineage principle is referred to as ideology indicates that it is taken to be, not merely an analytical concept (although it could be this as well), but a notion held by the actors; it is part of their conceptual universe. The same view is expressed by Middleton and Tait themselves (1958: 5). In his examination of the theoretical and methodological bases of the concept of segmentary lineage systems, M. G. Smith takes a similar position. He holds the postulate of corporateness and descent to be an ideology and refers to it as 'myth'. He criticises the segmentary lineage theory for equating the myth with the actual social patterns and considers this procedure to be its great weakness (Smith, M. G. 1956: 65, 76–7). Salzman (1978) clearly presents the notion of the segmentary lineage structure as the actors' ideology and analyses it as such. Seddon (1979) does the same and argues that other political ideologies can coexist with the segmentary lineage ideology in the same society.

Even those anthropologists who have either implicitly or explicitly held the concept of the segmentary lineage structure for a representation of ongoing social processes, specifically Evans-Pritchard and Fortes, presented it at the same time as a notion held by the actors themselves. Thus Evans-Pritchard suggested that the lineage model with its principle of segmentation and opposition between segments was the model held by the Nuer:

Thus a man of the Fadang section of the Bor tribe exemplified it when he told me, 'We fight against the Rengyan, but when either of us is fighting a third party we combine with them'. [The principle of segmentation and opposition between segments] can be stated in hypothetical terms by the Nuer themselves ... (Evans-Pritchard 1940: 143)

Of what he calls the paradigm of the lineage system of the Tallensi, Fortes says that

something of this sort, though less systematic and abstract, is in the mind's eye of every well informed native when he discusses the structure of his society and takes his part in the public affairs. (Fortes 1945: 30)

If we accept that the concept of the segmentary structure is a folk model, it follows logically that we are faced with the problem of explaining how is it possible that the actors hold a certain model of their political relations and at the same time engage in activities that are grossly discrepant with that model. Another logical possibility, of course, is that the folk model has been misread, and the problem therefore misconstrued. Hence, before trying either to suggest an explanation or to dismiss the problem, we have first to look very carefully at what the actors' notions or models actually are.

Apart from simply telling us that the 'principle of segmentation and the opposition between segments ... can be stated in hypothetical terms by the Nuer themselves', Evans-Pritchard provides further insights into Nuer notions of their social and political relations. Commenting on the Nuer way of depicting related 'lineages' in the form of lines running at angles from a common point, he says:

It is interesting to note how the Nuer themselves figure a lineage system. When illustrating on the ground a number of related lineages they do not present them the way we figure them ... as a series of bifurcations of descent, as a tree of descent, or as a series of triangles of ascent, but as a number of lines running at angles from a common point .... This representation and Nuer comments on it show several significant facts about the way in which the Nuer see the system. They see it primarily as actual relations between groups of kinsmen within local communities rather than as a tree of descent, for the persons after whom the lineages are called do not proceed from a single individual. (1940: 202–3)

If we superimpose the Nuer representation on the map of the Eastern Jikany tribal sections published by Evans-Pritchard (1940: 58), it becomes obvious that it depicts simply spatial relations between various *cieng* (tribal sections) (1940: 136, 204–5). What, in my view, is significant about the Nuer conceptualisation of the *cieng* is not so much the fact that in their model they are territorial units rather than lineages; this has been recognised by Evans-Pritchard himself. What is significant is that no notion of any differences in the order of segmentation of these territorial units is implied in their conceptualisation. Evans-Pritchard gives an account of actual hostilities and political alliances between the *cieng* mentioned in the Nuer diagram and their constituent *cieng* (1940: 145). It appears from this account that lineages of varying order of segmentation formed alliances and jointly fought lineages to which they were not related by the principle of balanced opposition. What is important about these hostilities is their relation to the folk model of the Nuer and to the model of the segmentary lineage structure as suggested by Evans-Pritchard. In the Nuer folk model, whose elements seem to be the various *cieng* and the spatial relations between them, these hostilities are unproblematic and the model is perfectly able to encompass them; they are fully meaningful within it. In Evans-Pritchard's model they are puzzling.

It could be objected that these instances of actual fighting do not disprove the adequacy of the model of segments in balanced opposition. It is a well-known fact that, when the realities of actual politics do not correspond with the genealogies which provide their charter, the genealogies are altered to tally with new relations (Bohannan 1952). There is a clear evidence that among the Nuer the genealogies were manipulated (Evans-Pritchard 1940: 241–6). It could be argued that the hostilities among the sections of Eastern Jikany tribes are a case of the genealogical charter lagging behind the realities of actual politics (cf. Gough 1971: 88 for a similar argument). But the adequacy of the segmentary lineage model can hardly be sustained by this argument. The alliances and enmities among the sections seemed to change so often that the genealogies would have had to be altered almost daily; that is hardly feasible.

It seems that the differences in the conceptualisation of the relations between tribal sections are not the only differences between the Nuer folk model and Evans-Pritchard's analytical model. Other differences obtain in the conceptualisation of the composition of local communities. In Evans-Pritchard's model, the local community, or *gol*, commonly consisted of brothers or a man and his married sons (Evans-Pritchard 1951: 3). It had a typical agnatic structure. The Nuer themselves obviously saw things quite differently. A statement of one Nuer whom Evans-Pritchard quotes, clearly indicates that the Nuer themselves conceptualised their local communities as *gaatwac* (children of the paternal aunt) or *gaatnyiet* (children of daughters) attached to a 'bull' (Evans-Pritchard 1950: 371, 1951: 12). The politically asymmetrical relationship between *gaatwac* and *gaatnar* (children of the maternal uncle) obtained not only at the interpersonal level within local communities, but at the intergroup level as well (Holy 1979b). There is some evidence to suggest that the specific character of the *gaatwac–gaatnar* relationship between sections was part of Nuer's own model: a reference to it justified political alliances and made them meaningful (Evans-Pritchard 1940: 144).

The Nuer themselves seemed to conceptualise the relationship between sections which stood in the *gaatwac–gaatnar* relationship to one another without any need to reconcile this relationship with their agnatic ideology. Gough, who treated lineages which stood in the relationship of *gaatnar* to lineages dominant in the tribe as being in the process of becoming themselves dominant in their respective tribal sections (1971: 90, 113), and who took this process as evidence of an 'attempt to maintain or to restore "the supremacy of the agnatic principle" at all levels' (1971: 91) was, like Evans-Pritchard, ascribing an importance to an ideological principle which greatly surpasses the degree of importance that this principle had in the Nuer's own cognitive and conceptual realm, as well as in the realm of actual social processes in which they engaged.

The information about how the Nuer conceptualised their political relations and processes is extremely scant, but what evidence is available indicates that the notion of the balanced opposition of the segments of an agnatic lineage was not the only part of it. Even when the Nuer might well have been able to state 'the principle of segmentation and opposition between segments in hypothetical terms', many more notions than this one were part of their own model of their political relations and processes. The same seems to be true of many other societies which were seen as organised on the principle of a segmentary lineage (Holy 1979a).

My brief outline of what I take the Nuer's model to be is not meant to suggest that the notion of the segmentary lineage was not part of their conceptual universe. But it is meant to suggest that besides this one, they had a number of other notions about their political relations and processes, which equally formed part of their own conceptual universe. My brief description of concepts, categories and norms which formed part of the Nuer notions is equally not meant to suggest that such a description accounts for the observed interactions. People's notions constitute merely a set of constraints within which decisions about the course of actions are made and individual choices exercised. However, notions do not only define constraints which people have to consider in their interactions. At the same time, they provide the framework within which the actors interpret the ongoing interactions, and on the basis of which they assign meaning to them. It is because of these notions that the actor is able to ascertain and understand what others do and why they do it.

It would be rather naive to assume that the actors' notions are all of the same order. Instead of simply talking about folk models, it is useful, following Keesing, to distinguish within the notional level of phenomena, the 'culturally postulated *things* and *relationships* from normative "rules" (usually implicit) that are phrased in terms of them and enable native actors to take decisions, behave appropriately, and anticipate one another's actions' (Keesing 1971: 126). Such a distinction parallels the philosophers' distinction between 'knowing that' and 'knowing how' and in anthropology it finds its expression in the distinction between cultural patterns as 'models of' and 'models for' (Geertz 1966) or in the distinction between representational models, corresponding to the ways actors think things are, and operational models, corresponding to the way they practically respond or act

(Caws 1974: 3). The Nuer, who were able to express in hypothetical terms the principle of segmentation and opposition between segments, might well have held the notion of the segmentary structure as the representational model of their political relations. In their actual political practice they seemed to operate a considerably different model, whose elements were the spatial relations between the various *cieng*, as well as the genealogical, but not only agnatic, relations between the dominant lineages associated with them.

The distinction between the actors' representational and operational models does not seem to derive so much from the difference in their bearing on ongoing social transactions, as rather from their differing degree of generality or from their differing roles in legitimising and interpreting the ongoing social processes.

The normative rules are always situation-specific in the sense that they are invocable in clearly defined situations which well may be seen as 'contingencies' (Peters 1967: 270) from the point of view of the representational model. The notions that society has a certain form do not necessarily have to be situation-specific. By referring to the enduring form of social reality persisting in spite of numerous contingencies taken into account on the operational level, they transcend specific interactional situations and have an existence above and beyond them.

The model of the segmentary lineage structure is thus not a model which the actors operate in their actual political processes. It is merely a representation of the enduring form of their society, or, as it has often been expressed, a kind of ideology (Smith, M. G. 1956: 76–7), Lewis 1965: 97, Peters 1967: 270, Salzman 1978, Seddon 1979). Instead of mistaking this ideology for actuality, it seems to be much more fruitful to inquire about its role and to investigate why the actors hold it when in numerous cases it is obviously at odds with their actual political processes. Peters suggests that the segmentary lineage ideology enables the Bedouin 'without making absurd demands on their credulity, to understand the field of social relationships, and to give particular relationships their raison d'être' (1967: 270). Salzman (1978) argues against this view and sees the segmentary lineage model as a 'social structure in reserve'. It provides a framework, not for commonsense understanding, but for social mobilisation in special circumstances, when the normally stable territorial relations between Bedouin groups are disrupted by population movements. In such circumstances, the territorial interests on which political relations between groups are normally based are suspended. Unlike Sahlins (1961), Salzman does not see segmentary lineage as an organisational form suited for predatory expansion, but rather more broadly as an organisational form which 'is especially suited to areas in which political conditions and productive activities result in an alteration through history of stable periods and periods of upheaval, periods of stable territoriality and periods of high spatial mobility and population mixing' (Salzman 1978: 68). However, the Tallensi, Gusii, Luo, Konkomba and others who did not display any, or at any rate, any high spatial mobility, also seemed to subscribe to segmentary lineage ideology. For what purpose?

According to M. G. Smith, one of the advantages of lineage ideology is its flexibility: 'It assumes invariance and uniformity in the constitution and relations of different units, while permitting their internal differentiation, cohesion, or development according to circumstances, and rationalising these departures as consistent with [it]' (Smith, M. G. 1956: 65–6, cf. also Southall 1952: 32). One important instance of the rationalising of departures from the ideology as consistent with it is especially worth mentioning. By ideologically defining any political action as an affair of segments in balanced opposition and not an affair of particular individuals, the notion of the segmentary lineage structure allows for the emergence of men entrusted with considerable authority and wielding great political power. As long as political leadership remains personal and does not become institutionalised into an office, it can be accounted for within the given ideology and the ideological dictum of egalitarianism upheld in spite of considerable political inequality on the ground. The Nuer who insisted on being equal to one another in their political status (Evans-Pritchard 1940: 181–2) were able to display a great deal of political inequality (Holy 1979b) and still uphold their ideology. The fact that so little attention has been paid to political leadership in societies classified as having segmentary lineage structures, and the fact that the observable inequality of status, political authority and power has been consistently underplayed in the analysis, are typical consequences of mistaking the ideology for actuality.

When considering the concept of the segmentary lineage structure as a set of notions, we have to bear in mind that not only do the actors have their ideas or notions but the anthropologists have them too. The concept of the segmentary lineage structure as an analytical model belongs clearly to the anthropologists' own set of ideas. Although there is no doubt that this analytical model corresponds to something in the actors' models, this correspondence does not need to be particularly close. After outlining the analytical model of the lineage structure, Fortes states that '*something of this sort, though less systematic* and abstract, is in the mind's eye of every well informed native' (1945: 30; emphasis added). His formulation clearly hints at the procedure involved in the construction of the anthropologists' analytical model: it is based on the native's own notions but these notions have been made more systematic and mutually consistent in terms of Western logic. A brief outline of the Nuer notions indicates some specific ways in which these notions were altered in the analytical model that Evans-Pritchard constructed as a system of logically interconnected concepts. In this outline of Nuer notions, consideration of the concepts of lineage, kinship, territorial group, corporation, social structure, and fission and fusion merits special attention.

From what little we know about the Nuer, it seems that they recognised three main categories of people in their conceptual system: those who lived together in a more or less permanent spatial proximity, those who were genealogically related, and those who shared agnatic descent from the same ancestor. In terms of relations rather than categories of people they conceptually distinguished spatial relations, kinship relations and relations of agnatic descent as obtaining between individuals as well as between categories of people. The case histories of actual enmities and alliances between territorial sections, that is between categories of people who lived together in spatial proximity, indicate that all three kinds of relations could have been brought to bear by them on their activities. Sometimes the spatial relations between territorial units were invoked in action, sometimes the kinship relations between the core members of the territorial units and sometimes the relations of agnation.

Unlike the Nuer, Evans-Pritchard conceptually distinguished only spatial relations and relations of agnatic descent as obtaining between the *categories* of people. He saw the Nuer system as consisting mainly of the territorial and lineage systems. The kinship relations, that is the recognised genealogical relations other than agnation, although considered by him as obtaining between *individuals*, were subsumed, in his model of the relations between groups, under the relations of agnatic descent; they were all seen as fitting into the lineage system.

Evans-Pritchard saw the lineage system in terms of the paradigm of hierarchically structured segments, each of which was a corporation (see also Fortes 1953: 25 for the same assumption and Smith, M. G. 1956: 62, 76 for further discussion of the problem of the corporateness of lineages). Is this notion of the lineage (of whatever order of segmentation) being a corporation an empirical fact, or is it merely the analysts' logical extension of observed empirical facts, or a consequence of their faulty assumption of the congruence of empirically observable social processes with their informants' description of them? If we disregard the fact that the Nuer, Tiv or Bedouin lineages were not isomorphic with the territorial political units of which they were the core (Bohannan 1958: 40, Peters 1967: 262) and consider the groups which crystallise in action to be lineages, what we typically observe empirically as groups, are lineages of the lowest order of segmentation. Peters reports that during his entire residence among the Bedouin in Cyrenaica, he did not see a group of agnates larger than a tertiary tribal section assemble for any purpose and that the feuds concern only two tertiary sections and not the opposed secondary sections of which they are a part (1967: 227–8). The Bedouin are probably not unique in this respect. Among the Gusii, for example, only particular clans belonging to two different tribes, not the whole tribes were involved in mutual conflicts which were conceptualised by the Gusii themselves as inter-tribal hostilities. This seems to have been empirically the case in spite of the fact that the Gusii themselves, when describing the inter-tribal hostilities, talked about them in terms of all clans of one tribe, which in different situations might have fought among themselves, fusing together and standing in opposition to the similarly fused clans of another tribe (Mayer 1949: 12). The danger involved in postulating corporateness is not only that anthropologists, during their brief field residence, may never see the latent corporative functions of lineages in operation, and thus miss and underestimate their importance, as Fried pointed out in his discussion of the Gusii (1957: 19). The danger is also that they might ascribe corporative functions to lineages, or overestimate their importance, through their faulty methodology. The lineages of the lowest order of segmentation may indeed be corporations in the sense that they are treated as internally undifferentiated by other lineages with which they have a specific relationship. Once they are perceived as such, the notion of corporateness is extended to segments of all orders because of their structural identity with the segments of the lower order (cf. Fortes 1953: 31, but see Gellner 1969: 48–9 for a different treatment of lineage corporateness). Although no corporateness has been empirically observed in the case of lineages of a higher order of segmentation, it is assumed on the basis of their structure and on the basis of the fact that the actors themselves present them in their model as corporations. Once they are taken for corporations, they are seen in the analytical model, not merely as categories of people, but as concrete groups which fuse in action and stand in balanced opposition to segments of the same order, perceived again as corporations. In the absence of any personified authority which could mobilise the segments for action and thus allow them to express their corporate identity, the conceptualisation of all lineage segments as corporations, and the notion of their fission and fusion according to the principle of their balanced opposition, is achieved at the expense of endowing the structural principles with intentionality of their own.

Although Evans-Pritchard himself realised that the lineages and the territorial divisions of the Nuer belonged to different areas of discourse (1940: 203), he saw them as parts of the same overall social system. Once a functional connection between the lineage and the territorial division was made at the level of the model, the lineage paradigm of hierarchically structured segments was extended to the territorial divisions. The notion of their functioning in terms of balanced opposition achieved through fission and fusion (mediated through the segmentary structure of the dominant lineage) was created. Three main errors seem to be involved in Evans-Pritchard's construction of the analytical model of the segmentary lineage structure: dismissing kinship relations from the model or ascribing to lineage relations a structural importance surpassing that of kinship relations, ascribing corporateness to what are empirically (and conceptually for the actors themselves) only categories of people, and postulating a functional fit between the analytically distinguished sub-systems of the overall system (particularly the lineage and territorial systems).

The segmentary lineage structure, as it has generally been understood by anthropologists, does not refer to actual social processes. It may refer to actors' representations of their political relations or to the anthropologists' representation of the actors' representations. Alternatively, it may refer to the set of anthropologists' ideas about the political relations in the studied society, that is, it may be their analytical model. These three sets of ideas, which are glossed over by the same term, can be three completely different things which might sometimes have very little in common. It is true that the model of the segmentary lineage structure has guided much excellent anthropological fieldwork. But it is also true that, because little attention has been paid to the problem of what this model is actually a model of, its use in description and analysis has occasionally been responsible for a direct misrepresentation of a considerable body of ethnography. It was also responsible for ascribing inflated importance to people's representations which, at least at the less systematic and abstract level, coincided roughly with the model guiding the research, and for not paying sufficient attention to people's other representations which the model does not subsume. The use of the model of the segmentary lineage was thus ultimately responsible for neglecting important areas of research into both the actual political processes and notions about them, existing in societies which have been classified as having segmentary lineage systems.

NEW GUINEA AND MELANESIAN ETHNOGRAPHY

The problem of the relation between social structure and the actual social processes could no longer be dismissed as non-existent when new ethnographic data, mainly from societies in the New Guinea Highlands and in Melanesia, became increasingly available from the late 1950s and early 1960s. The fieldwork during which the data were collected was governed by the modern requirements of detailed ethnographic recording, supplemented by quantitative information obtained through census techniques. The ethnographers working in the New Guinea Highlands pointed out that however much the ideology of patrilineal descent might have been normative there, the relation between the normative structure and the actually observable behaviour was highly problematic. They were able to identify major territorially based political units within New Guinea societies, which they usually described as 'clans'. They reported that the clans were conceived by the natives as groups of agnatically related men and that they functioned as corporate groups with respect to land tenure, war, ceremonial exchange and exogamy. The New Guinea ethnography demonstrated first of all that although the Highlanders might ideally recognise patrilineal descent as a principle of recruitment into corporate groups, in practice they disregard this principle to a considerable extent and freely admit cognates and affines into the local descent group and, after a relatively short period of time, treat them as full members. On the other hand, non-resident agnates are very soon forgotten and become lost to the local descent group. Not only the ties of agnatic kinship, but cognatic and affinal ties as well, give people access to land. Agnates, cognates and affines alike contribute to an individual's bridewealth. All this led to the characterisation of New Guinea societies as 'loosely structured' (Held 1957, Pouwer 1960).

The fieldwork in New Guinea was conducted by a new generation of anthropologists trained within the then current anthropological theory. As the result of the theoretical development in social anthropology in the 1950s, the most obvious model to apply in the New Guinea Highlands was the model of the corporate segmentary lineage system which envisaged the patrilineal lineage as the most important social group in the Highlands and as a segment of a more inclusive structure. One of the first monographs on the New Guinea peoples represented them in terms of this model developed by Evans-Pritchard, Fortes and others whose research was done in Africa (Meggitt 1965). The view that the basic groups in New Guinea were lineage segments and that the model of corporate segmentary lineage systems is applicable there was shared by others (Read 1954: 11, LaFontaine 1973). Yet on the whole, the quantitative data yielded through the research in New Guinea were not so easy to accommodate into the model of corporate segmentary lineage systems as had been the qualitative descriptions on the basis of which the model had originally been built in the 1940s. Some anthropologists conceptualised the basic groups in New Guinea as descent groups, and considered patrilineal descent to be the most important structural principle (for example, Salisbury 1956, 1962, Ryan 1958–9, Brown and Brookfield 1959–60, Brookfield and Brown 1963, Berndt 1964, Kaberry 1967), though they expressed reservations about the direct applicability to the New Guinea scene of the model of corporate segmentary lineage systems described for politically uncentralised African societies. Other anthropologists, however, not only considered the basic groups in New Guinea to be lineage segments, but also maintained that the model of corporate segmentary lineage systems is applicable in New Guinea without modification (LaFontaine 1973).

The debate about whether or not Highland groups should be described as patrilineal descent groups or as descent groups at all, which started in the late 1950s and continued well into the 1980s (Weiner 1982, Feil 1984, Scheffler 1985), was first of all a debate about the formulation of an analytic and explanatory model applicable to the 'loosely structured' Highland societies. What was being disputed was not only how the components of the structure are integrated into a system in the New Guinea Highlands but also what these components actually are. What was at issue first of all was what the most important social groups in the Highlands are and how they can properly be conceptualised. All ethnographers seem to be agreed that the most important social groups in New Guinea are the groups of co-residents in a given territory which, according to de Lepervanche (1967–8: 157) could better be described as 'parish groups' than 'descent groups'. The groups usually described as 'subclans' or 'subsubclans' are generally groups associated with a particular men's house in the 'clan' territory. Where there has not been an agreement, and what is the subject of controversy, is in terms of which ties, other than the territorial ones, do the natives themselves conceptualise these groups, and in terms of which ties, other than the territorial ones, can the anthropologists best conceptualise them. Immigrants seem to be quickly absorbed into the group and all male group members refer to one another as 'brothers' or as 'sons of one father' and to that extent think of themselves as a group. This suggested to many anthropologists that descent is an ideology in whose terms the solidarity of the local group is expressed.

However, even if descent stresses the unity of the local group, recruitment to it is through patrifiliation supplemented by using the ties of affinity and matrifiliation, the ties of common residence, participation in ceremonial exchanges, joining the following of a big man, etc. (Strathern 1969). This means that descent may well be the ideology in terms of which the unity of the group is conceptualised but it is not a guide to the actual behaviour of group members. In other words, there is a discrepancy between the ideology and actual behaviour or 'statistical norms' (Langness 1964: 182). The problem of this discrepancy was implied for the first time by Read (1951: 155) and Elkin (1952–3: 169), who stated with reference to the Gahuku-Gama and the Wabag of the Central Highlands that patrilineality is the most important structural principle, although deviations with respect to group recruitment, political relations and segmentation do exist. The problem has been explicitly formulated by Langness (1964) and Watson (1964) and recognised as such by Berndt (1964).

It is a problem which is of theoretical interest reaching far beyond the limits of New Guinea ethnography. De Lepervanche has noted that if the problem is formulated as 'the discrepancy between ideology and statistical norms', 'this sounds as if ideology descended from heaven upon a collection of Highlanders who did not conform to its demands' (1967–8: 168). What kind of confusion is involved here? Fortes pointed out that what is 'conducive to analytical confusion as well as to misinterpretation of the empirical data of kinship and social organization' is the 'diffuse and discursive usage of such key concepts as "descent" and "descent group"' (1969: 280). However, it seems to me that it is not so much the 'diffuse and discursive usage' of key concepts which leads to confusion and disagreement about the interpretation of empirical data, but rather the continuing use of concepts developed within the framework of the structural theory for answering questions asked outside this framework. The core of the confusion is not the interpretation of empirical data as such, or the disagreement about the definition of the concepts, but a failure to realise that a concept which had been defined in a specific way to cope with problems derived from a certain theoretical framework is not suitable for coping with problems formulated outside this framework. In other words, the core of the confusion is the failure to realise that a concept which might have its origin in a certain ethnography is not elevated to the status of an analytical concept because of its capacity to provide a kind of 'metalanguage' by which a wide range of ethnographic data can adequately be described, but because it enables analysts to organise their ethnographic data in such a way that they can accommodate these data within their theoretical model. In the final analysis, a concept is not derived from ethnography but from theory. It is defined in such a way as to enable analysts to explain their data within their theory.

The key concept in the formulation of the problem of discrepancy between ideology and actual behaviour is the concept of descent; the problem of discrepancy arises because social groups are ideally but not actually patrilineal (Langness 1964). In A. Strathern's words, '"the" ideology could thus be taken as read and sociological explanations advanced for the discrepancy between it and "actual" behaviour' (A. Strathern 1973: 25).

The problem could have been formulated in this way only because of the failure to realise that a concept of descent as a principle of recruitment into unilineal descent groups has not some universal heuristic value but is defined in this way 'in the interest of protecting a typology of segmentary system' and of 'the model of a segment as a physically distinct entity' (Schneider 1965: 75). If the Highlanders themselves use an agnatic idiom to express group solidarity, or if, as Watson puts it, patrilineal ideology provides 'an idiom in terms of which local groups may speak of others and of themselves to others' (1964: 14), the problem of discrepancy between ideology and actual behaviour can arise only (a) when it is assumed that the concept the natives use is the concept of descent, and (b) when it is assumed at the same time that descent refers to the principle of recruitment into groups (that is, when the analyst fails to realise that the recruitment meaning attributed to the concept of descent is not a universally valid generalisation of ethnographic fact but a meaning ascribed to the concept for the sake of maintaining consistency of a certain analytical and theoretical framework). The reasoning behind the formulation of the problem of discrepancy between ideology and actual behaviour (or statistical norm) is thus the following: the natives conceptualise group solidarity in descent terms; they then ideally conceptualise their groups as descent groups in the sense that descent is a principle of recruitment into them; descent, however, does not govern actual behaviour of living individuals which the anthropologist observed, hence the discrepancy between ideology of descent and actual behaviour.

In 1962, Barnes dismissed as a mirage the application of the model of African unilineal descent systems to New Guinea (1962: 4). According to him, the groups in the New Guinea Highlands cannot be seen as descent groups if 'we continue to restrict the category "descent group" to groups in which descent is the only criterion of membership' as Fortes argued (1962: 6). Because most men are affiliated at birth with their fathers' groups (although others whose fathers were not members of the group in question may acquire membership of it as well), when they have children of their own, these children become affiliated with their fathers' groups which will then also be their fathers' fathers' groups. Through this process of 'cumulative patrifiliation' a group may become similar 'in demographic appearance and *de facto* kinship ties' to a patrilineal group. But group ideology, processes of recruitment, and patterns of segmentation all make it doubtful whether

New Guinea Highland societies can be characterised by patrilineal descent (1962: 6). Similarly, Scheffler argued that native conceptualisations of the groups as composed of 'brothers' or the 'sons of one father' need not imply patrilineal constitution (1973: 778). He suggested that the New Guinea ethnographers wrongly assumed that the concept the natives themselves use to conceptualise solidarity of the local group is the concept of descent. According to him, a 'rule of descent' is only a special case of a 'rule of filiation'. In particular, it is a rule that specifies that patri- or matrifiliation is the necessary and sufficient condition for possession of a status. In the New Guinea Highlands, patrifiliation is a sufficient but not a necessary condition for group affiliation (Scheffler 1985). As a consequence, the position of fathers and sons and of brothers in a genealogical continuum is not an issue in New Guinea, and although the natives describe their groups as composed of 'brothers' or of 'sons of one father', the relations between and within groups are conceptualised simply in terms of kinship and not descent (Scheffler 1973: 778, 1985: 16). The principal structural framework of many Highland societies is provided by the genealogical and social relations of paternal and fraternal kinship. According to Scheffler, such groups might therefore be described as 'patrifilial kin groups' rather than 'patrilineal descent groups' (1973: 780, 1985: 16). According to Scheffler, the confusion involved in the formulation of the discrepancy between ideology and actual behaviour does not derive from the reification of the concept of descent in its limited meaning as the principle of recruitment, but from a more basic confusion of descent constructs with the simple recognition of several successive filial steps 'which is a more general phenomenon constituting the basis of what we call kinship' (1966: 543).

Although the discussion about the interpretation and understanding of New Guinea ethnography has far from achieved its aim in formulating a model, alternative to the model of segmentary lineage systems, which would be applicable to New Guinea societies, it has certainly had a positive result in formulating new problems for investigation. These problems could not have arisen in the framework of the structural analysis which treated all behaviour as determined by the demands of social structure. Their recognition clearly indicates the shift in emphasis in what is treated as problematic. The anthropologists working in New Guinea and Melanesia have been concerned not only with the formulation of the social structure and analysis of how this

structure works, but also with the formulation of the structure in such
a way that it would subsume not only the normative actions but all
the variations in the actual behaviour as well. In this way, what became
one of their main concerns was the explanation of the actual behaviour
of living individuals. This considerable shift in emphasis was probably
the result of the combination of two factors: (a) confrontation with
new data in need of explanation, and (b) new questions being asked
about the data. Proponents of the model of the segmentary lineage
system do not seem to have any difficulty in analysing and interpreting
these new data, so asking new questions about the data obviously must
have been a much more decisive factor. The whole shift of emphasis
is due to changing 'epistemological orientation rather than ethnographic
fact' (Buchler and Selby 1968: 90), or as LaFontaine observed, 'what
is involved here is a difference in emphasis which can be explained in
terms of the history of anthropological theory rather than the geography
of anthropological field-work' (1973: 41).

It may be true that if we restrict the analytical use of the term 'descent'
to a form of filiation that is a necessary and sufficient condition for
group affiliation, the ethnographic data from the New Guinea Highlands
are largely irrelevant to that body of theory formulated on the basis
of African ethnography accumulated during fieldwork carried out in
the 1940s and early 1950s, as Scheffler (1985) argued in his defence
of descent theory. But the fact remains that the debate about the
interpretation and understanding of New Guinea ethnography brought
into the foreground of theoretical interest not only the differences
between New Guinea and African societies but also numerous
similarities. When the debate was at its peak in the late 1960s, Kaberry
stressed that 'an analysis of some Nuer communities reveals that they
have a number of characteristics attributed by Barnes to many Highland
societies' (1967: 114) and Weiner later pointed out 'that "on the
ground" relationships in Africa and the New Guinea Highlands are
strikingly similar' (1982: 11). In his comparative study of Kwaio and
Tallensi ancestor worship, Keesing made the following observation:

The gulf between the way Kwaio (and I as their ethnographer) conceptualize
their system and the way Fortes and Goody conceptualize the African systems
seems far wider than the gulf between what the Kwaio and Africans *do*. And
if the gulf is generated more by the model than by the facts, we had better
look very carefully at the models. (1970: 765; original emphasis)

According to Fortes, patrilineal descent was a pervasive principle central to Tallensi social life. Patrilineal lineages were very important social groups in Tallensi society and membership in the lineage determined every individual's property rights and religious life. Tallensi lineages were exogamous groups which means that women married men from lineages other than their own. When sacrifice was offered to a lineage ancestor, not only members of that lineage but also people descended from women of the lineage were entitled to be present and partake of the sacrifice. Those descended from the women of the lineage were of course not members of their mothers' but of their fathers' lineages and they therefore belonged to different lineages than the one whose ancestor was being honoured. This led Keesing (1970) to argue that, apart from the rule of patrilineal descent, Tallensi also recognised the rule of cognatic descent and that any Tale individual belonged not only to an agnatic descent group, which Fortes explicitly recognised, but also to a multiplicity of cognatic descent categories, which Fortes failed to recognise. The children of the female members of the lineage did not participate in the sacrifice simply because their mothers participated in it but because they were cognatic descendants of the ancestor of the lineage. This is obvious from the fact that not only the children of the women of the lineage took part, but also the descendants of these children themselves. What was therefore involved in their participation was their relationship to the ancestor of the lineage, which was a relationship of cognatic descent and not merely a relationship of filiation. That the Tallensi recognised a cognatic descent rule was also manifest in their marriage rules. Marriage was prohibited not only between members of the same patrilineage but between any two people who were cognatically descended from the founder of the lineage. Unlike the patrilineal descendants of a common ancestor, his cognatic descendants did not form a group in Tallensi society, but they were clearly recognised as a distinct social category. In his re-analysis of Tallensi data, Keesing argues that it was the analytical concept of complementary filiation (subsuming both a culturally secondary descent principle and relationship of cognatic kinship) which prevented Fortes from recognising the operation of the cognatic descent principle in the Tallensi social structure (1970: 765, 767).

It is very likely that in a similar way the *gaatwac–gaatnyiet* relationship, which was often the basis of political alliances among the patrilineal Nuer, was not underpinned merely by the recognition of ties of cognatic kinship, but by the recognition of the cognatic descent of *gaatwac* and *gaatnyiet* from the same ancestor.

In his reassessment of the lineage theory, Kuper (1982) noted that the lineage model does not account either for the actual social processes or for the ideas which the natives themselves hold about them. This led him to deny it any value for anthropological analysis and to declare it theoretically bankrupt. It may well be theoretically bankrupt for even more profound reasons than those which Kuper has noted. Research conducted in New Guinea makes it clear that apart from the undisputed access to clan land and the observance of clan exogamy, hardly any other rights and duties accrue to particular individuals in virtue of their clan membership. There is little evidence that clans and subclans in the Highlands crystallise as groups in situations of warfare or ceremonial exchange, which have generally been considered the two most important aspects of the politico-jural relations in Highlands societies. Participants in these situations identify themselves in terms of their clan affiliations but clan members do not assemble for joint defence, aggression or ceremonial exchanges.

For example, Tombema-Enga groups of the western Highlands do not stress exclusiveness or boundedness through patrilineal descent or by any other means. Neither clans nor subclans are exchange units and ties between subclansmen are insignificant, in most cases, for the marshalling of exchange wealth; in exchange, it is every man for himself and there is fierce competition between subclan 'brothers'. As far as warfare and exchange are concerned, Tombema units do not confront each other and do not think of themselves as confronting each other as bounded entities or corporate groups. It is, in fact, purely interpersonal alliances that provide the most important ties in Tombema society (Feil 1984: 57–8). Considering societies like the Tombema-Enga, Feil raised doubts about whether exchange relations in the Highlands could be described as though they were between agnatic groups (1978) and Scheffler argued that 'the rights and duties of particular kinds of kin, especially fathers and sons and brothers, have been systematically misrepresented as the rights and duties of persons *qua* group members' in much of the ethnographic literature on New Guinea (1985: 15).

The research conducted in New Guinea brings into relief the unanalysed assumption that groups of one sort or another are essential to human life. This assumption, which lies at the very foundation of lineage theory, appears to be, like many other assumptions about kinship, a culturally specific Western assumption. If that is so, then the conception of society as a politico-jural order based on the existence of bounded and discrete groups integrated into a system is not necessarily a generalisation of the ways in which other peoples construct their sociality. It is the result of an imposition of culturally specific Western conceptualisations of social order, and of Western assumptions about sociality on others whose own ideas about these matters may be radically different.

As Wagner pointed out, there is no doubt that Westerners

live in a culture in which founding, joining, participating in, and integrating groups is a deliberate and important matter. The constitutional charters of our nations are founded on a notion of a 'social contract', a conscious act or event of some kind which initiated the existence of society. Citizens are members of these colossal 'descent groups'. Those who are not 'born to' them or within their clan territories must be 'naturalized', much as children may be legally adopted by foster parents. A society which emphasizes the citizen's duty to vote and be vigilant on behalf of his country is certainly insisting on conscious participation. And by making belonging to and participating in society conscious, this particular social form also makes it problematic. The problems of recruitment, participation and corporateness (economics) are *our* problems, but we take them with us when we visit other cultures, along with our toothbrushes and favorite novels. (Wagner 1974: 103; original emphasis)

Wagner argues that the Daribi in the eastern New Guinea Highlands create themselves socially in quite a different way. When a Daribi is asked, in a local idiom, who his 'house people' (*be' bidi*) are, he is likely to respond by a specific name denoting a category of people which the Daribi would designate in generic terms as *bidi wai'* – 'man-ancestors' – because its name is usually, although not always, based on a name of a genealogical ancestor. It would be easy to conclude from this that the specific names of various *bidi wai'* are descriptions of concrete, bounded and empirically existing groups. However, such a 'discovery' of groups with their concomitant politico-jural functions would be the result of projecting on the Daribi our own culturally specific ideas of order, organisation and consistency, and our own culturally specific notions of sociality. For the Daribi themselves, the names are significant not because they describe people who share certain characteristics – like being the descendants of specific forebears or belonging to shared lines of paternal substance, a common *bidi wai'* –

but because they contrast some people with others or differentiate some people from others. Any name is, first of all, a means of distinguishing, of including and excluding, and thus merely a device for drawing up boundaries.

When drawing boundaries by creating contrasts, the Daribi elicit social collectivities by alluding to them indirectly rather than deliberately organising them or consciously participating in them. Such elicitation of collectivities through indirect means is the most important aspect of Daribi creativity, most clearly brought to the fore in the exchange of wealth. This exchange also derives from the use of contrast and distinction to elicit social relationships. The contrast and distinction invoked in the exchange of wealth is the contrast and distinction between men and women. Men emphasise their 'maleness' and women their 'femaleness', each sex drawing a response from the other. Women are valued for their productive and reproductive capacity. Men respond to women's ability to do women's work and to bear children by negotiating exchanges of women and their progeny in return for items of male productivity, particularly pearl-shells, axes used in gardening, and meat, the eating of which augments the flow of semen.

Every legitimate acquisition of a woman – and since all persons are born of female creativity, perforce every acquisition of a person – must be accomplished through such an exchange. Every Daribi has *pagebidi* or 'people at the base'. A married woman's *pagebidi* are her brothers and other close kin; a man's or an unmarried girl's *pagebidi* are their close maternal kin. Every Daribi has also *be' bidi* or 'house people', who centre on the husband or paternal relatives. *Pagebidi* are entitled to receive male wealth from a man's *be' bidi* in exchange for his acquiring a wife in marriage and a child, the product of her creativity.

When talking about their marriages, the Daribi say that they marry the sisters and daughters of those to whom they give meat and that they cannot marry the sisters and daughters of men with whom they eat, or share meat. The distinction between the *be' bidi* and *pagebidi* is thus a distinction between those who share meat and other wealth and those who exchange meat or wealth. This distinction itself is much more significant than the categories *be' bidi* and *pagebidi* which it differentiates. The categories are left implicit; what is made explicit is only the distinction that separates or differentiates them.

Just as the specific names of various 'house people' elicit these social collectivities in the process of distinguishing them, the exchanges that allocate rights to a woman or child elicit specific instances of *be' bidi* and *pagebidi*. What most anthropologists, following their standard descriptive practice, would designate as 'groups' among the Daribi are thus never deliberately organised but only elicited through the use of names and through the exchanges which create differentiation among people (Wagner 1974: 105–12).

The ultimate demise of lineage theory, hailed in the middle of the century as a major theoretical breakthrough, is the result of anthropologists' growing sensitivity to natives' own conceptualisations. Once we started to pay due attention to how different peoples conceptualise their sociality instead of interpreting it in terms of our own analytical models, we became aware that the relationship between any peoples' ideology and their behaviour need not be one of simple congruence, that they may hold different models of their society which they may invoke in different contexts and for different purposes, and that they do not even have to have a concept analogous to our analytical concept of a group when they draw boundaries and create contrasts between various collectivities.

5   DESCENT AND THE PUBLIC DOMAIN II: MATRILINEAL AND COGNATIC DESCENT

Theoretical elaborations of lineage theory as well as all the criticisms of it have always been concerned either explicitly or implicitly with lineage systems organised in terms of patrilineal descent. Although the Trobriand Islanders, who in Malinowski's theorising stood for 'primitive society' in general, were organised in terms of matrilineal descent, and many more societies studied by functionalist anthropologists were matrilineal, little attention was paid to the particular problems and peculiarities of matrilineal systems until Audrey Richards (1950) drew attention to the 'matrilineal puzzle' – the problem of the position of men in societies divided into groups whose members trace descent in the female line. She specified the problem as the problem of 'combining recognition of descent through the woman with the rule of exogamous marriage' (1950: 246) in groups in which men are socially and politically dominant. Drawing on insights from Richards, Schneider (1961) formulated the characteristic features of matrilineal systems which set the agenda for their subsequent discussion. The extent to which patrilineal systems had become established as the paradigm of primitive social organisation is reflected in the fact that all that discussion was couched in terms of the fundamental differences of matrilineal descent groups from patrilineal ones.

MATRILINEAL DESCENT

Two universal aspects of human society, one of them natural and the other one social, are taken to account for the fact that matrilineal and patrilineal descent groups are not simple and straightforward mirror images of each other. The natural fact is the process of human reproduction, the consequence of which is that both matrilineal and patrilineal groups are reproduced through women for only women give birth. Whereas the husband–wife tie is the biologically procreative link in both systems, it is a socially procreative link only in a patrilineal one. In this type of system, it is not the female members of the descent group but the in-marrying wives who give birth to the future generation of group members. The women of the group, as they play no role in reproducing it, can be released from its control and given to other groups in 'exchange' for wives; their continuous association with their natal group is not essential and they can become fully incorporated into their husbands' group. In consequence, strong bonds of solidarity between husband and wife and stable marriages are fully compatible with the formation of groups on the basis of patrilineal descent.

In matrilineal systems, the socially procreative link is not that between husband and wife but between brother and sister for it is not the man's wife but his sister who gives birth to the next generation of group members. For this reason, Fortes (1959) suggested that it was misleading to speak of matrilineal descent as passing from mother to daughter and more accurate to conceptualise it as passing from a woman's brother to her son. In a matrilineal system, a woman's loyalty is not to her husband but to her brother and in consequence, the husband–wife tie is weak and the marriage brittle. Among the Nayar, where the brother–sister tie was the principle of household affiliation, the marriage tie, if one can speak of such a tie at all, was the weakest of all bonds. But marriage is in structural conflict to a greater or lesser extent with the principle of descent in all matrilineally organised societies and unstable marriages and a high divorce rate are characteristic patterns of many of them. In fact, in some types of matrilineal systems, the formation of socially viable descent groups is predicated on high divorce rate, high individual mobility and strong ties between mothers and their children.

The other presumably universal feature of human society which accounts for the basic differences between matrilineal and patrilineal groups is the fact that men exercise authority in both of them. When the presumed universality of male dominance and female subordination came to be challenged, many anthropologists turned to matrilineally organised societies in their search for societies in which women wield considerable power and authority. In particular, the matrilineally organised Iroquois Indians were seen as an example of a society in which women exercise considerable economic and political power (Randle 1951). There is, however, no agreement on how the high status of women in Iroquois society should be interpreted and even less agreement on the extent to which the high status of women could be seen as characteristic of all matrilineal systems. For all intents and purposes, men do seem to exercise political authority even in this type of society, even if they are not fully in control of its ritual activities.

The principle of male authority is perfectly compatible with tracing descent in the male line. A woman who does not exercise any authority in her natal patrilineal group and whose children are not members of her own but of her husband's group, can reside virilocally (that is, in the locality of her husband) and give birth to the new members of her husband's group. The fact that a group of agnatically related men with their in-marrying wives can easily be localised in one particular territory, is the result of the structural compatibility among marriage, male authority and tracing descent in the male line. Because of the principle of male authority, it is much more difficult for matrilineal groups to establish themselves as local groups and there are basically four ways in which a matrilineal descent group can organise itself on the ground.

The first way is through practising duolocal or natolocal residence. It is a form of residence when the husband and wife live separately in their natal homes, either permanently, as for example among the Nayar, or for a certain time after their marriage, as for example among the Ashanti. The advantage of this type of residence is that the female members, who perpetuate the group, and the male members, who exercise authority within it, are both kept in spatial proximity. But duolocal residence keeps the descent group together at the expense of the marital bond.

The second way in which members of a matrilineal lineage can be organised on the ground is through uxorilocal residence when the married couple live in the locality of the wife. This type of residence, practised, for example, among the Yao of Malawi (Mitchell 1956) keeps the female members of the lineage together in one village in which they live together with their husbands from other matrilineages, their married daughters and their unmarried sons, who upon their marriages move out to live with their wives in their respective villages. The disadvantage of this residential arrangement is that it disperses the male members of the lineage who hold authority within it.

The third possible type of residence is avunculocal, or more precisely viri-avunculocal residence, that is such residential arrangement when a woman lives with her husband who himself resides in the locality of his mother's brother. This type of residence automatically disperses the female members of the matrilineage and was practised, for example, among the Trobriand Islanders (Malinowski 1929). A boy grew up in the village of his father in which he had been born and where he was perpetually told that he did not belong. His proper home was the village of his own matrilineal group. This was the village of his mother's brother to whom he moved after his marriage. A Trobriand woman never resided in the village of her own matrilineal group. She also grew up in her father's village in which she had been born and after her marriage she moved from there to the village of her husband.

The fourth possible way in which members of a matrilineage can be organised on the ground is for women to move to the villages of their husbands upon marriage and for men to continue to live in the villages in which they were born. This type or residence – the virilocal one – disperses both male and female members of the matrilineage as children are born not in their mother's but in their father's villages. Men who live in the same village become eventually mutually related as fathers and sons and as brothers and patrilateral cousins. Nevertheless, matrilineal groups can remain vital and manage to remain localised in spite of a residence rule which ostensibly hinders their localisation. When virilocal residence is practised, it is the marriage tie which keeps a woman away from the village which is the home of her matrilineage. When her husband dies, or upon divorce, she and her children are free to settle in it. The coherence of the matricentric family of a woman and her children, brittle marriage and high individual mobility thus make possible the drift of lineage members back to the village which is regarded as the traditional centre of their matrilineage and their concentration there in spite of the centrifugal effect of virilocal residence. Societies like the Ndembu of Zambia (Turner 1957) or the Suku of Zaire (Kopytoff 1964, 1965) are examples of societies in which residence is virilocal and matrilineal descent has remained at the same time a strong organising principle.

Fox (1967) and Keesing (1975) discuss in detail the organisational problems faced by matrilineal systems and the underlying reasons for the differences between matriliny and patriliny. It would be superfluous to rehearse their arguments and I concentrate instead on the discussion of one particular difference between matriliny and patriliny which has received less analytical attention than the perceived structural differences between matrilineal and patrilineal systems but which is, nevertheless, closely related to the latter. This difference was stated in the observation that matrilineal systems are more liable to change than patrilineal ones when they are affected by modern economic development through absorption into the capitalist market system (Gough 1961b, Nakane 1967: 143). The argument usually put forward suggests that a change from production for subsistence to production for exchange leads to the emergence of the nuclear family 'as the key kinship group with respect to residence, economic cooperation, legal responsibility and socialization' (Gough 1961b: 631). The wealth controlled by its male head tends to be passed through inheritance to his sons rather than to his matrilineal kinsmen. A change like that or a growing tendency to such a change has been observed among many matrilineal peoples affected by economic development (Cardinal 1931: 84, Fortes 1950: 272, Meek 1957: 179, Colson 1958: 347, 1961: 95). Economic development everywhere means increased wealth. It has been implicitly assumed that once a man accumulates individual wealth, he holds on to it and transmits it through inheritance to his son, to whom he is bound by strong emotional ties (Colson 1958: 346–7, Gough 1961b: 649).

Affective bonds between fathers and sons exist, of course, in all matrilineal systems and these systems everywhere have to devise mechanisms for 'segregating and limiting the father's authority over his child so that it does not, and is not likely to, supersede the authority of the child's descent group' (Schneider 1961: 21). The hypotheses linking the shift to familial inheritance with the increase in individual wealth do not explain why these mechanisms suddenly fail to operate under the conditions created by economic development. Why should sons benefit from the wealth of their own fathers instead of from the wealth inherited from their own matrilineal kinsmen? The mere fact that there is suddenly more wealth to be inherited does not in itself explain why the norm of inheritance changes. The hypothesis that the wealthier the father is, the more inclined he is to provide for his own sons instead of fulfilling his jural obligation towards his uterine heirs rests on an unexplicated psychological assumption that the affective bond between the father and son becomes more binding if there is more wealth to be transferred than before. Goody avoids this pitfall of psychological reductionism and he ascribes the loosening of ties between the wide range of matrilineal kinsmen to the rise of property differentiation which upsets the reciprocity of the matrilineal inheritance pattern:

Among the LoDagaba the transfer of wealth outside the living-together group of distant uterine kin is based upon recognition of reciprocity, so that what is lost in one transaction can be regained in the next. Large inequalities of fortune render such a mode of inheritance difficult to work, because they upset the operation of equal exchange; and nowadays people are more inclined to hold on to wealth, since they can do more with it. (Goody 1962: 348)

Douglas suggests that Goody's emphasis is not entirely right in implying that differential access to wealth puts a strain on the system of matrilineal inheritance. She argues that 'it is not differential wealth, in itself, that causes rich men to favour their sons so much as scarcity in the basic resources' (Douglas 1969: 130):

On my view the enemy of matriliny is not the cow as such, not wealth as such, not economic development as such, but economic restriction. Many societies changing from production for subsistence to production for exchange find themselves entering a very restricted field. Economic restriction ... produces a movement to close the ranks and resist encroachment by other people. The emphasis is less on finding men to exploit resources than on an equitable sharing of a fixed amount within a limited group. (1969: 131)

However, economic restriction and a necessity to tighten the control of a narrow group over scarce resources do not have to lead inevitably to the shift from uterine inheritance. There are other means by which matrilineal systems can 'close ranks and resist encroachment by other people': the generation depth and span of the effective matrilineage may narrow, and the resources may be transmitted through inheritance only to the nearest uterine kin. Colson reports that among the Tonga, with the development of cash-crop farming and the increasing scarcity of fertile land, a tendency developed for matrilineal groups to break down, especially for purposes of inheritance, into small groups composed of uterine siblings and their immediate descendants through females (Colson 1961: 95, see also Colson 1958: 253). Fortes writes of the Ashanti that, as a result of intensive cash-crop farming, the maximal matrilineage or a major segment of it lost its significance for the inheritance of property; there emerged a tendency to pass the wealth on to the immediate descendants of the deceased's own mother (Fortes 1950: 261).

Goody's claim that wide distribution of wealth through a matrilineal system of inheritance to close as well as distant kinsmen is compatible only with a poor, egalitarian economy, has been confirmed by comparative research (Aberle 1961). However, it does not follow from this that an increase in wealth and the emergence of property differentiation are sufficient conditions for the change in the system of inheritance. They are relevant only insofar as they upset the basic principle of reciprocity which underlies all ongoing social transactions. Accumulation of wealth which can be put to use, and particularly the emergence of considerable property differences, are incompatible with a wide distribution because any group which has produced the wealth through the joint efforts of its members, opposes its transfer to those who have not contributed to its production. It tries to secure at least a greater portion of it, if not all of it, for the group members. It is therefore this tendency for the members of the productive group to keep the fruits of their own labour to themselves, which works against the principle of wide distribution. Among the Ashanti, Fortes noted severe criticism 'of the tendency of matrilineal heirs to eject their predecessor's widows and children from the enjoyment of properties in the building up of which they have often assisted' (1950: 272). The tendency to pass on the property to the man's sons therefore develops when the basic productive group is the household formed by the members of the nuclear family and particularly when the cooperation in production between the father and his son continues when the son, after his marriage, establishes his own household in his father's village. In other words, the transmission of wealth from father to son seems to occur when they have produced it through their joint cooperative efforts (Holy 1986). If the production group consists of matrilineally related kinsmen, however rich any male member may be, no tendency will arise towards the transmission of the wealth to his own sons instead of his matrilineal heirs (Hill 1963: 82). A change from uterine to agnatic inheritance can only be generated by the emergence of previously non-existent conditions which bring fathers and sons into close cooperation and into the formation of joint productive teams. In his analysis of the LoDagaba system of inheritance, Goody stresses a similar point when he argues that the mode of uterine inheritance is disharmonic with the residential pattern in which the domestic group is formed around an agnatic core (Goody 1962: 423) and the productive group consists of agnatically related men (Goody 1958).

Matriliny is of course more than the matrilineal system of inheritance. According to Poewe, it is a 'total system and consists of the combination of matrilineal ideology and those social actions and relations which are meaningfully informed by it' (1981: 55). Transmission of property through inheritance is the practice most obviously informed by, or embodying, matrilineal ideology in that it equates those who have a right to one another's property with those who share a common substance. But the defining feature of matriliny is not a single social practice meaningfully informed by matrilineal ideology, but that ideology itself, that is, the assignment of individuals to culturally recognised categories whose membership is defined by descent traced through females (Aberle 1961: 656, Douglas 1969: 124). Any explanation of the decline or demise of matriliny must therefore satisfactorily account not only for the change in the transmission of property through inheritance but also for the general decline or demise of the tracing of descent exclusively through females. There is, of course, no logical reason to assume that a change in the system of inheritance has invariably to be accompanied by a change in the conceptualisation of descent. Why cannot men inherit property from their fathers while considering themselves members of a category of people who are descended in the matrilineal line from a common ancestress? After all, among the Tonga, Nayar and Minangkabau, the practice of the transmission of individually earned property to one's own children has not affected the tracing of descent in a matrilineal line (Fuller 1976, Colson 1980, Kato 1982).

The demise of tracing descent in a matrilineal line has generally been ascribed to 'the institutionalisation of very strong, lasting or intense solidarities between husband and wife' (Schneider 1961: 16–18). As economic development invariably leads to the strengthening of familial ties at the expense of ties of wider kinship, it also automatically leads to the demise of matrilineal descent groups (Lewis 1955: 14, Bauer and Yamey 1957: 66, Gough 1961b: 649, Smelser 1963: 39).

It is readily understandable that if the nuclear family takes over all the functions formerly discharged by a descent group, the very notion of tracing descent from a common ancestor or ancestress would itself become irrelevant: there is simply no activity left which would revalidate it and thus keep it in existence. This has empirically been the case in some matrilineal societies, for example among the Luapula, where the businessmen and -women find their obligations arising from the notion of shared matrilineal descent an obstacle to economic growth. They sever their relations with their close kin in an attempt to temper their demands; they justify their behaviour by substituting the religious ideology of the Seventh-Day Adventists for the traditional matrilineal ideology (Poewe 1981: 80–1). However, at least three other ways can be detected in which matrilineal descent has been affected under the conditions of modern economic development.

First, matrilineal descent may be invoked less frequently than before and thus become applicable in a gradually diminishing range of situations. For example, among the Gwembe Tonga resettled after the construction of the Kariba dam, daily interaction among the lineage members within a neighbourhood declined and the notion of common matrilineal descent ceased to be invoked in claims to land. Fellow members of the lineage ceased to respond to demands for assistance with elopement damages and bridewealth payments made by young men who were unable to find employment in towns; their requests for assistance were usually heeded only by their own fathers, brothers and mother's brothers (Colson 1971: 90–1).

Second, the size of groups whose members are recruited on the basis of matrilineal descent may decrease. Only matrilineal descent from closer ancestors may be given recognition as a criterion defining membership of a culturally recognised category and, in consequence, the generation depth and span of effective matrilineage narrows. As I have mentioned before, this process has taken place for example among the Tonga or the Ashanti.

Third, the range of activities and the size of groups whose members are recruited on the basis of descent does not change, or at least not dramatically, but matrilineal descent ceases to be recognised as a valid principle of recruitment into them. The notion of descent as such does not become obsolescent but the mode of tracing descent through females becomes replaced by tracing descent through males or through both sexes.

Presumably, the significance of the nuclear family has increased, and the father–son bond strengthened, in all matrilineal societies absorbed into the capitalist market economy. To treat this general factor as a cause of the particular changes in descent conceptualisation is thus clearly inadequate. There must obviously be other factors which influence the way in which matrilineal descent becomes affected when the society is exposed to modern development.

Following Lowie (1920: 70–6, 122–37, 157–62, 166–85), Murdock (1949) and Fox (1967: 109–11) stress the role of residence rules in the process of social change. According to Murdock, it is patrilocal residence which inevitably leads to the decline of matrilineal mode of tracing descent as 'patrilocal residence involves a man in lifelong residential propinquity and social participation with the father's patrilineal kinsmen' (Murdock 1949: 202). It follows for him that 'bit by bit, ties with patrilineal kinsmen are strengthened and ties with matrilineal relatives undergo a diminution in importance' (1949: 202).

In his analysis of the Suku residential arrangements, Kopytoff criticises Murdock's evolutionary model for equating the concept of 'residence' with a specific point in physical space. He makes the valid point that the concept of residence should concern 'a person's relationship to various social fields' and in consequence should not refer to 'the *spot* at which one lives but the *zone* within which one resides' (Kopytoff 1977: 555; original emphasis). A man can 'reside' patrilocally in his father's locality and at the same time his 'residence' is still avunculocal in the residential zone, within which his relations to its other inhabitants are important principles of recruitment into various activities. Patrilocal residence does not then need to pose a threat to matriliny·as Murdock's model predicts.

It has to be noted, however, that the avunculocal residence within the residential zone is the product of the in-gathering process by 'which lineage members drift "back" directly into the lineage center or, indirectly, to the subsidiary loci as they grow older' (Kopytoff 1977: 549). Such an in-gathering process is at work in some Central African matrilineal and virilocal societies like, for example, the Ndembu (Turner 1957) or the Tonga of Malawi (van Velsen 1964). In none of them is matriliny threatened by patrilocal residence, for men have not been brought into '*lifelong* residential propinquity and social participation with the father's patrilineal kinsmen' (emphasis added) which Murdock's model stipulates as the initial condition for the diminution in importance of ties with matrilineal relatives. In all of them, matrilineally related men are kept in spatial proximity within individual villages because of their inter-village mobility.

Such mobility can become inconvenient for a variety of reasons: perhaps men have invested in a brick-built house in their father's village which they would have to leave if they changed residence, they may have established cooperative relations with their fathers and their father's kin and would find it difficult to enter into new cooperative relations in a different village, or they may find it difficult to gain access to land elsewhere. If mobility decreases and village residence becomes stabilised, the main mechanism through which matrilineally related men were kept in spatial proximity ceases to operate. The changed social composition of villages hinders the tracing of descent in a matrilineal line for the simple reason that people related matrilineally live dispersed in different villages and areas, and the spatial distance between them prevents them from being jointly recruited into groups which crystallise in various situational contexts. When this becomes empirically the case, that is, when the membership of a descent category which defined an individual's entitlement to membership of various social groups can no longer do so because people cannot, for practical reasons, activate their entitlement, their membership of the descent category becomes, for all practical purposes, meaningless and consequently the descent, which defined their membership of the descent category also becomes meaningless.

This interpretation subscribes to Murdock's view (*pace* Fortes 1958: 3) 'that an alteration in the prevailing rule of residence is the point of departure for nearly all significant changes in social organisation' (Murdock 1949: 202) in that it stipulates the spatial distribution of people resulting from particular residential arrangements as the most important restraint on the practical possibility of the invocation of the existing notions of descent. However, even if people can no longer invoke the existing notions of descent, it does not mean that categories of which people are members in virtue of their common descent from a particular ancestor, will inevitably disappear as culturally meaningful categories. What may happen is that a matrilineal mode of descent reckoning changes either into a cognatic or patrilineal one.

A change like that took place among the Toka of southern Zambia (Holy 1986) among whom descent traced in a matrilineal line has recently been replaced by tracing descent through either males or females in consequence of newly increased residential stability which brought into spatial proximity men mutually related through their fathers. But the notion that everybody belongs to a descent category called *mukowa* (pl. *mikowa*) has persisted and the *mikowa* continue to perform the same activities as they did when they were conceptualised as descendants in a matrilineal line from a common ancestor. The members of a *mukowa* are called *basimukowa*. In virtue of being *basimukowa*, people participate in common rituals which are conceptualised as *mukowa* affairs, jointly hold the right to a certain territory, have a right to inherit a part of the property of any deceased *basimukowa* and have a say in the selection of a successor to anyone of them. In this respect, a *mukowa* can be conceptualised as a community, that is a circle of people who live together, who belong together and who share a whole set of common interests. Analytically, we may best view the change in the principle of recruitment into the *mukowa* as a change in only one sphere of community relations. The sphere of genealogical relations has changed as a consequence of changed residential structure and people conceptualise their *basimukowa* not only as those who trace descent from a common ancestor in a matrilineal line; anybody who can trace descent from the ancestor of the *mukowa* in any line, including a mixed one, counts as a member. The territorial, ritual and other relations within the community have endured. People attend funerals of their *basimukowa* who are at the same time their neighbours, they have a say in choosing successors to the dead *basimukowa* with whom they lived in spatial proximity and they have a right to inherit from them. Together with their *basimukowa* with whom they live in the same area they participate in rain-making rituals and they recognise the senior headman in the area as the head of their *mukowa*. As before, people interact in the same way with other individuals who have two qualities: they are genealogically close and they are close in spatial proximity. What has changed are the conditions under which those who see themselves as genealogically close were brought into close spatial proximity. In other words, we may say that what has changed is the type of genealogical relations which recruit people into the community; on the level of descent categories, this means a change in the mode of tracing descent from matrilineal to cognatic.

Dalton has remarked that '[e]mpirical studies of modernisation teach us a good deal about traditional societies that was not obvious before they began to modernise' (1971: 26). This is because such studies enable us to evaluate the relative significance of different sets and types of relations in the totality of social relations in which each individual is involved. For an anthropologist who is interested in studying small-scale communities as ongoing systems of social relations, activities and institutions, a changing society offers a unique opportunity for analytical isolation of social relationships that persist in the process of social change. The strategic significance of such relationships for the shaping of the total social structure can then be determined in the process of analysis; a similar analytical procedure is often difficult under traditional conditions.

Low-level technology combined with small scale and relative isolation of a community results in an ingrained mutual dependence among people sharing many relations: those with whom one is economically involved are at the same time those with whom one is involved through neighbourhood, religion, polity and kinship. Any of these relationships are part of the overall community relationships. In a stable system, it is much more difficult to isolate analytically these different sets of community relations; it is virtually impossible to ascertain any causal connections among them and the ways in which they mutually affect, reinforce or modify one another.

Anthropologists have traditionally studied societies as stable systems. Even when these societies were affected by modern economic development (and almost all societies studied by anthropologists were so affected at least to a certain extent), the effects of this development were usually not their primary concern. Most leading ideas, concepts, specifications of functional relationships and analytical conclusions and generalisations which constitute the body of anthropological theory of kinship, were formulated as a result of the empirical study of societies as stable systems. This had its effect on the conceptualisation of kinship as an irreducible domain of social relations, which was explicitly formulated by Fortes (1969), but which is implicit in all anthropological studies of simple societies: economic, political, ritual and other relationships are perceived as being embedded in kinship relationships. It was this reducing of political, economic and ritual relations to kinship ones which gave rise to the notion of the irreducibility of kinship.

The analysis of the changes in the conceptualisation of descent in matrilineal societies affected by modern economic development suggests that kinship relations are embedded in other community relations in almost the same way as anthropologists have traditionally perceived economic, political or ritual relations to be embedded in kinship ones. This analysis further indicates that while kinship relations may determine the nature of political, ritual, economic or other relations, it is the residential structure of the community which determines the nature of kinship relations. In this sense, kinship relations are not an irreducible principle of social structure. Their treatment as such may lead to the misapprehension of the significance of kinship ties in the totality of social relations. It would rather appear that, although many other relations are expressed in the idiom of kinship, the content of every kinship relationship itself is dependent on the spatial proximity or distance between the participants in the relationship. If that is the case, it is probably misleading to focus on the change in kinship structure when studying the social consequences of technological and economic development.

COGNATIC DESCENT

That societies can be organised not only in terms of patrilineal or matrilineal descent but also on the basis of cognatic descent was discovered comparatively late in the development of kinship studies. As Bohannan pointed out, this was perhaps because a cognatic descent group is 'obvious and therefore not easy to see' (1963: 129). Goodenough (1955) drew the anthropologists' attention to the existence of cognatic descent groups, which he called 'unlimited decent groups', in the Gilbert Islands. In the late 1950s and 1960s, when anthropologists became seriously interested in non-unilineal forms of organisation, they spent a great deal of effort in formulating a theory of cognatic systems which in its rigour would parallel their theoretical understanding of unilineal descent systems (Firth 1957, 1963b, Davenport 1959, Peranio 1961, Forde 1963, Scheffler 1964, 1965, Sahlins 1965). But it soon became clear that it was not possible to specify the forms or principles of social organisation which could be applied to all cognatic societies as their characteristic or defining features. As Needham pointed out, cognatic descent systems were classed together primarily because of what they lack in comparison with societies with unilineally defined descent groups: 'In other words, cognatic societies constitute a negatively defined class, and are thus recalcitrant to any comparative investigation into what possibly typifies them' (Needham 1974: 103).

Conceptualisation of cognatic systems largely arose in opposition to the conceptualisation of segmentary lineage systems. As a result, what came to be seen as a characteristic feature of cognatic systems was their apparent inability to form enduring corporate descent groups.

When descent is traced unilineally through an unbroken chain of links which are exclusively either male or female, each person is a member of only one descent category and nobody can simultaneously be a member of two or more categories. As a result, unilineal descent categories are clearly bounded, exclusive and do not overlap. Corporate descent groups, whose members are recruited from among members of descent categories, can easily crystallise. As some anthropologists have expressed it, in unilineal descent systems it is descent alone which defines group membership or closes the group. One is a member of a lineage because one is unilineally descended from its apical ancestor and remains a member irrespective of whether one lives in the lineage territory or not. Other criteria, like the place of residence, do not enter into consideration of descent group membership which is solely defined on the basis of descent.

The situation is quite different when descent is traced cognatically. All those who trace descent from a common ancestor through male or female links, or a mixture of both, are regarded as members of a cognatic descent category. Like unilineal lineages, cognatic descent categories are therefore also ancestor-focused units and include all those who happen to be descended from a particular common ancestor. Obviously, each person has many ancestors; he or she may trace descent from all of them and therefore be a member of several cognatic descent categories simultaneously. Everybody has four great-grandfathers, two on the father's side and two on the mother's side. One can trace descent from each one of them and thus be a member of four different descent categories. If one traces descent from male ancestors one generation above one's great-grandfathers, one can be a member of eight different descent categories; and if one goes one generation further back in tracing descent, one can be a member of sixteen different descent categories. If one considers both male and female ancestors, the number of descent categories of which one can be a member doubles.

If one belongs to more than one descent category, these categories overlap similarly as kindreds overlap because each person is a member of several kindreds. And if descent categories overlap, it follows that action groups limited in their duration in time can be formed by those who belong to a specific descent category, again like the way in which action groups can be formed by the members of a kindred. But the formation of enduring social groups, and even more so of corporate groups recruited from among members of a specific descent category is obviously quite difficult.

Yet, in cognatic descent systems, more or less clearly bounded and exclusive descent groups do form because of certain mechanisms which operate in every cognatic descent system and which quite effectively prevent the proliferation of descent categories. The Toka who nowadays trace descent cognatically are an example of how the number of descent categories with which people can affiliate themselves becomes considerably restricted in practice. As I have mentioned before, a descent category among the Toka is called *mukowa* (pl. *mikowa*). Although it is not unusual for a *mukowa* to have a depth of six or seven generations counted from the members of the youngest adult generation, the average depth of a *mukowa* is about five generations. Basing the calculation on a five-generational depth, and taking into account that it is always male forebears who are recognised as apical ancestors of *mikowa*, any Toka may ideally trace his or her descent back to eight different ancestors and thus potentially exercise a choice of affiliation with eight different *mikowa*. However, in practice the choice is much more limited.

An important factor reducing the number of *mikowa* with which people can affiliate themselves derives from the fact that not all the eight ideally recognisable forebears are in fact recognised as apical ancestors of existing *mikowa*. It is usually the founders of villages, and particularly of large villages, who become recognised as apical ancestors of *mikowa* whose members are their cognatic descendants. Others are simply forgotten and therefore nobody can trace descent from them. Although the choice of any individual's *mukowa* affiliation is considerably restricted in this way, it is not altogether eliminated. Another important factor which restricts it, is people's residence and the residence of their forebears. For example, if ego's paternal grandmother resided virilocally in ego's father's natal village, ego will affiliate himself or herself with his or her father's father's *mukowa*. If, on the other hand, ego's paternal grandfather resided uxorilocally in ego's father's natal village, ego will affiliate himself or herself with his or her father's mother's *mukowa*. A person's own place of residence determines first of all whether one will consider oneself and be considered by others a member of one's father's or one's mother's *mukowa*. If one lives in an area inhabited by members of the mother's *mukowa*, one will count as one of them and cognatic descent traced through one's mother will substantiate one's membership. If one lives in an area inhabited by members of a *mukowa* of which one's father is or was a member, one will count as a member of that *mukowa*. The fact that only some of an individual's forebears are recognised as *mikowa* founders combined with the fact that one's own and one's forebears' place of residence determines to a great extent one's actual *mukowa* affiliation, makes it possible for the Toka to talk about their *mukowa* membership in much the same way in which people who trace descent either matrilineally or patrilineally are able to talk about their lineage membership.

Considering that in societies with cognatic descent an individual can be effectively limited to being a member of just one descent category, this category, like a unilineal descent category, can be more or less exclusive in membership in spite of the fact that the boundaries of a cognatic descent category are inevitably somewhat blurred. And descent groups can then crystallise from among its members rather like they do in unilineal descent systems. But it is not descent alone which defines the category or the group; among the Toka, the cognatic *mukowa* is defined by combining the principle of cognatic descent from a recognised ancestor with the principle of an individual's and his or her forebears' actual residence.

Especially in Oceania, where cognatic systems are most common, there is very often another principle at work than an individual's residence which operates as a mechanism for closing the cognatic descent group. In addition to the principle of cognatic descent, there is very often simultaneous recognition of the principle of patrilineal descent. This is the case, for example, among the Kwaio of the Solomon Islands (Keesing 1970). Although all cognatic descendants from the founding ancestor of the descent group are entitled to membership, those who are patrilineally descended from him occupy a privileged position in it and have much stronger rights. Alternatively, there may simply be a cultural preference for affiliation with one's father's group. This results in patterns of affiliation which are predominantly patrilineal, or at least patrilateral. Under normal circumstances, a Kwaio will grow up with his or her father's people and affiliate with them. Because of cumulative past affiliations, most members of the descent group will be agnates. To break this pattern means to weaken one's status and the status of one's descendants.

In societies in which descent groups are ranked, people tend to affiliate with the group which has a higher status. For example, the Maori of New Zealand affiliate themselves with their father's cognatic descent group, provided that it has a higher status than their mother's group and with their mother's group when it has a higher status than their father's group (Scheffler 1964).

Although discrete or relatively discrete corporate groups are formed in societies which trace descent cognatically, cognatic systems provide individuals with greater choice and exhibit a greater degree of flexibility than do unilineal descent systems. People cannot live everywhere at the same time: they have to have their home in a specific place and in consequence, they usually become members of that group on whose land they live and farm. Among many groups of which they potentially can be members on the basis of cognatic descent, they activate their membership of only one. The unilineal descent systems also offer a certain choice as far as descent group affiliation is concerned. But in unilineal systems, individuals can change their lineage affiliation only if the genealogy, which legitimises their membership, is edited or reinterpreted. It is, however, never left to any particular individuals to reinterpret their genealogy in the way which suits them. The members of a lineage to which any particular individual aspires, also have their say in the matter. It is ultimately up to them to accept new members by accepting as valid their version of their genealogy. This imposes a considerable limitation on the choice of an individual's affiliation·and the change of lineage membership is usually a long-term process, accomplished over several generations, when the knowledge of genealogical relations of relevant forebears fades and can be opened to different interpretations which suit the momentary political or economic circumstances of the people involved. In a cognatic system, an individual's group affiliation is not genealogically limited to the extent that it is in unilineal systems. On the basis of their genealogy, people qualify as members of several groups and they can more easily change their group membership if they so wish. If they are members of their father's group and if land, for example, becomes scarce in their father's community, they may move to a less densely populated area if they can claim cognatic connection to those living there and thus effectively change their descent group membership. In a cognatic system, one can therefore identify with the group which offers most advantages without jeopardising one's potential membership of other groups. This flexibility is particularly advantageous in situations of conflict and in times of scarcity. If a particular group outgrows its resources or faces difficulty as a result of some disaster, its members can seek help from many different groups. This led some anthropologists to argue that cognatic descent systems are better equipped to cope in situations of scarcity than unilineal ones and that there is a tendency for unilineal systems to change to cognatic ones when the pressure on land increases because the cognatically traced descent, which offers a wider choice of group affiliation, makes possible the necessary demographic adjustments. Such a hypothesis has been advanced, for example, by Goodenough (1955) who suggested that cognatic systems may be regarded as functionally advantageous in situations of high population density and heavy pressure on land resources (see also Brown and Brookfield 1959–60: 75).

But not all anthropologists share this view. Meggitt suggests that 'where the members of a homogeneous society of agriculturalists distinguish in any consistent fashion between agnates and other relatives, the degree to which social groups are structured in terms of agnatic descent and patrilocality varies with the pressure on agrarian resources' (Meggitt 1965: 266, 280; see also Reay 1971). He argued that where land was scarce, the agnates, as it were, closed their ranks against their cognates: the allocation of land to sisters' sons would be rare, movement of individuals between local groups would be restricted, and the composition of local groups would tend to be determined by agnatic descent. Allen, on the basis of his research among the Nduindui in the New Hebrides (1971) reconciles Meggitt's and Goodenough's hypotheses by trying to measure the degree of scarcity. He argues that the tendency of a local group to be composed of men related to one another through patrilineal ties ceases to appear once a certain level of population density and land shortage is reached. Beyond this point the adaptation of groups to the fluctuation of resources, and to the population increase in some of these groups, cannot be resolved by warfare, and the only alternative is to employ mechanisms of adjustment based on the utilisation of all available ties of kinship and affinity, leading to the crystallisation of groups of co-residing cognates.

As in all societies with cognatic descent groups, filiation is only a necessary but not a sufficient condition for the possession of a status which is held simultaneously by a set of persons, Scheffler revised his original view that such sets could be described as 'cognatic descent groups' (1964, 1965) and subsequently argued that there were no cogent reasons to support such a description (1985: 9–11, 18). Ultimately, the difference between unilineal and cognatic descent groups boils down to the permanency of group membership. Cognatic descent as a principle of ascription of status as a group member allows for the possibility of change in group membership, whereas in unilineal descent systems group membership can be changed only through legal fiction, that is, by acquiring a new genealogy. Refusing to recognise cognatic descent as a principle of group formation thus derives ultimately from the ethnocentric Western assumption that 'blood is thicker than water' and that a status ascribed on the basis of a genealogical relation is for life because it is established 'in nature' and hence cannot change unless by a legal fiction.

DOUBLE DESCENT

I have mentioned above that only three descent rules exist: the rule of patrilineal descent, the rule of matrilineal descent and the rule of cognatic descent. A society need not recognise only one specific way of tracing descent which would be applicable in all situations and to all people. Different people may sometimes trace descent in a different way or the same people may trace their descent in different ways for different purposes.

A widely quoted example of a society in which different people trace descent in different ways are the Mundugumor of New Guinea where daughters have been reported to trace descent through their fathers and sons through their mothers (Mead 1939: 176–9). What seems to be involved is that movable property, including the sacred flutes to which the Mundugumor ascribe great importance, are passed from father to daughter and from mother to son. These lines of inheritance are called 'ropes' by the natives but it is questionable to what extent the 'ropes' can be seen as descent categories; all that is probably involved in their formation is the notion of filiation rather than descent. Among the Apinayé of Brazil (Maybury-Lewis 1960), descent lines are gender specific: women trace descent matrilineally and men patrilineally which means that women are members of matrilineal groups which consist only of females and men are members of patrilineal groups which consist only of males. This is a perfectly feasible arrangement provided that the purposes for which the female groups and the male groups exist are fairly limited.

While among the Apinayé rules of matrilineal and patrilineal descent apply to different individuals, in other societies patrilineal and matrilineal descent is traced simultaneously by the same person. In such societies there also exist patrilineal and matrilineal descent groups but all people belong simultaneously to both: they are members of the patrilineal groups of their fathers and matrilineal groups of their mothers. The best-known society in which this situation obtains are the Yakö of eastern Nigeria (Forde 1950). They lived in unusually large villages averaging about 4,000 inhabitants. Land was the property of patrilineal lineages (*yepun*) and men who were related patrilineally usually lived together in one ward of the village. Cattle, money, tools, weapons and all objects of daily use were inherited by the members of the deceased's matrilineal group (*yajima*) who were also collectively responsible for each other's debts. Because they inherited the movable property of the deceased, matrilineal kin also performed all funerary rituals. Also various social positions were inherited in the female line, typically, for example, the membership of various cult associations. The priests of fertility spirits, associated with each village, were recruited from among the members of matrilineal groups. Whenever a priest performed a ritual to honour the fertility spirit of his matrilineage, members of the matrilineage, who lived scattered in the different wards of the village assembled for the performance of the ritual. During the harvest, all priests of the village performed a ritual to ascertain the wellbeing of the village and people attended this ritual in virtue of their membership of the priest's matrilineage. In this way the ties of matrilineal descent cross-cut the ties of patrilineal descent, which divided people into different wards, and bound together members of different wards within one village.

The Yakö society has usually been seen as having double descent, variously described also as double-unilineal descent, duolineal descent or bilineal descent. The Mundugumor way of descent reckoning has often been described as that of cross or alternating descent and the Apinayé were characterised as practising parallel descent. Distinguishing double descent, cross descent and parallel descent as special modes of tracing descent besides the rules of patrilineal, matrilineal and cognatic descent (see for example Barnard and Good 1984: 70) involves a confusion between the particular mode of tracing descent and the classification of the social system in terms of descent. A society may perfectly well be classified as having double descent in the sense of having simultaneously patrilineal and matrilineal descent rules and forming both patrilineal and matrilineal descent categories. But double descent, or cross and parallel descent for that matter, are not special ways of tracing descent; they merely mean a simultaneous recognition of patrilineal and matrilineal descent rules as the basis for the formation of specific descent categories or groups.

Not only may patrilineal and matrilineal descent rule be simultaneously recognised in the same society, but unilineal and cognatic descent rules may coexist as well. I have already alluded to societies which trace descent cognatically but recognise at the same time the rule of patrilineal descent as a secondary principle of differentiation and I have also already mentioned that the opposite is probably true of many societies which have traditionally been presented as organised on the basis of patrilineally traced descent. There is of course a difference between the prevailing mode of tracing descent in any particular society and the way in which it orders social relations in terms of the genealogical ties among specific individuals. Nevertheless, very often the whole system of genealogical relationships is characterised in terms of the descent system of the given society. We thus talk about the Tallensi or the Nuer as patrilineal societies, or about the Trobriand Islanders as a matrilineal society. Not only is the descent system of the given society elevated to classify the whole society, but one specific mode of tracing descent or one specific type of a descent category is seized upon and used to classify the whole descent system. We talk about the Tallensi as being a patrilineal society in spite of the fact that patrilineal descent is just one mode of tracing descent which they recognise. It might be the socially most prominent one but it is not the only one and this should be kept in mind. What also has to be kept in mind is the fact that every society which orders the recognised genealogical connections in terms of descent, orders them also in terms of kinship. Sometimes only dyadic relations between particular persons in the kinship system are of any practical significance, but sometimes wider categories of kinsmen may be recognised for various social purposes. A society which culturally recognises categories or groups of people who have an ancestor in common, may also recognise categories of people who have a kinsman in common. Expressed differently, it means that societies which have lineages may also have kindreds and that, as Leach pointed out a long time ago (1961a: 4), classifying societies as patrilineal, matrilineal or cognatic may hide as much as it may reveal.

6   MARRIAGE AND ALLIANCE

Reproduction is obviously a biological process essential for the survival of humans as a species. But kinship is not a system of social ties based on acknowledging actual biological relations among people brought into being by physiological acts of mating, engendering and giving birth to offspring. It is everywhere culturally defined (Barnes 1961: 298), including the West. This is not only because 'true' biological links are mostly unknowable but, more importantly, because the assumed biological relations among the members of any given population are not the result of random mating as not all types of mating are allowed, equally preferred or occur with the same degree of probability. The assumed genealogical relations which are seen as arising out of procreative activities are therefore culturally constructed. They are a socially structured set of relations culturally conceptualised as natural relations (Harris 1990: 29).

The most important social rules which regulate mating are the rules of incest, that is, rules which prohibit sexual intercourse between certain categories of persons. In the West, incest is defined rather narrowly as the sexual relation between parents and children, and between siblings. By contrast, the Nuer concept of *rual* which Evans-Pritchard glossed as 'incest', prohibited sexual relations between members of the same clan, between cognates within six generations and between a man and the women who married other men of his lineage (Evans-Pritchard 1951: 30–1, 37).

However widely or narrowly the rules of incest may be defined in different societies, they have one common consequence. Although one can have sex without marriage, one cannot, or at least one is not expected, to have marriage without sex. From this it follows that if two people are forbidden to have sexual relations, they are also automatically prohibited from getting married.

The rules of incest are, however, by no means the only rules which regulate who can marry whom and for this reason alone, rules governing sexual relations have to be distinguished from rules governing marriage. Very often these two sets of rules do not coincide: in some societies, sexual relations between certain categories of kin are allowed, or at least tolerated, but marriage between them is prohibited.

One of the most important rules governing marriage is the rule of exogamy which prohibits marriage within a specific group or category, usually defined in terms of kinship, descent or locality. Expressed in positive rather than negative terms, it is a rule compelling people to choose their marital partners from some other group or category than their own. The obverse of exogamy is the rule of endogamy which stipulates the group or category within which a person should or must marry.

Brushing aside the essential distinction between rules governing sexual relations and those governing marriage (Leach 1970: 103–4, 1982: 186), Lévi-Strauss considers the essence of incest taboos to derive not from the fact that they prohibit marriage between certain persons but rather from the fact that they force men to seek spouses from another category than the one which is prohibited. In his explanation of the imposition of the incest taboo, he basically follows Tylor whose observations on exogamy anticipated by some sixty years the discussion of the significance of marriage alliances for the cohesion of society. Tylor argued that in early human societies, an isolated family could not have survived for it lacked sufficient manpower to organise collective hunts of big animals and to defend itself against attacks by enemy groups. To survive economically, it needed to cooperate with other families and friendly relations with other families were at the same time the only guarantee of its security. These friendly relations were established through exogamic marriages, that is, through marriages of women of one family to men of another. As Tylor put it himself: 'Again and again in the world's history, savage tribes must have had plainly before their minds the simple practical alternative between marrying-out and being killed-out.' He emphasised that exogamy

cements ... uncultured populations ... into nations capable of living together in peace ... till they reach the period of higher military and political organisation .... By binding together a whole community with ties of kinship and affinity, and especially by the peacemaking of women who hold to one clan as sisters and to another as wives, it tends to keep down feuds and to heal them when they arise, so as at critical moments to hold together a tribe which under endogamic conditions would have split up. (Tylor 1889: 268)

Lévi-Strauss similarly argues that the incest prohibition is first and foremost a rule obliging the sister or daughter to be given in marriage to others rather than a rule prohibiting marriage with the sister, daughter or mother, and he points out that the actors' own notions directly confirm this interpretation. In support he cites Margaret Mead's research among the Arapesh. When she asked her informants whether a man ever sleeps with his sister, they found her question totally absurd:

Certainly not, they reply: 'No, we don't sleep with our sisters. We give our sisters to other men, and other men give us their sisters'. The ethnographer pressed the point, asking what they would think or say if, through some impossibility, this eventuality managed to occur. Informants had difficulty placing themselves in this situation, for it was scarcely conceivable: 'What, you would like to marry your sister! What is the matter with you anyway? Don't you want a brother-in-law? Don't you realize that if you marry another man's sister and another man marries your sister, you will have at least two brothers-in-law, while if you marry your own sister you will have none? With whom will you hunt, with whom will you garden, whom will you go to visit?' (Lévi-Strauss 1969: 485)

This anecdote illustrates well Lévi-Strauss's basic thesis that incest prohibitions are prohibitions only secondarily and derivatively. Rather than being a prohibition on a certain category of persons as marriage partners, they are a prescription directed towards another category of persons as marriage partners.

Although Lévi-Strauss stresses the positive aspect of the rule of exogamy, this rule, nevertheless, defines only the group or category from which a marriage partner cannot be chosen. It does not specify the group or category from which it must or should be chosen and in that sense it can be classified as a negative marriage rule. Some societies operate not only negative marriage rules but also positive ones which define the group or category from which a spouse should be appropriately selected. Lévi-Strauss considers societies with positive marriage rules to have 'elementary structures' of kinship and those which have only negative marriage rules to have 'complex' ones.

MARRIAGE PRESTATIONS

However marriage is defined or conceptualised, it means a significant change in the status of any person entering it and the creation of a whole range of new social relations. These are not only the relations between the spouses themselves and their relations to the other's kin, but also the relations between their whole kinship or descent groups. In this respect, marriage is, as Radcliffe-Brown expressed it, 'essentially a rearrangement of social structure' (1950: 43). It seems that only some hunter-gatherer societies did not have specific ceremonies and rituals which sanctioned the conclusion of a new marriage which was simply assumed to have occurred when a man and a woman started to live together (Hoebel 1954: 83, Thomas 1959: 159) or in which the change of status from an unmarried to a married person was a gradual process (Collier and Rosaldo 1981: 285–6). In most societies, the change of status and relations which every marriage entails is marked by a ceremony or ritual ('wedding') and usually validated and sanctioned, or at least accompanied, by specific marriage prestations.

Various types of marriage prestations and their social significance and functions have been widely discussed by anthropologists (Goody and Tambiah 1973, Goody 1976, Sharma 1980, Comaroff 1980). Two of the most common forms of marriage prestations are bridewealth and dowry; the former involves the transfer of valuables from the bridegroom's group to that of the wife and the latter the transfer of valuables from the bride's father or group to the couple or to the bride herself. Goody (1973a, 1976) sees dowry as a form of pre-mortem inheritance and his comparative study of marriage prestations suggests that the bride is endowed with a dowry usually in societies with pronounced economic differentiation in which a distinction is drawn between male and female property.

Early writers assumed, and it is still a widespread popular belief, that where marriage is legalised by the transfer of bridewealth, the husband is buying his wife. Even if the purely economic aspect of bridewealth cannot be completely eliminated, particularly nowadays when bridewealth is often paid in cash, anthropologists have insisted that the woman herself is not regarded as a commodity to be purchased. They have pointed out that at marriage certain rights in the woman are transferred from her natal group to that of her husband and that bridewealth can be seen as a compensation for their transfer. First of all, the husband and his group acquire the rights in the woman's labour which until then have been vested in her natal group. The transfer of rights in the woman's labour is strikingly demonstrated particularly in those cases where the woman leaves her natal home upon marriage and goes to live with her husband and his kin. The logical consequence of this aspect of bridewealth is that upon divorce, when the woman returns to her natal group, the bridewealth is very often returned to her husband. Another important right which the husband acquires is the right in the woman's procreative services and bridewealth can be seen as compensation to the wife's group for the children she bears for her husband and for the rights which he and his group acquire over them. In line with this aspect of bridewealth is the fact that in many societies, the bridewealth is returned when the wife is barren, or that her group has a duty to replace her with another woman who can bear children for her husband. Other facts also support the explanation of bridewealth as a prestation paid for acquiring rights in the woman's offspring. Some peoples on Sumatra and in eastern Indonesia distinguish two types of marriages. If the whole bridewealth has been transferred, the children affiliate with their father's group but if the whole bridewealth has not been paid, they belong to their mother and her kin.

In many patrilineal societies, in which it is important for a man to have legitimate offspring, various mechanisms exist through which children begotten by one man count as legitimate offspring of another. They all follow from the principle that children borne by the woman for whom bridewealth was paid count as legitimate offspring of a man on whose behalf it was transferred. One particular outcome of this principle is that marriage established through the transfer of bridewealth does not come to an end upon the death of the husband. The husband's brother who has inherited the deceased's estate and succeeded to his position lives with the widow in a relationship called levirate (from the Latin *levir* – husband's brother). The children whom he begets with the widow do not count as his but as those of his deceased brother in whose name the bridewealth was transferred. Very often the widow is not forced to cohabit with her husband's brother. But even when she goes to live with another man and has children with him, they still count as the legitimate offspring of her late husband.

It is obvious that the explanation of bridewealth as husband's compensation to the wife's kin for the children she bears for him holds only in patrilineally organised societies. Bridewealth cannot fulfil this function in matrilineal societies where children affiliate with the wife's and not the husband's group. Similarly, bridewealth can function as compensation to the wife's group for its loss of a working member only in those societies where the bride leaves her natal group after her marriage and takes up residence with the group of her husband. In those matrilineal societies where the woman continues to live with her own group after her marriage, bridewealth obviously cannot fulfil this function. It is hence not surprising that in matrilineal societies, if bridewealth is paid at all, it is usually small. Nevertheless, the fact remains that the transfer of bridewealth – however small it may be – legalises marriage in quite a number of matrilineal societies in which bridewealth obviously cannot fulfil some of its functions so far mentioned.

To appreciate the meaning of bridewealth we have to realise that marriage is not simply an affective bond between a man and a woman but a relationship which links together two families or groups of kin. In simple societies, the exchange of valuables is used to establish and maintain friendly relations between members of separate social groups. This exchange is not so much guided by the insistence on the equivalence of what is exchanged as by the notion of reciprocity; the fundamental rule is that a return must be made for whatever is received.

Obviously, if one group gives a woman in marriage to another one, the group which received the woman is in debt to the one who gave her to it and very often this debt is offset by the payment of bridewealth. The bridewealth provides the bride's group with the means to obtain wives for the men of the group. For example, among the Lovedu of Transvaal, marriage was contracted in such a way that a man's patrilineage transferred cattle to his wife's patrilineage. The cattle which had been received for the woman were then used by her brother to obtain a wife for himself from another lineage than the one into which his sister had married. Having used as bridewealth the cattle received for his sister, the man became her cattle-linked brother. The cattle received for his cattle-linked sister were said to 'build his house' and his house 'had a gate which the cattle sought' in the next generation. This metaphor expressed the principle that each lineage married off its women to the same lineage in each generation and that men of each lineage received their wives from the same lineage in each generation. Women therefore moved in marriage between the same two lineages and bridewealth passed between them in the opposite direction. It meant that each man married where his father had married and, as the Lovedu expressed it, a woman went upon marriage to her father's sister, that is, married where her father's sister had married.

The marriage system of the Lovedu can be seen as a system of the exchange of women between groups. However, a group which had given away a woman in marriage did not receive another woman from the group into which the first woman went, but received bridewealth instead. By passing this bridewealth to another group, the original group received a woman who replaced the daughter and sister the group had originally lost. Women were thus exchanged for bridewealth and bridewealth was exchanged for women. In this system of marriage, bridewealth becomes an additional element in the system of exchange and of the creation of alliances between groups.

The result of this system of the exchange of women and cattle between groups is a marriage between cross-cousins, that is children of the opposite-sex siblings: a man marries his mother's brother's daughter and a woman marries her father's sister's son. Among the Lovedu, the fundamental rule was that a man must not marry a daughter of any brother of his mother, but only the daughter of that brother who used the man's mother's marriage cattle to obtain a wife for himself, that is, his cattle-linked cross-cousin. The Lovedu said that the children of the cattle-linked brother and sister were 'born for one another' (Krige and Krige 1943: 142–5).

The Kriges did not take the cross-cousin marriage as the starting point of their analysis of the marriage system of the Lovedu but saw it as the result of the exchange of women and bridewealth between patrilineal lineages. In their view, 'that is the complex network in which cross-cousin marriage is enmeshed' (1943: 144). Their analyses thus anticipated the explanation of marriage as an exchange of mates between exclusive groups and as the source of social solidarity which has become known as 'alliance theory' and which is most closely associated with the names of Lévi-Strauss (1963, 1969), Dumont (1953, 1957, 1968), Leach (1951, 1957, 1961a) and Needham (1958, 1960a).

MARRIAGE ALLIANCE

Marriage alliance 'refers to the repetition of intermarriage between larger or smaller groups' (Dumont 1968: 19), typically descent groups. The concept of marriage alliance was developed principally by Lévi-Strauss (1969) to deal specifically with societies which practice various forms of cross-cousin marriage. According to him, such forms of marriage are but specific aspects of systems of the exchange of women between groups which create perpetual marriage alliances between them.

As already mentioned, Lévi-Strauss sees the prohibition of incest as a universal rule which prevents marriage within the family and therefore creates society. It does so by forcing men to give their sisters and daughters in marriage to men of other families and to seek their own wives in these other families. This exchange of women links families together into a group of interrelated families and creates solidarity between them which simply would not exist if men were not obliged to seek their wives from families other than their own because there would be nothing which could possibly make these families mutually interdependent. The function of the rule of exogamy is thus to establish exchange between families and to integrate them into a larger social system. In some societies, as for example among the Lovedu, the mutual dependency between exchange units is achieved by the exchange of women for bridewealth, but in others women are exchanged directly or indirectly for each other. Following Mauss (1954), Lévi-Strauss considers the exchange of gifts between groups to be a symbolic expression of their mutual interdependence within a larger societal whole. The obvious question of course is, why families and kin groups should exchange women and not something else. Lévi-Strauss's answer is that the exchange of women is not simply an alternative to the exchange of valuables but that it is the primary form of exchange because in the case of women, the object of the exchange itself constitutes the relationship which it at the same time symbolises and no separation is yet involved in it between the relationship of solidarity itself and the symbolic means of the gift exchange through which it is expressed. In his view, the exchange of women is the most elementary form of exchange which must have preceded the exchange of goods with its distinction between the symbol itself (the goods exchanged) and the relationship of inter-group solidarity which it symbolises (Leach 1970: 104–5).

Lévi-Strauss distinguishes between two main types of exchange of women in marriage. The first one is a direct exchange of women between two exogamous groups. For example, among the Tiv of Nigeria, it was usual for a man to marry a sister of the husband of his own sister. That the two families saw the mutual marriages of their children as an exchange was plainly indicated by the fact that a wife took over the name of her husband's sister. This custom made it clear that she was considered to be a replacement for the woman lost to the family through her marriage. Among the Tiv, this exchange of women was more or less haphazard and was carried out between families who agreed on it, but in many other societies it was a regular practice which linked two exogamous groups through mutual intermarriages.

If an exchange of women between two families is consistently practised over generations, the result is that one's wife is simultaneously one's cousin and, furthermore, that cousin marriage is necessarily symmetrical since one's wife can be either a matrilateral cross-cousin (MBD) or patrilateral cross-cousin (FZD).

What is significant about this type of exchange is that each family simultaneously gives women to and receives women from the other. As far as giving and receiving of women is concerned, there is no functional specialisation between the families. In consequence, this kind of marriage generates mechanical solidarity between the two exchanging units as they are both functionally equivalent and unspecialised: they are both wife-givers and wife-takers with respect to each other.

Lévi-Strauss classified the marriage system in which two groups directly exchange women between themselves as restricted exchange, because the exchange of women is restricted to two groups only: for a woman that a group gives away, it receives another woman from the group to which it gave one.

As a rule, the boundaries of exogamy enclose much wider groups than a family, usually clans or lineages, and it is these exogamous groups which exchange women between themselves. If the whole society is divided into two exogamous groups, these groups are called moieties and the social system based on two moieties is referred to as a dual organisation of society. Irrespective of whether descent is patrilineal or matrilineal, parallel cousins, that is to say the children of the father's brother and of the mother's sister, belong to the same moiety as ego, while cross-cousins. that is, the children of the father's sister and of the mother's brother, always belong to the other moiety. Lévi-Strauss points out that cross-cousin marriage is far more frequent than exogamous moieties and that it exists even where exogamous moieties do not. Evolutionist anthropologists assumed that the cross-cousin marriage occurs either in societies with extant dual organisation or in societies in which dual organisation existed in the past, and they considered cross-cousin marriage to be derived from this form of social organisation. Lévi-Strauss is not interested in posing problems of derivation of this type of marriage from dual organisation or vice versa. According to him, it is not the hypothetical succession of the two institutions which should be considered, but rather their structure (Lévi-Strauss 1969: 101–3, 106). For him, cross-cousin marriage and dual organisation are connected on a different level: 'As their functional value (viz. to establish a system of reciprocity) is identical, it can indeed be understood how the absence of dual organization can be compensated for by the presence of cross-cousin marriage' (1969: 103).

Whilst the restricted or direct exchange of women promotes mechanical solidarity between the exchanging units, the second type of exchange promotes organic solidarity among them in that it binds together functionally specialised and therefore dissimilar units. The units engaged in the second type of exchange are specialised in the sense that they are either wife-givers or wife-takers with respect to each other. Such specialisation of exchanging units arises from a situation when a group does not give women to a group from which it has taken them but when it receives women from one group and gives its own women to another, different group. Each group is thus linked with two others: with the one from which it receives women and with the one to which it gives them. Lévi-Strauss classifies this exchange of women in marriage as generalised or indirect exchange of women because groups do not exchange women between themselves directly but indirectly within a circle. It is obvious that at least three groups are necessary to make this system of exchange possible: group A gives women to group B, B to C and C to A. But many more groups than three can form such a cycle in which women are indirectly exchanged among the groups which are mutually linked within the cycle. Moreover, every group tends to find itself in a number of different cycles and at any moment in time it can start giving women to groups to which it did not give them previously. In reality, there may thus be many actual groups to whom, let us say, A gives women; B is merely a model shorthand for all of them. This 'openness' of the system as a whole lies at the root of its enormous strength and resilience. When practised over generations, the system of indirect or generalised exchange produces a marriage in which the man's wife is his matrilateral cross-cousin (MBD). Whilst the system of restricted or direct exchange gives rise to a symmetric marriage rule, that is a rule according to which both the matrilateral and patrilateral cross-cousins are marriageable, the system of generalised or indirect exchange gives rise to an asymmetric marriage rule which allows marriage of a man only to his matrilateral but not his patrilateral cross-cousin. The marriage of a man to his father's sister's daughter is proscribed. If he married her, he would be taking back a wife from the group to which his group previously gave one, thus contravening the basic asymmetric rule.

The opposite of the asymmetric rule of marriage with a matrilateral cross-cousin is the rule which prescribes or deems as preferential the marriage of a man to his patrilateral cross-cousin (FZD). The existence of such rule has been reported from 'between two and six societies' in the world, 'depending on how strict your criteria are' (Buchler and Selby 1968: 126). It comes into existence when group A gives women to group B, group B to group C and group C to group A. Again, the cycle does not have to be limited to three groups only but can be much longer and it again does not matter whether the groups exchanging women among themselves are patrilineages or matrilineages. On the level of one generation only, the system is the same as the system of indirect or generalised exchange which produces the matrilateral cross-cousin marriage. However, the picture changes in the next generation. In the matrilateral case, the wife-takers never give women back to their wife-givers, remaining thus in a certain sense perpetually in debt to them. In the patrilateral case this debt is wiped out in the next generation when the group gives women back to the group from which it received them in the previous generation. Unlike in the matrilateral case when women move in the same direction in each generation, in the patrilateral case they move in one direction in one generation and in the opposite direction in the next generation. This seemingly complicated arrangement is easily achieved by following a simple rule that a woman should marry into the group from which her mother came. When this rule is followed, it automatically produces a man's marriage to his father's sister's daughter.

Like the system of the indirect exchange of women which produces matrilateral cross-cousin marriage, the system which produces the patrilateral cross-cousin marriage is also asymmetrical as during one generation the groups involved are clearly in an asymmetrical relationship and can only be linked in a cycle; the marriage rule as such is also clearly asymmetrical. But according to the nature of the exchange relationship between groups, this system is symmetrical or direct: women go from group A to group B in one generation and from group B to group A in another. There is thus a direct exchange of women between groups A and B. This exchange, however, is not immediate as in the case of the direct exchange which produces the symmetrical marriage rule, but delayed in the sense that the debt is repaid only in the next generation, that is after a delay (Fox 1967: 206–7).

The discussion of what is basic to these various types of exchange led, on the one hand, to numerous modifications of Lévi-Strauss's theory (Needham 1962, Dumont 1966, 1968, Fox 1967, Barnard and Good 1984: 95–104) and, on the other hand, to its extensive and often severe criticism (Josselin de Jong 1952, Schneider 1965, Leach 1970: 95–111, Scheffler 1970a; 1973: 782–6). The question of how the various marriage rules should be explained to which the different types of exchange give rise generated an acrimonious debate in the 1950s and 1960s. Perhaps its most important result was the realisation that it is a mistake to presuppose that marriage alliances of various types concern people who are already genealogically related (typically as cross-cousins) and that the units exchanging women consist of people related to each other by common descent. In fact, the exchanging units need not be descent groups at all; very often they are local residence groups (Leach 1961a: 56) and marriage rules may be formulated in terms of 'genealogical connexion, relationship category, locality, descent group, social class, prior affinal alliance' and so on (Needham 1973: 173).

Among the Kachin, who are frequently cited as a typical case of a system of generalised exchange, the preferred marriage

is not between mother's brother's daughter and father's sister's son, but between *classificatory* mother's brother's daughter and *classificatory* father's sister's son (Kachin *nam* and Kachin *gu*). It is only among the chiefs, whose circle of kinsfolk is necessarily somewhat restricted, that an orthodox marriage with *nam* implies marriage with a 'real' mother's brother's daughter or any near relative. A commoner male normally has a wide range of *nam* to choose from, including for example any lineage sister of the wife of any of his father's lineage brothers. In many cases the actual relationship between *gu* and *nam* is very remote, but in Kachin eyes *any gu–nam* marriage is strictly orthodox. (Leach 1961a: 87; original emphases)

A Kachin ... must marry a *nam*, that is a girl junior to Ego who is a member of any wife-giving lineage with respect to Ego. There will ordinarily be at least half-a-dozen such lineages and there is no statistical likelihood that the chosen bride will be of the same lineage or even of the same clan as Ego's own mother. (Leach 1963: 77)

It is obvious that to gloss Kachin terms *gu* and *nam* in genealogical terms as father's sister's daughter and mother's brother's daughter would clearly be wrong. Who at any particular time would stand in the relation of *gu* and *nam* to each other depends on previous marriages of the lineages and on the number of local lineages from which a marriage partner can be chosen. If that is the case, the explanations of cross-cousin marriages or of the relations between wife-giving and wife-receiving groups as being determined by genealogical relations, are clearly misleading.

The debate between the proponents of the 'alliance theory' of Lévi-Strauss, Dumont, Leach and Needham, and the proponents of 'descent theory' developed mainly by Radcliffe-Brown (1952) and elaborated by Fortes (1953, 1959, 1969) and Goody (1959), which dominated the anthropological study of kinship in the 1960s, was concerned with the old sociological problem of explaining social cohesion. Underlying the dispute was an agreement on societies existing as systems held in a state of equilibrium, and on actual physical segments (descent groups) as component parts of these systems. If members of different segments intermarry, over time they become linked by a web of mutual kinship ties. However, individuals who are linked to each other by ties of mutual kinship, are at the same time also mutually separated in virtue of their descent which places them into separate segments, the membership of which legitimises their rights to various forms of property and determines their political and jural status. The ties of descent thus keep separate what ties of kinship unite and the cohesion of the whole social system is achieved by a balance between the unifying principle of kinship and the dividing principle of descent. This is the view of the descent theorists. The alliance theorists see the unifying principle to lie not in the balance of kinship and descent but in the exchange of women between segments which links them into perpetual alliances. As Schneider pointed out

[t]wo different kinds of system, each made up of identically structured segments, are really at issue. In one system, the segments are articulated into a logically interrelated system by the descent rule, the mode of classification of kinsmen, and the relationship of perpetual alliance between segments. In the other, the segments are defined by the descent rule, exogamy and the variable bounding of the segments in terms of special functions (domestic, jural, political, residential, territorial, and so on). (1965: 58)

On the ethnographic level, the debate between descent and alliance theorists was basically a debate between ethnographers working predominantly in Africa on the one hand and in Southeast Asia on the other. The notion of the complementarity of descent and kinship or filiation as the main structural principles derives mainly from African ethnography accumulated during fieldwork carried out in the middle of the century. Ethnographers who subsequently worked in India, Burma, Sri Lanka, Indonesia and South America discovered that, in an explanation of the social structure of many societies in these areas, the main structuring principle could not be ascribed to the interplay of kinship and descent ties. They saw the structuring principle as inherent in enduring alliances between groups, whose members were related to each other as affines.

It seems therefore to appear that neither descent nor alliance theory can claim to be a universally valid theory of social cohesion but that each of them is merely a generalisation of different ethnographic 'facts'. Such a conclusion is also supported by the fact that neither of them can satisfactorily account for the social systems of many Middle Eastern societies where segments are defined by descent rule but no rule of exogamy relates these segments in marriage exchanges with other segments of the same kind. Allowed or preferred marriages between patrilateral parallel cousins, that is marriages between the children of two brothers, challenge the basic assumptions of descent theory in that these marriages occur between members of the same descent group and in consequence blur the distinction between descent and kinship which descent theory emphasises. They also challenge the basic assumptions of alliance theory because they clearly negate the importance of exogamy, alliance and exchange on which this theory is built (for cousin marriages in the Middle East see Holy 1989).

MEANING OF MARRIAGE

The taxonomy of the different forms of exchange is based on the assumption that relations between men who receive wives and women who become wives are everywhere of the same kind. It fails to note the differences in the social context and significance of marriage for men and women and the different ways in which men and women experience marriage.

In their study of gender, economic and political relations and ritual symbolism in hunter-gatherer and hunter-agricultural societies in which marriage is not legitimised by bridewealth but by 'brideservice' or gifts of labour by the groom to his in-laws, Collier and Rosaldo (1981) point out the different meaning which marriage has for men and for women.

For a man, marriage is a precondition of his adult status which makes him equal to other adult men and differentiates him sharply from bachelors who have no direct and privileged access to female sexuality and to the products of female labour. Marriage therefore marks a critical transition in the life career of a man; it enables him to attain a public position and to acquire the independence which makes him equal to other adult men. Loss of a wife significantly undermines this achievement. While a man thus considerably gains from marriage, marriage marks a decline in a woman's status and autonomy. A newly married woman does not gain a more privileged access to male products than that enjoyed by her unmarried sisters, and sexual access to a husband often does not outweigh the loss of personal and sexual freedom which she enjoyed before her marriage. Whereas for a man marriage is a desirable achievement, women often are reluctant to marry and have to be forced into marriages by their brothers and parents. It is mainly the anticipation of grown children that endows marriage with positive significance in the eyes of a woman: as she becomes a mother of marriageable daughters, she starts enjoying special access to the labour and products of prospective sons-in-law (Collier and Rosaldo 1981).

In simple societies, where productive relations are expressed in terms of kinship relations, 'marriages create not only families but also those patterns of cooperation, obligation and expectation that organize productive activity' (1981: 316). It is therefore different roles of men and women in productive activity, most sharply marked in the sexual division of labour, which lend different meanings of marriage to men and women. Among the Berti, there are tasks which can be, or customarily are, performed by only one sex. Only men slaughter animals, attend to camels and sheep at pasture, spin cotton, sew, and make leather bags, ropes and wooden utensils. Only women husk millet in wooden stamps, grind flour, cook meals and brew beer. They also harvest and winnow the threshed grain although a man can perform these two tasks if no woman is available.

However, the mutual dependence of the sexes on each other for the performance of specific tasks is not symmetrical and it is this asymmetry which women emphasise. They invariably stress that a woman can easily live on her own, as indeed many do, either temporarily when her husband is away from the village, or permanently if she is divorced or a widow. If there are only women present in the household when they want to kill a chicken, they either ask a neighbour or any man passing by to do it for them. Furthermore, meat can always be purchased from the butchers in the market without resort to one's own slaughtering. The dependence of women on men is thus only occasionally made manifest in the existing division of labour; moreover, it can easily be alleviated through the culturally recognised alternatives. When a woman who lives on her own needs a leather bag, a rope or a utensil which only men manufacture, she can again buy it in the market. If she has camels or sheep which have to be grazed outside the village, she is certainly wealthy enough to be able to hire a herder.

Unlike a woman, a man cannot live on his own. Although he could harvest his own field and thresh and winnow the grain all by himself, he cannot cook his own food and brew his own beer. It would be a clear indication that he failed to maintain a woman who would care for him as a woman should for a man. As food and beer have to be prepared daily, the men's dependence on women for the performance of these tasks is made manifest continually and more directly than the women's dependence on men. Moreover, there are no culturally accepted alternatives to the preparation of food in the household: although beer can be obtained from the market, cooked food cannot.

The asymmetry in the mutual interdependence of the sexes that women emphasise, manifests itself in yet another important way that the women are ready to point out. The man's status as an elder who has a right to take part in settling disputes, that is, his status in the public domain, depends on his being *rājil be bētu* (a man with a house), that is, on being head of his own household, in which his daily sustenance is provided for him by his wife.

The model of gender relations explicitly expressed by Berti men is that of male dominance and female subordination. It emphasises the men's role in the public domain and sees men as dominant because women hold no position of authority in the public domain in which they are represented by men, either fathers or husbands, under whose protection they are.

The women's model clearly privileges the domestic domain; women have power over men not only directly because of their monopoly over the processing of food but also indirectly in that it is the man's status within the domestic domain that is the basis for the ascription of his status in the public domain. For this reason women can see themselves as making the men what they are. A man without a wife has no status in the public domain. He acquires it only after he has married and established his own house. If he subsequently gets divorced, he does not lose his status as an elder but his prestige does become significantly impaired. The source of the woman's power is her monopoly over the processing of food. A woman acquires this power, and thus becomes a fully adult member of her sex only through marriage, for only as a newly married woman does she acquire her hearth which is the symbol of her independent existence. Until her marriage she was not a woman (*mara*) but a girl (*binei*). An adult unmarried man is not referred to as a boy (*walad*) but as a bachelor (*'āzib*). As such, he is not yet a full man; he becomes one only when he has his own house. Women acquire their power and men their authority only through marriage; women thus depend for their power on men and men for their authority on women. But this relationship is again not symmetrical. The status of a woman as a mistress of her own hearth, which enables her to lead an independent existence, is not affected by her subsequent divorce; after her divorce she does not revert to the status of a *binei* fully subjected to the authority of her father. She becomes *'azaba* (divorcee) who can maintain her own independent household (as most divorcees do) virtually for the rest of her life and who controls all her economic transactions as well as all her subsequent relations with men, either as lovers or future husbands. Unlike a woman, a man after divorce reverts to what he was before his marriage – an *'āzib* (bachelor) with a concomitant loss of prestige awarded to proper elders, that is, *rujāl be bētum* (pl. of *rājil be bētu*).

Whereas a woman only needs to be married once to be forever a fully adult member of her sex, and in fact as a divorcee gains a considerable degree of economic autonomy which a married woman does not enjoy, a man has to be perpetually married to qualify as an adult member of his sex. If he does not have his own house, he can regain his full status in the public domain only with advanced age, when the fact that he is an elder of a group of his own descendants (even if he lives as a dependent in a household of one of his children) is more important than the fact that he has no house of his own; and when his status as a *shāib* (an old man) becomes more significant than that he is technically an *'āzib*.

Within the context of the women's model of power relations between the sexes and the male model of authority relations it also makes sense that polygyny and a great number of children are seen as the signs of a man's prestige for they are at the same time the signs of his successful management of his relationship to a particular woman or women made possible through his effective control of female power. A woman displays this power effectively when she refuses to cook or sexually cohabit with her husband. Although the manifestations of women's power are limited, the means by which a man is able to cope with a woman who refuses to yield her power are even more restricted. He has no monopoly of control over anything a woman cannot obtain without his cooperation. He can, of course, withhold sex as a woman can, but then he is harming himself and not the woman, for he is refusing himself the children, who, as the Berti say, belong to their father and not their mother and whose patrilineal affiliation is the expression of this fact. If everything fails, he can divorce his wife. The asymmetry of the divorce right, which accrues only to the husband but not to the wife, has been seen by a number of analysts as a manifestation of male dominance. Such a meaning of divorce is construed on the basis of specific cultural experience according to which divorce leaves the woman destitute, and on the unwarranted presupposition of its universality. The Berti cultural experience is distinctly different. For them divorce is the ultimate sign of the man's failure to control his wife. It is the sign of the victory of her power over his authority. He has lost and he also suffers most. While a divorced woman can go on living on her own, a divorced man has to attach himself to his mother or sister, at least for sustenance, if not in terms of his actual residence in her household. He can manage his sustenance from his own household only if there is an adult daughter in it who can cook and brew beer for him. Whatever the case, the divorce for him means changing his dependence on one particular woman for dependence on another.

I have mentioned before that contemporary thinking about the significance of descent groups and lineage systems has been greatly modified as a result of anthropologists' growing sensitivity to natives' own conceptualisations. The thinking about marriage has been similarly affected. The ethnographic examples of 'brideservice societies' and of the Berti of the Sudan suggest that it would be a misguided enterprise to generalise about the significance which marriage invariably has in all societies. The interpretation of the observed relationships in terms of the concepts, premises and values which are culturally significant in the studied society, has made it abundantly clear that the meaning of marriage may differ not only from one society to another, but even for different categories of people within the same society. The present-day anthropological interest in people's own conceptualisations and constructions has an effect on our conceptualisations not only of descent groups or marriage but of the whole field of relations which we call kinship. The next chapter addresses this issue.

The study of kinship, from its very inception, has been based on the assumption that kinship creates divisions in society by conceptually separating those who are genealogically related to each other from those who are not so related. This separation is grounded in the difference between people resulting from the natural facts of procreation. The anthropological concept of kinship is thus built on links established in the process of engendering and bearing children, that is, on the basis of immutable natural facts which are given and can be seen as preceding the activities and processes through which a particular cultural expression of these natural facts is elaborated. As kinship has thus 'to do with tracing natural ties' (Strathern 1992a: 52), it is grounded in something that is ontologically different from sociality or, expressed differently, it is a cultural recognition of something that precedes sociality and something that sociality has to take into consideration in one way or another. As Strathern expressed it, kinship is the social construction of natural facts (Strathern 1992b: 27) while the 'natural facts' of life are seen as natural in the sense of belonging to the biology of the species (Strathern 1992a: 119).

This basic assumption that people everywhere ascribe cultural significance to natural facts of procreation has recently been challenged by a number of anthropologists (Schneider 1984, Strathern 1992a, 1992b, Bouquet 1993) who argue that the ascription of significance to the facts of procreation may well be the result of projecting onto others a view which is particular to Western culture. What this culturally specific view is, has been summarised succinctly by Meigs in the following way:

who one is related to, is established in the popular American view
prenatal act of conception. By the time one is born, in fact at the moment
conception, it is established who one's 'real' kin are. The use of such terms
'real mother' and 'real father' attests to the importance in this ideology of
the presence or absence of what is understood as an actual physiological
connection, as does the cultural fascination with genealogy. (Over fifty do-
it-yourself genealogy books are currently in print in the United States. The
recent phenomenon of adopted children searching for their 'real' parents is
additional testimony to the power of the notion that 'real' kinship is determined
by birth.) Kinship, according to this ideology, is a matter of shared blood (or
genes) by which one is eternally and immutably related. (1989: 36;
reference omitted)

We were able to talk about kinship in different cultures as a system
of social ties based on the acknowledging of relations resulting from
engendering and bearing children because we projected on to them
our culturally specific conceptualisation of what are universal 'natural'
facts with which all cultures have to cope, even if they may impose
different cultural meanings on them. This projection was sustained by
the method by which the students of kinship gather the 'data' from
which they construct their theoretical generalisations.

GENEALOGICAL METHOD

The method of inquiring into the way in which people see themselves
as related is the 'genealogical method' developed by Rivers during the
Torres Straits expedition of 1898–99 (Rivers 1910). As Bouquet
recently noted, this method 'aimed to establish ethnology as a science
as exact as physics or chemistry' (1993: 114). She points out that Rivers
formulated his scientific methodology by borrowing and translating
the English aristocratic idiom of pedigree (1993: 21, 218) and she
discusses in detail how the concept of pedigree is grounded in the English
ideas about animality, personhood and distinction on the one hand,
and on the other hand how the culturally specific English assumptions
about kinship led to the formulation of the genealogical method and
to the subsequent development of kinship theory.

The genealogical method was described by Rivers in the 4th edition
of *Notes and Queries in Anthropology* published in 1912 and his description
was incorporated with certain modifications into the last edition of
this fieldwork manual published in 1951. Although the method was

devised by resorting to the notions which gave rise to the English concept of pedigree, built into it is a conceptual distinction between pedigree and genealogy. While pedigree refers to indigenous knowledge of relatedness expressed in oral or written form, genealogy refers to that knowledge systematically rendered as the '"scientific" … record made in standard format by the anthropologist, with random errors removed, evidence duly verified, and the testimonies of different informants combined and consolidated' (Barnard and Good 1984: 21). As Bouquet noted, obtaining basic information on relatedness through the use of the genealogical method amounts to translating the culturally specific notions of relatedness into our own terms (1993: 208). The fieldworker is warned that even those vernacular terms which may be glossed as 'mother', 'father', 'brother' and 'sister' may be used to refer to a wider range of relatives than those which are designated by these terms in English. The method recommends ascertaining first the name of 'the woman from whose womb [the informant] was born' and the name of the man 'who begot him' (*Notes and Queries* 1951: 54). The collection of kinship data thus begins by eliciting names of biological parents and proceeds to elicit the reciprocal terms of address and reference. By using names as the concrete means of access to an abstract system of relationships (Bouquet 1993: 147, 178, 205) and by employing the elicited vernacular terms for F, M, H, W, S and D, the genealogical method proceeds to record the ties of consanguinity and affinity which are recognised between people in the studied population.

The authors of a guide to the study of kinship published in 1984 whose aim is 'to explain … how kinship may be most effectively studied and analysed' (Barnard and Good 1984: 15) stress that the fieldworker should not prompt or constrain their informants to express their ideas in etic, genealogically based terms, adding the caveat 'at least until after you have mastered their own idiom' (1984: 26). They are critical of the implicit lineal bias of the genealogical method which considers terms for lineal relatives (F, M, S, D) potentially less ambiguous than the terms for collateral relatives like 'brother', 'sister', 'aunt' or 'cousin', and stress that the idiom of collecting genealogical information has to conform with local usage and local circumstances should be taken into consideration (1984: 27, 28). Nevertheless, they still present the genealogical method as a standard technique of investigating kinship (1984: 26–33) and emphasise that all possible relationships should be explored 'in a reasonably systematic way' (1984: 31).

Bouquet noted that the genealogical method 'contains an empirical injunction: it is an invitation to collect comparable materials' (1993: 18). The materials become comparable due to 'the translation from "local dialect" to standard, global idiom' (1993: 140–1). As everywhere children are borne by women and the role of the father is usually culturally recognised, everybody everywhere can point out their mother and most people in most societies can point out their father. As a result, 'one really can collect a genealogy from any people … and expand that genealogy as far as the informant's memory will carry him' (Schneider 1980: 13–14). But it does not follow from this that links between parents and children (or genealogical relations generally) are necessarily ascribed the same cultural significance which they have in Western societies. Obtaining basic information on relatedness through the use of the genealogical method results invariably in imposing the notion of kinship as a system of genealogical relations on societies whose own cultural notions of relatedness may be quite different. When collecting kinship terms by using Rivers's genealogical method, Margaret Mead elicited from her Samoan informants a different system of terms for relatives than the one which the Samoans actually used when they were not prompted by her to think about their mutual relatedness in genealogical terms (Mead 1969: 126–9).

The genealogical method cannot but confirm that genealogical relations constitute the basis of the notions of relatedness in all societies. This assumption about what kinship is all about is already built into the method of inquiry into the field of relations we call kinship. Another ethnographic example may illustrate this important point. People on the island of Yap in the West Caroline Islands (Schneider 1984) address each other by kinship terms only in special formal and ritual situations and they call even their fathers and mothers by their names. But if asked about the term of reference for 'the woman from whose womb he was born' and 'the man who begot him', a Yapese would give them as *citiningen* and *citamangen*. Those to whom he refers by these terms, refer to him as *fak*. Not only the father but also his brothers and his male patrilateral parallel cousins are referred to as *citamangen*. The term *citiningen* is similarly extended. This is in no way unusual and is common in many cultures. What is rather special for Yap is that relational terms are used to refer only to one's own living relatives and that at any one time one can have only one *citamangen* and one *citiningen*. Thus if one's own real father is alive, only he is referred to as *citamangen*. After his death, when he is succeeded by one of his brothers or cousins, his successor will be referred to as *citamangen*. Likewise, if one's mother is alive, only she is referred to as *citiningen* and after her death only that particular woman who has taken her position will be ego's *citiningen*. Everybody thus has only one *citamangen* and one *citiningen* at a time but is also never without one because there is a reservoir of people to replace the original *citamangen* and *citingen* when he or she dies.

Although this 'reservoir system', as Schneider has called it, is unusual, it does not detract from the fact that the terms *citamangen*, *citiningen*, *fak* and other relational terms which the Yapese use, are terms for people who stand in specific genealogical relations to ego. Ego calls a particular man *citamangen* either because he is the man who begot him or because he is a man who is genealogically related to the man who begot him. And he calls a particular man *fak* because he either engendered him or he is genealogically related to the man who engendered him. When reaching this conclusion, it may easily escape us that it is the result of our mapping of the relational terms on the genealogical grid in the first place: we started by inquiring about the terms of reference for a father and mother. But from the Yapese point of view, this is a wrong, or at least, irrelevant question, which they can, nevertheless, answer, because a Yapese, like everybody else everywhere, was borne by a particular woman and begotten by a particular man. However, what is significant about *citamangen* for the Yapese is not that he is the father or some other man who succeeded the father to his position, but that he is the figure of authority and superiority while the one referred to by the reciprocal term *fak* is dependent, obedient and respectful.

We can gain an insight into the culturally specific content of the *citamangen–fak* and other ostensibly 'genealogical' relations on Yap by briefly considering some of the cultural units within which these relations acquire their meaning. If we assume without question that genealogical relations must be as significant on Yap as they are in Western culture, the cultural unit on Yap called *tabinau* may be seen as corresponding to two groups which can be characterised as a patrilineal lineage and a patrilocal extended family. The core of the patrilocal extended family is formed by co-residing men who are all members of the same lineage which has a clear structure of authority and a clear set of rules for the succession to the office of the head of the *tabinau*.

Although land is nominally held by the head of the *tabinau*, the patrilineage (*tabinau*) may be considered to be a landholding corporation. It is a major unit of production, distribution and consumption and it is also a basic political unit in that it provides the offices of the village and the district.

The *citamangen—fak* relationship provides the model for the relationship between the office holders in the village and the village members which are described as those of *citamangen—fak*, or father and child. Similarly, the relationship between the district and its constituent villages is described as a *citamangen—fak* relationship. Should a person or village in the position of *fak* not behave in a respectful, subservient and obedient fashion, the *citamangen—fak* relationship will be terminated.

If one abandons the assumption that the social relations on Yap are either determined by or modelled on the genealogical relations, the cultural unit called *tabinau* can be seen as having a number of meanings. This term can be used to refer to the house or dwelling, to a person or persons who are tied to the speaker through ties to the land, or to a group of people who live together and who have different ties to the same land. In the latter sense it may be used to describe a group consisting of a man who holds the land, the woman who lives with him and the children whom she bore or whom they have jointly or separately adopted. People who do not have a relationship through land cannot constitute a *tabinau* and if there are no people, land alone also does not constitute a *tabinau*. One also does not become a member of a *tabinau* by virtue of one's birth into it. The Yapese stress residence and activity and the relationship of child to *citamangen* rather than birth as the principles of recruitment into a *tabinau* and they talk about a child being 'formed on the *tabinau*'. According to the Yapese, all rank and all offices adhere in the land and a person who holds an office is merely a voice of the land. In their conceptualisation, the land holds the office, has rank and is the voice which speaks through a person who has the right to speak for it. The essence of their conceptualisation of the *tabinau* is that it is people who belong to the land and not the land that belongs to the people.

It was work that made the land of the *tabinau* and it is work that makes and maintains it; people gain rights in the *tabinau* in exchange for their work. After her marriage, a woman lives with her husband on his *tabinau* where she works: she tends the gardens, cooks the meals and takes care of her husband's ageing parents as well as of her children.

When the woman's children are young, their mother's husband (*citamangen*) takes care of them. As they grow progressively older, they begin to work for the *tabinau* to secure their rights in it, following the instructions of their *citamangen*. As he grows into maturity, the woman's son provides the old people with care and help which they require and which he is expected to provide as an obedient and supportive *fak*. If the woman or her children fail to carry out the work which is expected of them, they can be 'thrown away' from the *tabinau* and lose all their rights in it.

For the Yapese, the relationship between *citamangen* and *fak* is a relationship of authority and dependency. *Citamangen* takes care of his *fak* when they are young, but when the *fak* become adult, they take care of and provide for their *citamangen*. Typically a woman's husband is a *citamangen* to her child who is his *fak*, but when he is old and incapacitated he becomes a *fak* of her son who is then referred to as his *citamangen*. But other people besides the woman's husband and her child may stand in the *citamangen–fak* relationship to each other. If the woman's husband is neglected in his old age by her son, another man may take care of him becoming thus the old man's *fak*. In that case, the woman's son loses his right in the *tabinau* and after the old man's death his new *fak* succeeds to his position and holds the *tabinau*.

Like the term *citamangen*, the term *citiningen* does not denote a state of being or a set of attributes but a role that is performed. Under normal circumstances, a woman who is married and bears a child is that child's *citiningen*. But it would be inaccurate to gloss the term *citiningen* as 'mother' for if the woman becomes divorced from her husband, leaves his *tabinau* and returns to the *tabinau* of her own *citamangen* and *citiningen*, she ceases to be a *citiningen* to her child. Her husband's new wife, or if he does not remarry, his sister becomes the child's new *citiningen*.

The head of the *tabinau* allocates plots of land to those who have the right to them. These rights, however, do not depend on genealogical ties. Those who fail to perform appropriately the role of *fak* may lose their rights even after many years of work. A person who assumes that role and pleases the *citamangen* or landholder becomes a new *fak* even if there is no genealogical relation between him and his *citamangen*. The new *fak* becomes the landholder after the death of his *citamangen*. The membership of a *tabinau* is thus not a state of being and is not predicated on the notion of common descent or consanguinity. It depends on the continuous process of the work of building the land, on being respectful and obedient and on performing one's duty of caring for the elders.

If one assumes that genealogical relations are ascribed the same cultural significance on Yap as they are in Western culture, all the different kinds of relations encompassed in the attitude and conduct between *citamangen* and *fak* can easily be interpreted as kinship relations within which the political, economic and ritual relations between *citamangen* and *fak* are subsumed and in terms of which they are constituted and expressed. But such interpretation would grossly distort the Yapese's own understanding. For them, it is not kinship but land which is culturally salient. Rather than seeing the right to land as deriving from specific kinship ties among people, the kinship relationship is encompassed in the idiom of land. Thus the *citamangen–fak* relationship is not a kinship relationship but a relationship between those who hold land and those who acquire rights in that land if they work on it, are respectful and obedient and look after the elders properly. The same applies to the relationship between those who are referred to as *wolagen*, typically siblings, paternal half-siblings and children of the male patrilateral parallel cousins. If we privilege genealogical relations as an idiom in which all other relationships are expressed, *wolagen* could be glossed as siblings. However, what is culturally salient about *wolagen* for the Yapese are not their mutual genealogical relations but the fact that they are those who share equal rights in land.

In their conceptualisation of *citamangen–fak* relationship, the Yapese stress doing rather than being; the relationship is constituted by what the *citamangen* does for *fak* and what *fak* does for *citamangen*. The Western and anthropological conceptualisation of kinship and descent, by emphasising certain inherent attributes, is, in a sense, a direct opposite of this Yapese conceptualisation, for it rests on the notion of a state of being, rather than on doing (Schneider 1984: 11–33, 63–4, 72). The gist of Schneider's argument is that anthropologists imposed this conceptualisation on all peoples in their insistence on kinship as being grounded in the process of reproduction which in all societies creates ties of consanguinity between people which are then universally attributed social significance. The presumed universality of kinship is the result of our ethnocentrically derived assumptions and of the practice of the study of kinship which is grounded in these assumptions. This practice is based on the use of the 'genealogical method' which axiomatically presupposes that the ties resulting from the engendering and bearing of children are everywhere endowed with special social significance and which therefore perpetually confirms its own guiding assumptions. Once we abandon these assumptions, it becomes highly questionable to what extent the *citamangen–fak* relationship could be regarded as a kinship relationship. As Schneider put it, '[k]inship cannot be regarded as the "base" of Yapese society, nor as the idiom in terms of which land or any other relations between *tabinau* members are formulated' (1984: 75).

Although Schneider's rejection of the importance of genealogical ties on Yap has been questioned by some anthropologists (Lingenfelter 1985), his critique of the whole practice of kinship studies is, nevertheless, a valid one. It challenges the generally accepted assumption that kinship, as it has been conceptualised by anthropologists, is postulated as a distinct domain of social relations in all societies. Schneider argues forcefully that kinship need not be universally recognised in all cultures as a culturally constituted domain or that the genealogical grid need not be universally culturally constituted, though it may be possible to impose such a grid on all cultures by using analytical anthropological concepts. He thus expresses strong doubts that kinship, as anthropologists understand it, is a human universal, in spite of the fact that anthropologists have always treated it as such. Since the time of the founders of kinship studies – Maine, Morgan and McLennan – through the functionalists and structural-functionalists like Malinowski, Radcliffe-Brown, Fortes and Goody among others, to Marxists and structuralists and beyond them to scholars like Goodenough (1970) or Scheffler and Lounsbury (1971), the conceptualisation of kinship as a distinct domain which is universally recognised as existing in every culture, rests on three assumptions.

The first one is that together with economics, politics and religion, kinship constitutes one of the institutional domains which are conceived to be universal components or building blocks of every society. The view that every society can be said to have its kinship system, economic system, political system and its system of belief has dominated anthropological study from its very inception. The crucial difference between the kinship system of a society and its other systems lies in the privileged position which kinship occupies in the overall social system in which it functions as an idiom for the articulation of the institutions pertaining to the remaining three systems. Whilst the economic system can be conceptualised as ordering the production, distribution and consumption of goods and services, the political system as being concerned with the distribution of power and the maintenance of law and order, and religion as being about the relation between people and the supernatural, kinship has no content. It is true that there were attempts to define kinship in terms of 'what it is all about', the most celebrated being Fortes's (1969) notion of the axiom of amity. But amity conceptualised as the presumed contents of kinship does not easily separate what we understand as kinship relations from any other kind of relations: people who love each other, support each other and altruistically help each other need not necessarily be kin.

Since anthropologists started to pay systematic attention to people's own cultural conceptualisations, we have realised that economics, politics or religion need not be conceptualised as separate and distinct domains of activity and values in every society. They are meaningful domains into which Western culture carves social reality but they are not necessarily meaningful domains in many non-European cultures. In them, kinship is the *idiom* through which economic, political or religious values and activities are expressed. In many non-Western societies, people cooperate economically because they are kin, they form a political group because they are kin and they perform religious rituals together because they are kin. We conceptualise their society as kin-based. The notions of kin-based society and kinship as an idiom thus depend on the distinction between kinship, economics, politics and religion, that is on the distinction between functionally different systems constituting a society, which are culturally conceptualised as different in the West but not necessarily so in many non-Western societies. This of course raises the following question: if kinship is an idiom for economics, politics and religion – and in consequence the society is kin-based – how can kinship as such be understood and separated from the other domains as a domain in its own right?

Whatever may be the particular conceptualisation of kinship by any particular anthropologist, the whole idea of kinship is based on the premise that kinship has to do with the reproduction of human beings and the relations between human beings that are the concomitants of reproduction. This premise represents the second assumption on which the study of kinship and the presumed universality of kinship are based. The reproduction of human beings is a biological process, to which of course various social and cultural attributes may be attached. The social and cultural attributes – although they are the primary subject matter of anthropologists – are nevertheless derivative and of lesser determinate significance than the biological relations. The biological relations have special qualities in that they create and constitute bonds, ties and solidary relations.

The third assumption on which every conceptualisation of kinship rests is the assumption that every society utilises for various social purposes the genealogical relations which it assumes to exist among people. Schneider calls it the Doctrine of the Genealogical Unity of Mankind. This doctrine is derived from the other two axioms about kinship, which are mostly left unspelt out in kinship studies: the first one is that kinship is universal and the second one that it has to do with human reproduction and the relations concomitant to that process. In every culture, the process of reproduction yields a father, mother, husband, wife, son and daughter. How far out the genealogy is then extended and how it is apportioned varies of course from culture to culture. Every culture recognises a father, mother, husband, wife, son and daughter, but not all of them trace genealogical relations to more distant relatives in the same way.

As anthropology developed, a difference between social and physical kinship has become established and we are now fully aware that social kinship does not simply mirror physical kinship. For anthropologists, kinship means genealogical relations as they are defined by the folk theory of procreation (Schneider 1984: 114). But the view that natural, biological processes constitute a major determinant, or at least a constraint on any direction that social kinship might take, has persisted. Even more importantly, it could not have really been abandoned. For if kinship is purely social and in no way physical, how is it to be conceptualised? To have a notion of kinship at all, we have inevitably to conceptualise it as being essentially about reproduction. The question which nevertheless remains, is why reproduction is so salient that it is given a central place among the other institutional domains seen as universally present in all human societies.

Schneider's answer is that kinship has been defined by European social scientists and that this definition derives from what kinship means in European folk culture with its notion that 'blood is thicker than water'. What are called 'blood ties' or ties of consanguinity can be understood as bonds of solidarity that are caused or engendered by actual biological connectedness. Kinship is defined as having to do with reproduction because reproduction is seen as a distinct and vitally important feature of social life. Its distinction is given in anthropologists' experience of their own culture with its notion of the mother's love for her child and the child's love for her, the notion of the father's innate or unconscious preference for his own real child, or the notion of the perpetuation of one's self in one's own children. According to Schneider, the view that all people ascribe to reproduction as high a value as the Westerners do is unsupported. This view persists simply because the assumption that the genealogical grid is universal, and especially that it has the same meaning in all cultures, has never been challenged in spite of occasional reports that genealogical relations in various cultures are not as culturally salient as they are for the Westerners. In the Solomon Islands, for example, the bonds of solidarity are not seen as arising from procreative activities as such. According to Levy, 'children are kept by their parents not because of the natural, given order of things, but because the parents happen to wish to, and are allowed to by others in the community. That is *all* parents–children relationships will tend to be seen as contingent' (1970: 82; emphasis altered) and 'relationships between all parents and children are fragile and conditional' (1970: 84).

In spite of reports like this, in the whole practice of kinship studies the view that the genealogical grid has the same salience in all cultures has never been treated as a mere assumption but always as a fact because men everywhere beget children and women bear them and these 'facts of life' – whatever any particular culture may say about them – must have the same meaning and importance as they have in Western culture. But the fact that everywhere men beget children and women give birth to them yet does not mean that every culture in the world must ascribe the same meaning and importance to genealogical relations as Western culture does. Even if a culture recognises the commonality of blood among some people, it does not need to ascribe the same meaning and importance to genealogical relations as Western culture does or – to use a specifically Western metaphor – it does not need to postulate that 'blood is thicker than water'.

In essence, Schneider argues that postulating 'kinship' as a special and separate domain of social relations is the result of the anthropological practice of mapping social relations on the genealogical grid, generated by the use of the 'genealogical method' which axiomatically presupposes that the ties resulting from the engendering and bearing of children are everywhere endowed with special social significance. It was thus the genealogical method that led to the 'discovery' of the importance ascribed to genealogical relations in societies in which such importance may not be culturally salient at all. The method constructs the notion of relatedness as relations established through procreation for this is what is being recorded through it. It already presupposes the importance of procreation as generating the notion of relatedness. In brief, postulating 'kinship' as a special and separate domain of social relations is not so much the result of the generalisation of empirical 'facts' or 'data', as rather the result of the methodology for recording and analysing those 'facts' or 'data'. In studying kinship as a system of genealogical relations, anthropologists were studying something that may be simply the product of their methodology rather than what may be the culturally specific constructions of relatedness in the societies studied.

PARTIBLE PERSONS

The basic assumption that kinship is the social recognition of natural relations logically implies other assumptions about kinship. The conceptualisation of kinship as the recognition of genealogical relations is the 'scientific' formulation of the English adage that 'blood is thicker than water'. As blood is not something one can choose, it implies that genealogical relationships are involuntary or, as another English saying goes, 'one can choose one's friends, one cannot choose one's relatives'. This is because kinship is not the result of any specific interactions in which people may be involved but results from their very being, that is, it is perceived not as socially constituted but as grounded in nature. Kinship status is thus an ascribed status. It is non-negotiable for it automatically ensues from an individual's birth. Although in the Western conceptualisation, individuals are certainly not seen as physiologically and psychologically fully developed at the moment of birth, their genetic make-up is, nevertheless, fully established and who their kin are is fully determined at that point. In this conceptualisation, reproduction understood as a physiological process terminates at birth. Whatever people may subsequently do has no effect on kinship resulting from the 'natural' process of human reproduction. Irrespective of how much, for example, the adoptive parents nurture the child, that child's 'real' mother is the woman who gave birth to it and the 'real' father is the man who engendered it (Meigs 1989: 36). The Yapese conceptualisations of relatedness as the result of doing rather than being challenge the cross-cultural applicability of the view that inherent attributes give rise to the types of relatedness which we call kinship.

Other ethnographic cases call into doubt the notion that birth universally determines a person's status or that maternal or paternal parentage ascribes to a person rights in groups whose members see themselves as descendants of specific ancestors. Writing of the Merina of Madagascar, Bloch (1986) makes a distinction between 'biological kinship' of an interpersonal nature and the 'kinship of descent'. The Merina imagine their descent groups as undivided and enduring. They are ideally endogamous and associated with specific territories, each such territory containing a collective tomb of the deceased members of the group. The tombs not only contain the remains of the group members but may actually be seen as creating the group for in practice most members of the group actually reside elsewhere than in the group territory. After death, however, they are returned to it to be buried in the tomb in the second funeral. The Merina imagine the 'kinship of descent' not as the result of birth but as the product of the blessing that flows from the dead in the tomb, through the elders, to the new generation. Descent has thus not that much to do with birth as with the ancestral blessing and a person's attachment to a specific tomb. A person's identity as a descent group member is established according to where he or she is finally buried. As a consequence, neither birth nor death but the burial determines a person's descent status. The general point that birth need not necessarily determine a person's status was made by Fox (1987: 174–5) who argues that in Austronesian societies, a person belongs to a kin group only after death. Writing of the Zafimaniry of Madagascar, Bloch observed that if one's identity is not given at birth and biological parentage does not determine status, it is meaningless 'to ask whether Zafimaniry use patrilineal descent to form groups or whether they practice cross-cousin marriage since all these questions imply that birth and parentage are relevant for status' (1993: 119).

The fact that genealogical relations are involuntary and beyond a person's control means that they are also unalterable and permanent. Once established, they cannot be undone, they are forever until death:

The fact that there is no society without a kinship system of some kind means that in the first place there is overt allowance made for sentiments generated by parturition, sex union and common residence (to put it at its lowest, even where male procreation is not understood); in the second place that these physical phenomena provide a simple base, usually easily recognizable and usually unchallengeable, on which other necessary social relationships may be erected. Moreover, the kinship tie is permanent until death – unless diverted by the fiction of adoption. In small societies, such as Tikopia, then, it can be readily grasped why kinship is at the root of much of the social structure. (Firth 1963a: xiii)

It is certainly part of Western notions that kinship ties are unalterable and permanent (Schneider 1980: 25). But the Yapese notions of relatedness as resulting not from one's birth but from one's interactions with others again challenge the cross-cultural validity of this view. As Yapese relationships depend on doing rather than being, not only can new relationships be created where none existed before but they can also be terminated in ways other than through a person's death.

All the specific assumptions, on which the nature and character of kinship has been predicated throughout the long history of kinship studies, are ultimately grounded in the Western conceptualisation of personhood and relationships. According to this conceptualisation, it is people's individual statuses and not their relationships that guarantee their own personhood (Strathern 1992b: 26). In the West, the individuality of persons is imagined in terms of their uniqueness as functioning organisms. Individuals are thought of as discrete, skin-bound physical entities that exist outside each other and that have between them absolute boundaries. A person's social life is regarded as extrinsic to his or her physical discreteness and relations are imagined as existing between individuals (Strathern 1992a: 50). In his or her interactions with others, the individual person is influenced or affected by them, but such interdependence often appears negotiable (Strathern 1992b: 25). The fact that one can pose the question about one's 'real' relatives – as, for example, when the adopted children ask about their 'real' parents – implies that individual persons exist prior to any relationship:

The child was there, according to this view, as an outcome of the acts of other individuals, whatever relations they may claim afterwards. From such a perspective, then, *individuals reproduce individuals* .... Relationships, in this English model, were not reproduced in the very act of procreation. (Strathern 1992a: 53; original emphasis)

Due to research done in Melanesia, we have become increasingly aware that in other cultures, persons and relations can be construed differently from how they are construed in the West. Rather than taking individuals as cultural givens, we now pay more attention to whether people think about themselves as discrete individuals, clearly bounded and separated from others, or whether they appeal to more relational idioms. In particular, Marilyn Strathern's comparative work on kinship and gender in Melanesia and on the Euro-American concepts revealed in debates about the new reproductive technologies has brought into relief the difference between Western and Melanesian discourses on personhood.

Melanesians understand personhood as the effects of relationships rather than their origins, in that the self is defined and experienced through an array of significant relationships with others. Whereas in the West, individuals are seen as irreducibly unique and are imagined as conceptually distinct from the relations that connect them to each other as parts of a society, Melanesian persons are frequently constructed as the plural and composite site of the relationships that produced them. Far from being regarded as unique entities, they are often conceived as 'dividuals' rather than individuals (Strathern 1988: 12–13).

The contrast between individuals and 'dividuals' has been formulated by Marriott in relation to the conception of personhood in South Asia, where

persons – single actors – are not thought to be 'individual', that is, indivisible bounded units, as they are in much of Western social and psychological theory as well as in common sense. Instead, it appears that persons are generally thought by South Asians to be 'dividual' or divisible. To exist, dividual persons absorb heterogeneous material influences. They must also give out from themselves particles of their own coded substances – essences, residues, or other active influences – that may then reproduce in others something of the nature of the persons in whom they have originated. (Marriott 1976: 111)

Melanesian persons are essentially multiple beings produced as the object of multiple relationships. In being multiple, they are also partible: entities that can dispose of parts in relation to others (Strathern 1988: 185). Aspects of one's identity can be detached, circulated and used in ceremonial exchanges to extend relationships. Persons are revealed in the context of these relationships to the extent that persons reveal relationships that composed them as inherently multiple constructs (1988: 274). They also objectify aspects of themselves in these relationships and their identity lies in the effect that this objectification produces in others. In contrast to the Western individual, there is no autonomous starting point for the Melanesian 'dividual' whose self is realisable only by way of others and constituted through relationships with others, past and present, living and dead. In Western conceptualisations, children are born as natural, asocial beings and social relations are constructed after this 'natural' event through posterior socialisation. In this conceptualisation, persons gradually accumulate identity throughout their life, adding experiences and relationships to their personal biography by creating relationships between persons. The Melanesians start off with the relationships in and through which they were constituted and brought into being, and spend their lives contextually detaching parts of themselves in order to achieve particular effects in the world, extending the influence of their relationship to others by objectifying and circulating aspects of themselves. While the Western notion of the individual emphasises the unity of the person, the Melanesians emphasise the plural and multiple composition of persons.

Conceptualisations of personhood as a relational phenomenon have been repeatedly reported from various parts of Melanesia as the result of ethnographic research sensitive to people's own notions. But I deliberately introduce an African example to suggest that notions of personhood radically different from Western ones may well not be confined to that part of the world.

The Nuer asserted that with the birth of children, affinal links between husband and wife and between their respective kin eventually became transformed into kinship ones (Evans-Pritchard 1951: 12, 45, 72, 98, 104, 139, 156). One of Evans-Pritchard's informants made the point in the following way: 'Now she [your wife] is like your mother; she cooks for you and milks the cows and performs the other services which your mother once performed for your household. She is a real kinswoman. She is like your mother' (Evans-Pritchard 1949: 100). Evans-Pritchard himself summarised the Nuer view by saying that '[t]he birth of a child gives the wife kinship with her husband's people and the husband kinship with the wife's people. They say that *ruagh*, in-law relationship, becomes *mar*, kinship' (1951: 96).

After two or three children were born to the couple, the man ceased to observe prohibitions on eating with his parents-in-law or appearing naked in their presence (1951: 99–101). The woman gradually ceased to use the expression *jigoala* (people of my home) in reference to her natal family and kin and used it to refer to the people of her husband's home. In speaking to her husband's kin, she used the same terms of address as he did and he used the same terms of address for her kin as she did. She came under the protection of his lineage spirits and ancestral ghosts and since she had been accepted by them, she might invoke them in rituals which she performed for her husband's lineage (1951: 98–104, 170).

A clear indication that kinship existed between a man and his wife's kin was the fact that after the wife had borne her husband a child, an incest prohibition applied to the relationship between a man and his wife's sister. Evans-Pritchard noted that there was no consanguinity between a man and his wife's sister (1951: 44) but the Nuer view of the matter was obviously quite different:

When I argued that there was no kinship tie between a man and his wife's sister, Nuer said that this was not true. 'What about the child?' they asked. They regard a man and his wife's sister as related through the child of the wife – for a woman is only fully married when she has a child and comes to live with her husband's people as their 'kinswoman', as they say, since her child is their child. Her sister is therefore also a kind of kinswoman, seeing that she is also the mother of their child. Your wife's sister being your child's maternal aunt is your sister (as we say, sister-in-law). (1951: 33)

But if the Nuer assertion of kinship between a man and his wife's sister was only a figure of speech as Evans-Pritchard intimated in describing it as a 'kind' of kinship and in maintaining that it was only an in-law relationship, why did the Nuer find the incest taboo appropriate to the relationship? In-law status or figurative kinship could hardly justify the incest taboo (Evens 1989: 331). The Nuer clearly meant what they said when they asserted that with the birth of children affinity became kinship and implied in what they said is the notion of the conversion of one substance into another (1989: 334) which, in its turn, implies that the Nuer did not think of bodies as discrete entities. We do not know how they themselves imagined the transmission of substance but in not thinking about bodies as discrete entities, they may well be similar to the Melanesians. Many anthropologists working in Melanesia, who paid particular attention to native theories of conception, personhood and bodily growth and to their consequences for the conceptualisations of kinship and gender, have pointed out the importance of the transmission of substance for such a conceptualisation. I shall limit myself to describing briefly just one such conceptualisation.

The Hua of the Eastern Highlands of Papua New Guinea consider *nu* to be the essence of life and growth. *Nu* can be glossed as 'vital substance' and in Hua thinking it is associated with blood, sweat and sexual fluids but also includes other bodily substances like hair, nail parings and flesh itself as well as any products of the body like faeces, footprints or shadows. Consistent with this conceptualisation is the notion that it also includes the products of one's labour. In the Hua view, reproduction results from the mixture of the *nu* of semen with the *nu* of menstrual blood but it is not seen as a discrete physical act which terminates at birth. Throughout their lives, individuals develop and change through further transfer and mixing of *nu*. Germane to their conceptualisation of kinship is the notion that *nu* is a substance that is transmitted among individuals. The role of parents is to pass *nu* to their children both before and after their birth and husbands pass *nu* in the form of semen, sweat, body odour and breath to their wives during sexual intercourse.

The Hua understand a group of kin (*bgotva' auva* – one skin, one body) as a group whose members share *nu*. Common residence leads inevitably to sharing *nu*. When people live together, they exchange *nu* among themselves and transmit it to each other in the course of their everyday living. They inhale each other's odour, absorb some of each other's sweat and body oil through their mutual contact, ingest some of each other's saliva when sharing food and utensils, come into contact with each other's excreta when sharing restricted domestic space and, above all, exchange *nu* among themselves when eating food they have produced, prepared or served. All these exchanges of *nu* create kinship in the same way as birth leads to shared *nu* and hence creates kinship. Conversely, those who do not share *nu*, are non-kin or strangers. Strangers possess an alien *nu* which is potentially dangerous and any contact with it is hence proscribed.

The Hua usually marry women from outside the Hua community and a wife is specifically supposed not to be *bgotva' auva*. Her *nu* is potentially dangerous to her husband and the members of his community and to prevent its harmful effect on them, a married woman is subject to numerous prohibitions. No initiated man in her husband's community, including her husband himself, can eat any food which she has produced, prepared or served, or eat from an earth oven into which she has placed leafy green vegetables, lest they lose health and strength or their growth be stunted. Numerous other rules proscribe the contact of the members of her husband's community with her menstrual fluids, shadow, hair, sweat, body oil, etc. Once the woman has borne a child, the number of these proscriptions decreases and they gradually cease to be observed with the birth of further children. When her children have begun to grow up, men may eat the vegetables which she has picked although this prohibition still applies to her husband. After about fifteen years of marriage, the husband and wife undergo an informal ceremony in which the proscription on eating leafy vegetables is removed from her husband. After the menopause, if she has borne more than three children, the woman is formally initiated into the men's house and like male initiates, she has herself to follow the proscriptions of which she was formerly the target.

The gradual decrease of the prohibitions and their eventual complete or near complete cessation suggests a gradual development of kinship between the husband's community and his wife brought about by the mixing of her *nu* with that of her husband's community. Such mixing results not only from the sexual congress between husband and wife but also through commensality. Production, preparation, serving and eating food inevitably involves a transfer of *nu* as each piece of food contains the *nu* of the one who has produced, prepared and served it. Eating food inevitably involves receiving somebody else's *nu*. Through eating, people take into their body a small bit of somebody else's *nu* and through this process they alter their kinship (Meigs 1989).

I would suggest that kinship between a husband's and a wife's people could be imagined by the Nuer in a way which was in many respects similar to Melanesian conceptualisations of kinship identity as established through the transfer of substances through eating, sexual intercourse and everyday casual contact and that what underlay this conceptualisation was the construction of personhood which, again, was in many respects similar to Melanesian constructions.

Evans-Pritchard made clear the overwhelming preoccupation of the Nuer with their cattle. As he stated it, they 'tend to define all social processes and relationships in terms of cattle. Their social idiom is a bovine idiom' (1940: 19). He also pointed out the identification of men and cattle (1956: 255–60). Nuer boys were initiated into manhood through a ritual in which '[t]heir brows are cut to the bone with a small knife, in six long cuts from ear to ear' (Evans-Pritchard 1940: 249). Between this operation and the boys' emergence from seclusion, they were known as *cot*, which is the word used for a hornless cow or ox, and the operation itself was explicitly compared to the cutting of the horns of favourite oxen (Evans-Pritchard 1956: 256). The distinction between paternal and maternal kin was expressed through cattle. The cattle of married brothers, though owned by them separately, were often tethered in the same kraal (Evans-Pritchard 1951: 128, 159) but a man and his maternal uncle might not tether their cattle together in the same kraal (1951: 164).

The identification of man and beast was particularly apparent in Nuer sacrifices. According to Evans-Pritchard's interpretation, when the Nuer sacrifice their oxen, what they surrender

are living creatures, gifts more expressive of the self and with a closer resemblance to it than inanimate things, and these living creatures are the most precious of their possessions, so much so that they can be said to participate in them to the point of identification.

But it is not only in this rather general sense of identification of men with cattle that Nuer can be said to offer up themselves in offering up their cattle in sacrifice ... one of the chief features of their sacrifices is the rubbing of ashes along the backs of the victims. It is true that this may be regarded as an act of consecration but it is also, to a greater or lesser degree, an act of identification. (Evans-Pritchard 1956: 279)

The identification of man and beast suggests that for the Nuer a person is not a discrete skin-bound entity. Being regarded not as a unique entity but as exceeding entitative boundaries (Evens 1989: 336), a person was also imagined as partible. This notion of personhood was also hinted at in Evans-Pritchard's analysis of sacrifice: 'When Nuer give their cattle in sacrifice they are very much, and in a very intimate way, giving *part of themselves*' (1956: 279; emphasis added).

Marriage among the Nuer was established through the gradual payment of bridewealth cattle and through the performance of a sequence of rituals. The marriage union was seen as finally established when the wife gave birth to the child and husband and wife started living together in their own home (Evans-Pritchard 1951: 58–9). Most of the cattle which the bridegroom's family transferred to the bride's father (who then distributed it to the bride's paternal and maternal kinsmen) came from a common family herd in which the bridegroom's brothers had equal right with himself. If their father was dead, his brothers were the trustees of the animals. In the words of Evans-Pritchard,

the cattle belong to the lineage, to the sons as a whole, who are links between the ancestors and its as yet unborn members. If the sons are men when their father dies they ought to go on living together round a common kraal ... [although] they frequently do not do so. Whether they do so or not, the cattle belong to all of them and should be used, when the herd is large enough, to obtain wives for them in order of seniority ... (1951: 128)

The Nuer themselves saw marriages as lineage affairs. They 'often speak of the lineage marrying a wife with its cattle or giving their daughter in marriage to another lineage for cattle' (1951: 97). As an object of transaction between previously unrelated lineages or groups of agnates, cattle were detachable from the group and, given the close identification of men with cattle, they could be seen as a part of them which was detached from themselves and attached to another group.

If cattle were a detachable part of man's identity which could be attached to another group than his, the detachable part of a woman was her child. In the form of her child, her fertility was detached from her group and appropriated by her husband's group. A woman bore her first child in her parent's home where she was still living, for only when the first-born had been weaned would the husband build a hut for his wife in his father's homestead. The detachment of the child from its mother's group and its attachment to her husband's group was made visible in a ritual performed shortly after the birth of the woman's first-born: she brought the baby to her husband's home and laid it in the ashes of the hearth in the centre of her husband's father's byre (1951: 73). This was the place of the herd in which her husband and his close agnates had joint rights; it symbolised the unity of their group (1951: 125). Children became attached to this group for they were '"children of the cattle" and therefore of the man in whose name they were paid', and they became 'joints in his branch of descent' (1951: 98). They remained with the father if their mother died or if she left her husband. In the latter event, any children which she might subsequently bear were his, irrespective of their physiological paternity (1951: 91–3, 98).

What was exchanged between the two intermarrying groups was apprehended as extracted from one and absorbed by the other (Strathern 1988: 178). Their singularity and mutual exclusiveness was obliterated through detachment of their parts and their attachment to the other.

Through this detachment and attachment the two groups transferred substances between themselves and converted one substance into another in a similar way in which the Hua transfer substances through eating, sexual intercourse and everyday casual contact. It was the resulting transubstantiation that created kinship between them. It makes sense that in the Nuer view, affinity was not converted into kinship until a child was born. For until then, part of the bridegroom's group and part of its substance (cattle) had been attached to the bride's group but no part of the bride's group had yet been attached to the bridegroom's group. The mutual transubstantiation — the basis of mutual kinship — remained incomplete until the substance of the bride's group was transmitted to the bridegroom's group and each group could be said to be the source of the other's identity. This was achieved through the birth of the child and its attachment to the father's group.

CONTEMPORARY CONCEPTUALISATIONS OF KINSHIP

The most significant development in the study of kinship has been the growing awareness of the cultural specificity of what were previously taken to be the natural facts on which all kinship systems were presumed to be built. As a result of Schneider's critique, we are left with the following problem: we either have to abandon the assumption that kinship as a system of genealogical relations arising out of procreative activities is a cultural universal, or adopt a wider definition of kinship than a system of relations deriving from the engendering and bearing of children.

To abandon the use of kinship as an analytical category, as Schneider suggests, does not appear to be a realistic proposition. Too much theoretical effort has been invested in it for that. Schneider's book is a critique of the way in which generations of anthropologists have tacitly accepted their own culturally specific views of kinship as a social or cultural construction of natural facts and have conceptualised kinship everywhere in terms of this culturally specific construction. But underlying Schneider's criticism is also the recognition that this is the defining feature of kinship as it has been constructed in anthropology from its very beginning (Strathern 1992a: 45).

If we maintain the conceptualisation of kinship as the system of genealogical ties, we will have to revise our theoretical assumption that kinship is a human universal and to acknowledge that there may be societies where people do not ascribe the same cultural significance to the ties established in the process of reproduction as we do and where they do not necessarily conceptualise relatedness as rooted in the biology of human reproduction. We would also have to realise that we might have created the illusion that kinship is universal by describing as kinship those relations which have nothing to do with genealogical connections.

Scheffler pointed out that the conceptualisation of kinship as a human universal is the by-product of the liberal-humanitarian voice of anthropology which sees itself as speaking for the 'other'

to the extent that we do that we have a strong interest in assimilating that 'other' to ourselves and, in the process, to a common humanity equally entitled to the same human rights. In the past that effort took the form of a search for the elements of the 'psychological unity of [hu]mankind' or for 'the universal categories of culture', one of which was 'kinship'. (1991: 375)

To adopt a wider definition of kinship than a system of relations arising from procreation is grounded in the realisation that we cannot treat alternative concepts of kinship as differing cultural elaborations of universal natural or biological facts as this precludes the possibility that different societies might conceptualise differently what makes people related to each other. Anthropologists have of course long recognised that people who do not see themselves as genealogically related address each other by kinship terms and treat each other as kin. That their relationship is conceptualised as a kinship one is typically expressed in a ban on marriage between them. Adoption and godparenthood (*compadrazgo*) to which anthropologists have paid considerable attention (Pitt-Rivers 1968, Caroll 1970a, Gudeman 1972, Brady 1976, Goody 1982) are typical examples of these types of relationships which have usually been glossed in literature as 'fictive', 'ritual', 'artificial', 'pseudo-' or 'quasi-' kinship. All these terms suggest that, although these relationships do not involve a recognition of shared substance and are not based on genealogical relations, they are, nevertheless, modelled on them. In his study of what he calls 'created kinship' in the Truk District of Micronesia, where the differentiation between those who share substance and those who share land, food, labour, residence or support is distinctly blurred, Marshall (1977) shows that various people who do not share substance mutually acknowledge each other as kin.

Although the Trukese do not go as far as the Yapese by not ascribing any importance to genealogical relations, they nevertheless conceptualise close significant personal relationships as those established through performance as well as those resulting from procreation. In this respect, they are certainly not alone. The emphasis on performance and code of conduct in determining who is and who is not a relative has been reported from other societies like the Melanesian Fore (Glasse 1969), the Micronesian Banaban (Silverman 1970), various societies in Polynesia (Caroll 1970b, Feinberg 1981), or the Navajo (Witherspoon 1975). This led Marshall to suggest that what was common to kinship was not merely the shared physical substance but the concept of sharing itself which could be 'expressed through a variety of culturally specific symbolic and interactive media' (1977: 655).

Although the studies which suggest that kinship in many cultures is defined not only by genealogy but also by a code of conduct, particularly conduct expressing sharing of food, land and services, may seem to challenge the anthropological conceptualisation of kinship as a system of ties established through procreation, they are, in fact, parasitic upon it. If people who do not share substance mutually acknowledge each other as kin, how do we know in the first place that they acknowledge each other as *kin* and not as something altogether different? We are able to classify relationships established through particular performance and code of conduct as kinship relationships simply because the natives apply relational terms in these relationships which we know are kinship terms because they are also applied in relationships established through sexual reproduction. The argument that in various societies people do not differentiate between those who share substance and those who share land, food, labour, residence or support does not thus challenge the definition of kinship as a system of genealogical relations and social ties modelled on them. In fact, we are able to say that in this or that society the differentiation between those who share substance and those who share other things is blurred precisely because we operate with the model of kinship as a system of genealogical relations in the first place.

A more radical attempt to get away from the definition of kinship to which reproduction is central is made by those anthropologists who explicitly emphasise the point that kinship, as it is culturally conceptualised in different societies, need not necessarily be built on the recognition of genealogical connections. They prefer to talk about relatedness and notions of relatedness rather than about kinship (Bouquet 1993: 157, 173, 179, 215, Carsten 1995: 224, 236). Bouquet characterises relatedness as a 'concept which allows for different nuances' and 'does not presuppose that genealogical relations are necessarily the most important' (Bouquet 1993: 157). Carsten uses 'the term "relatedness" to indicate indigenous ways of acting out and conceptualizing relations between people, as distinct from notions derived from anthropological theory' (Carsten 1995: 224). But an obvious drawback of the concept of 'relatedness' is that it cannot be separated in any precise way from the general notion of the social and thus endowed with a meaning which would prevent it from becoming analytically vacuous. The main problem is that the concept of relatedness does not specify what precisely 'relatedness' is meant to involve, how it is to be defined and how it should be distinguished from any other kind of social relationship. For Carsten, the central question in the study of kinship should be

how do the people we study define and construct their notions of relatedness and what value and meaning do they give them? It seems to me that we would do better to use the term 'kinship' to characterize the relatedness that people act and feel. In this way we may arrive at a new and more flexible study of kinship in anthropology. (1995: 236)

People everywhere 'act and feel' numerous kinds of relatedness. They are related to each other as friends, neighbours, citizens, fellow-worshippers, producers and consumers, members of the same ethnic group and in myriad other ways. If we are to 'arrive at a new and more flexible approach to the study of kinship', our study of the way people in different societies 'define and construct their notions of relatedness' has to be concerned with particular and specific kinds of relatedness. To avoid equating the concept of relatedness with any kind of social relationship, those who advocate its usefulness restrict it to relationships which resemble those of traditionally defined kinship. Replacing the concept of kinship with that of relatedness thus amounts in practice to a semantic solution of the difficulties involved in the definition of kinship. But renaming a phenomenon does not solve the problems involved in its conceptualisation. If we insist on talking about relatedness rather than kinship, we shall soon be debating what we mean by relatedness as we have been debating for decades what we mean by kinship.

Similar problems are also faced by those who follow Needham's (1971) critique of the standard anthropological conceptualisation of kinship. For example, Barnard and Good argue that it is impossible to define kinship substantively because all substantive definitions tend to be monothetic in that they specify some ultimate defining feature or features which the phenomenon in question has to possess. Instead they propose a polythetic definition of kinship and suggest an admittedly not exhaustive list of twelve features or characteristics of kinship. They take a relationship as pertaining to kinship if it displays some of these features or characteristics (Barnard and Good 1984: 188–9). However, their 'polythetic' definition of kinship is so wide that virtually any relationship could be classified as a kinship one if one so wished. When comparing cross-culturally kinship polythetically defined, we may end up comparing relationships which have altogether nothing in common, for example relationships which involve 'the making of prestations without expectation of immediate or direct return' – which may well include relationships of friendship (Pitt-Rivers 1973, Leyton 1974) – with relationships which assign 'the parties to an "in" group or category, in opposition to persons not so assigned' – which may well be relationships of ethnicity. As this example indicates, polythetic definitions of kinship will make it impossible to distinguish, even within one culture, relationships of kinship from those of friendship or ethnicity. If kinship 'involves the nurture and upbringing of small children', on which grounds do we then distinguish roles and statuses which persons occupy in the process of socialisation from kinship roles and statuses? Are we to conclude that nursery staff and kindergarten teachers are the kin of their charges, particularly as the children may call them 'aunts' and 'uncles'?

Those who advocate a polythetic definition of kinship are right in reminding us that different cultures may be working with conceptions of relatedness which are not simply different cultural elaborations of immutable natural or biological facts. The examples above were adduced to show that a polythetic definition of kinship will inevitably lead to the notion of 'kinship' as coterminous with any cultural conceptualisation of relatedness and difference. As we would no longer be able to differentiate kinship conceptually from, say, friendship or ethnicity, we would ultimately have to dissolve not only kinship as an analytical category, but a number of other analytical categories (for example ethnicity and friendship) as well. This would of course not preclude our concern with how people in different cultures conceptualise their mutual relatedness and difference, but it would make questionable whether we are really comparing like with like cross-culturally.

The current debate about how kinship should be conceptualised and defined has made it abundantly clear that in many cultures the system of relationships, which resemble what we would commonsensically call 'kinship', is not necessarily based on the tracing of genealogical connections. What the debate about the culturally specific extra-genealogical conceptualisations of kinship seems not to have sufficiently appreciated is that genealogical relations, which are central to the traditional anthropological definition of kinship, are a specific Western way of imagining relatedness among people resulting from their sharing of substance and its transmission over generations. In the Euro-American conceptualisation this sharing of substance is the result of the process of biological reproduction. It is an idea whose origins can be traced to the mid-nineteenth century when the current definition of 'biology', understood as a matter of genetic transmission, emerged (Ingold 1990: 209–11, 1991: 359). This conceptualisation replaced an earlier view that an individual was not determined solely at conception but as a result of a much longer process in which characteristics were passed on to children not only in the womb but also through the milk which they suckled after birth (Marvick 1974, Ross 1974).

If we are to preserve kinship as a meaningful analytical category, kinship of course cannot be conflated with 'social' generally or with *any* kind of relatedness; it has to be conceptualised as a *particular* type of social relationship. This is the view taken by Kelly who defines kinship as

social relations predicated upon cultural conceptions that specify the processes by which an individual comes into being and develops into a complete (i.e. mature) social person. These processes encompass the acquisition and transformation of both spiritual and corporeal components of being. Sexual reproduction and the formulation of paternal and maternal contributions are an important component of, but are not coextensive with, the relevant processes. This is due to the ethnographic fact that a full complement of spiritual components is never derived exclusively from the parents. Moreover, the sexually transmitted ingredients of corporeal substance are frequently transmitted in other ways as well .... Foods may also constitute essential ingredients in the spiritual or corporeal completion of personhood .... Finally, maturation frequently entails purging, replacing, adding, and/or supplementing spiritual and corporeal components of personhood. There is no analytic utility in artificially restricting the category of kin relations to relations predicated on some but not all of the constitutive processes of personhood because these processes are culturally formulated as components of an integral system and the social relations they predicate are all of the same logical type, i.e. relations of shared substance or shared spirit. (1993: 521–2)

I would similarly suggest that to be meaningful as a concept, kinship has to be understood as a culturally specific notion of relatedness deriving from shared bodily and/or spiritual substance and its transmission. In the West as well as in many non-Western cultures this may be seen as resulting from the process of sexual reproduction; in yet other cultures this may well be seen as resulting from sharing the same food, living on the same land, or whatever. In Western terms, the latter processes would of course not be classified as biological but social and therefore not 'kinship' within the traditional anthropological definition. Carsten has addressed this issue and writing of the Malays on the island of Langkawi she points out that

it makes little sense in indigenous terms to label some ... activities as social and others as biological. I certainly never heard Langkawi people do so. It is clear that the important relationships of kinship involve what we would regard as both. If blood, which is the stuff of kinship and to some extent of personhood, is acquired during gestation in the uterus and, after birth, in the house through feeding with others as people in Langkawi assert, is it, then, biological or social? The impossibility of answering this question merely underlines the unsatisfactory nature of this distinction. (1995: 236–7)

If the separation of the 'social' from the 'biological' which underlies the traditional anthropological definition of kinship is a specifically Western contrast which is not drawn in all cultures, the adherence to the conceptualisation of kinship as shared substance and its transmission (rather than the much narrower conceptualisation of it as genealogical relations) would have more far-reaching consequences for our analytical practice than we have so far realised. One of these consequences would be that we also 'abandon the ... "Western", and logically prior, distinction of the biological from the social on which the definition of kinship as a biological process rests' (1995: 236).

On the level of actual research practice, the conceptualisation of kinship as a human universal is the result of the genealogical method which enabled anthropologists everywhere to map categories of people on the pre-existing genealogical grid without first ascertaining that the locally recognised categories refer in fact to relations established in the process of reproduction or to relations which are specifically modelled on them. It was the presumed objectivity of the data collected through this method that made possible the generalisations about kinship and the formulation of what has become known as kinship theory. Once we have realised that data about relatedness that were collected through the genealogical method were far from objective but our own constructions which might have been at odds with the constructions of the people studied, we have become critical of almost every aspect of the received kinship theory and we have abandoned the once fashionable formulations, reformulations and refinements of the basic analytical concepts in the study of kinship. Recent reviews of anthropological theory and of the current state of anthropology (Ortner 1984, Clifford and Marcus 1986, Marcus and Fisher 1986, Borofsky 1994) make hardly any references to the theoretical problems in the study of kinship which exercised the imagination of our predecessors.

The main shift in the study of kinship is evinced by the fact that the study now concentrates on people's own conceptualisations and constructions and not on the assumed system of genealogical relations. It concentrates on investigating the meaning of the observed relationships in terms of the concepts, premises and values which are culturally significant in the studied society. Analyses of kinship which begin from native categories and are sensitive to the ways in which sharing of substance and its transmission are conceptualised in different cultures clearly show how inadequate it is to describe native conceptualisations in terms of our analytically derived concepts of descent, affinity (Rivière 1993), filiation and such like. If such concepts prove inadequate for describing any particular native conceptualisations, it also follows that it will become increasingly difficult to formulate any cross-culturally valid generalisations about descent, affinity, filiation and indeed the whole area of relations which we call kinship. Recent studies of kinship eschew the static and abstract theoretical models of traditional kinship theory as a result of the growing realisation that the study of kinship, as well as other traditional fields of anthropological interest like politics, economics or religion, cannot be pursued in the isolated terms of these functionally defined institutions. Contemporary studies of kinship tend to be historically grounded, emphasising how local experiences of kinship have been affected by state politics, trade, colonialism or nationalist discourses, and tend to focus on people's everyday experiences, understandings and representations of power, inequality and difference. They emphasise the importance of ethnicity, class and gender in local conceptualisations pertaining to kinship, family and household (Peletz 1995).

The realisation that the objectivity at which we aimed was nothing more than an imposition of culturally specific Western assumptions and constructions on others had one inevitable result. Rather than looking for regularity in social processes we are now much more sensitive than ever before to cultural specificity and tempted to analyse every case as different. We are less willing than ever before to formulate cross-cultural generalisations. If we compare, it is not to formulate generalisations but to show the cultural specificity of particular constructions. Marilyn Strathern's work is a case in point. She uses the Melanesian material to bring into relief the manner in which the English construe relations (1992a). The tendency to shy away from 'kinship theory' is noticeable in present-day anthropology. But the temptation to analyse every case as different may be as problematic as viewing kinship everywhere as a particular cultural response to a universal human predicament.

The merit of studies that explicitly reject the culturally specific Western assumption that guided the study of kinship since its very inception is undeniable and the move towards the description of the cultural logic which underlies the notions of relatedness in specific societies is undoubtedly a move in the right direction. But present-day anthropological discourse on kinship is a discourse which has its own antecedents in the traditional discourse of which it is openly critical. This seems inevitable as it is the traditional discourse which equipped us with many concepts without which the act of cultural translation, which lies at the root of all anthropological endeavour, would not be possible. The perpetual recourse to these concepts indicates the importance of the work of those generations of kinship theorists of whose theories and assumptions we are now openly critical. We could not get on with what we are currently doing if they did not provide us with the vocabulary through which we can communicate the sense of any particular culture to an audience in another culture. And in that, if not in anything else, lies the lasting importance of kinship studies for anthropology.

REFERENCES

Aberle, D. F. 1961. Matrilineal descent in cross-cultural perspective. In D. M. Schneider and L. Gough (eds), *Matrilineal kinship*. Berkeley and Los Angeles: University of California Press.

Adams, R. N. 1960. An inquiry into the nature of the family. In G. E. Dole and R. L. Carneiro (eds), *Essays in the science of society in honor of Leslie A. White*. New York: Thomas Y. Crowell.

Alexander, J. 1978. The cultural domain of marriage. *American Ethnologist* 5: 5–14.

Allen, M. 1971. Descent groups and ecology amongst the Nduindui, New Hebrides. In L. R. Hiatt and C. Jaywardena (eds), *Anthropology in Oceania: essays presented to Ian Hogbin*. Sydney: Angus and Robertson.

Arensberg, C. M. and S. T. Kimball. 1968. *Family and community in Ireland*. Cambridge, MA.: Harvard University Press.

Bachofen, J. 1861. *Das Mutterrecht*. Stuttgart: Krais und Hoffmann.

Barnard, A. and A. Good. 1984. *Research practices in the study of kinship*. London: Academic Press.

Barnes, J. A. 1961. Physical and social kinship. *Philosophy of Science* 28: 296–9.

—— 1962. African models in New Guinea Highlands. *Man* 62: 5–9.

—— 1964. Physical and social facts in anthropology. *Philosophy of Science* 31: 294–7.

—— 1973. Genetrix : genitor :: nature : culture? In J. R. Goody (ed.), *The character of kinship*. Cambridge: Cambridge University Press.

Bauer, P. and O. Yamey. 1957. *The economics of underdeveloped countries*. Cambridge Economic Handbook. London: Cambridge University Press.

Beattie, J. 1964a. *Other cultures: aims, methods and achievements in social anthropology*. London: Cohen and West.

—— 1964b. Kinship and social anthropology. *Man* 64: 101–3.

Bell, N. W. and E. F. Vogel (eds) 1960. *A modern introduction to the family*. New York: Free Press.

Bender, D. R. 1967. A refinement of the concept of household: families, co-residence and domestic functions. *American Anthropologist* 69: 493–504.

—— 1971. De facto families and de jure households in Ondo. *American Anthropologist* 73: 223–41.

Berndt, R. M. 1964. Warfare in New Guinea Highlands. In J. B. Watson (ed.), *New Guinea: the Central Highlands. American Anthropologist* 66, No. 4, part 2, special publication: 183–203.

Berreman, G. D. 1978. Ecology, demography and domestic strategies in the Western Himalayas. *Journal of Anthropological Research* 34: 326–68.

Bloch, M. 1986. *From blessing to violence: history and ideology of the circumcision ritual of the Merina of Madagascar.* Cambridge: Cambridge University Press.

—— 1993. Zafimaniry birth and kinship theory. *Social Anthropology* 1: 119–32.

Bock, P. K. 1969. *Modern cultural anthropology.* New York: Alfred A. Knopf.

Bohannan, L. 1952. A genealogical charter. *Africa* 22: 301–15.

—— 1958. Political aspects of Tiv social organization. In J. Middleton and D. Tait (eds), *Tribes without rulers.* London: Routledge and Kegan Paul.

Bohannan, P. 1963. *Social anthropology.* New York: Holt, Rinehart and Winston.

Bohannan, P. and L. Bohannan. 1968. *Tiv economy.* Evanston, IL: Northwestern University Press.

Boon, J. A. 1974. Anthropology and nannies. *Man* (N.S.) 9: 137–40.

Borofsky, R. (ed.) 1994. *Assessing cultural anthropology.* New York: McGraw-Hill, Inc.

Boserup, E. 1970. *Woman's role in economic development.* London: Allen and Unwin.

Bouquet, M. 1993. *Reclaiming English kinship: Portuguese refractions on British kinship theory.* Manchester: Manchester University Press.

Bourdieu, P. 1977. *Outline of a theory of practice.* Cambridge: Cambridge University Press.

Brady, I. A. (ed.) 1976. *Transactions in kinship: adoption and fosterage in Oceania.* ASAO Monograph No. 4. Honolulu: University of Hawaii Press.

Brookfield, H. C. and P. Brown. 1963. *Struggle for land: agricultural and group territories among the Chimbu of the New Guinea Highlands.* Melbourne: Oxford University Press in association with the Australian National University.

Brown, P. and H. C. Brookfield. 1959–60. Chimbu land and society. *Oceania* 30: 1–75.

Buchler, I. R. 1966. On physical and social kinship. *Anthropological Quarterly* 39: 17–25.

Buchler, I. R. and H. A. Selby. 1968. *Kinship and social organization.* New York: Macmillan.

Burton, C. 1985. *Subordination: feminism and social theory.* Sydney: George Allen and Unwin.

Capra, F., D. Steindl-Rast and T. Matus. 1991. *Belonging to the universe: explorations on the frontiers of science and spirituality.* San Francisco: Harper.

Cardinal, A. W. 1931. *The Gold Coast.* Accra: Government Printer.

Caroll, V. (ed.) 1970a. *Adoption in Eastern Oceania.* ASAO Monograph No. 1. Honolulu: University of Hawaii Press.

—— 1970b. Adoption on Nukuoro. In V. Caroll (ed.), *Adoption in Eastern Oceania.* ASAO Monograph No. 1. Honolulu: University of Hawaii Press.

Carsten, J. 1995. The substance of kinship and the heat of the hearth: feeding, personhood, and relatedness among Malays in Pulau Langkawi. *American Ethnologist* 22: 223–41.

Caulfield, M. D. 1981. Equality, sex and mode of production. In G. Berreman (ed.), *Social inequality*. London: Academic Press.

Caws, P. 1974. Operational, representational and explanatory models. *American Anthropologist* 76: 1–10.

Chock, P. P. 1974. Time, nature and spirit: a symbolic analysis of Greek-American spiritual kinship. *American Ethnologist* 1: 33–46.

Clay, B. 1977. *Pinikindu: maternal nurture, paternal substance*. Chicago: University of Chicago Press.

Clifford, J. and G. Marcus (eds) 1986. *Writing culture: the poetics and politics of ethnography*. Berkeley: University of California Press.

Clignet, R. 1970. *Many wives, many powers: authority and power in polygynous families*. Evanston, IL: Northwestern University Press.

Cohen, M. L. 1976. *House united, house divided: the Chinese family in Taiwan*. New York: Columbia University Press.

Collier, J. F. and M. Z. Rosaldo. 1981. Politics and gender in simple societies. In S. B. Ortner and H. Whitehead (eds), *Sexual meanings: the cultural construction of gender and sexuality*. Cambridge: Cambridge University Press.

Collier, J. F. and S. J. Yanagisako. 1987. Introduction. In J. F. Collier and S. J. Yanagisako (eds), *Gender and kinship: essays toward a unified analysis*. Stanford, CA: Stanford University Press.

Colson, E. 1958. *Marriage and family among the Plateau Tonga of Northern Rhodesia*. Manchester: Manchester University Press.

—— 1961. Plateau Tonga. In D. M. Schneider and K. Gough (eds), *Matrilineal kinship*. Berkeley and Los Angeles: University of California Press.

—— 1971. *The social consequences of resettlement: the impact of the Kariba resettlement upon the Gwembe Tonga*. Manchester: Manchester University Press.

—— 1980. The resilience of matrilineality: Gwembe and Plateau Tonga adaptations. In L. S. Cordell and S. Beckerman (eds), *The versatility of kinship: essays presented to Harry W. Basehart*. London: Academic Press.

Comaroff, J. L. (ed.) 1980. *The meaning of marriage payments*. London: Academic Press.

Coward, R. 1983. *Patriarchal precedents*. London: Routledge and Kegan Paul.

Cucchiari, S. 1981. The gender revolution and the transition from bisexual horde to patrilocal band: the origins of gender hierarchy. In S. B. Ortner and H. Whitehead (eds), *Sexual meanings: the cultural construction of gender and sexuality*. Cambridge: Cambridge University Press.

Dalton, G. 1971. Introduction. In G. Dalton (ed.), *Economic development and social change*. New York: American Museum of Natural History.

Davenport, W. 1959. Nonunilinear descent and descent groups. *American Anthropologist* 61: 557–72.

Delaney, C. 1986. The meaning of paternity and the virgin birth debate. *Man* (N.S.) 21: 494–513.

De Lepervanche, M. 1967–8. Descent, residence and leadership in the New Guinea Highlands. *Oceania* 38: 134–58, 163–89.

Douglas, M. 1969. Is matriliny doomed in Africa? In M. Douglas and P. Kaberry (eds), *Man in Africa*. London: Tavistock Publications.

Drummond, L. 1978. The transatlantic nanny: notes on a comparative semiotics of the family in English-speaking societies. *American Ethnologist* 5: 30–43.

Dumont, L. 1953. The Dravidian kinship terminology as an expression of marriage. *Man* 53: 34–9.

—— 1957. Hierarchy and marriage alliance in South Indian kinship. *Occasional Paper of the Royal Anthropological Institute* No. 12. London: Royal Anthropological Institute.

—— 1966. Descent or intermarriage: a relational view of Australian descent systems. *Southwestern Journal of Anthropology* 22: 231–50.

—— 1968. Marriage alliance. *International Encyclopedia of Social Science* 10: 19–23.

—— 1971. *Introduction à deux theories d'anthropologie sociale.* The Hague: Mouton.

Elkin, A. P. 1952–3. Delayed exchange in Wabag Sub-District, Central Highlands of New Guinea. *Oceania* 23: 161–201.

Engels, F. 1884 (reprinted 1972). *Origin of the family, private property and the state.* New York: Pathfinder Press.

Evans-Pritchard, E. E. 1940. *The Nuer: a description of the modes of livelihood and political institutions of a Nilotic people.* London: Oxford University Press.

—— 1949. Nuer rules of exogamy and incest. In M. Fortes (ed.), *Social structure.* London: Russell and Russell.

—— 1950. Kinship and the local community among the Nuer. In A. R. Radcliffe-Brown and D. Forde (eds), *African systems of kinship and marriage.* London: Oxford University Press.

—— 1951. *Kinship and marriage among the Nuer.* London: Oxford University Press.

—— 1956. *Nuer religion.* Oxford: Clarendon Press.

Evens, T. M. S. 1989. The Nuer incest prohibition and the nature of kinship: alterlogical reckoning. *Cultural Anthropology* 4: 323–46.

Fallers, L. A. and M. J. Levy, Jr. 1959. The family: some comparative considerations. *American Anthropologist* 61: 647–51.

Feil, D. K. 1978. Straightening the way: an Enga kinship conundrum. *Man* (N.S.) 13: 380–401.

—— 1984. Beyond patriliny in the New Guinea Highlands. *Man* (N.S.) 19: 50–76.

Feinberg, R. 1981. What is Polynesian kinship all about? *Ethnology* 20: 115–31.

Firth, R. 1957. A note on descent groups in Polynesia. *Man* 57: 4–8.

—— 1963a (1936). *We, the Tikopia: a sociological study of kinship in primitive Polynesia* (abridged edn). Stanford, CA: Stanford University Press.

—— 1963b. Bilateral descent groups: an operational viewpoint. In I. Schapera (ed.), *Studies in kinship and marriage.* Royal Anthropological Institute Paper No. 16. London: Royal Anthropological Institute.

Firth, R., J. Hubert and A. Forge. 1969. *Families and their relatives: kinship in a middle-class sector of London.* London: Routledge and Kegan Paul.

Forde, D. 1950. Double descent among the Yakö. In A. R. Radcliffe-Brown and D. Forde (eds), *African systems of kinship and marriage.* London: Oxford University Press.

—— 1963. On some further unconsidered aspects of descent. *Man* 63: 12–13.

Fortes, M. 1945. *The dynamics of clanship among the Tallensi.* London: Oxford University Press.

—— 1949a. *The web of kinship among the Tallensi.* London: Oxford University Press.

—— 1949b. Time and social structure: an Ashanti case study. In M. Fortes (ed.), *Social structure.* London: Oxford University Press.

—— 1950. Kinship and marriage among the Ashanti. In A. R. Radcliffe-Brown and D. Forde (eds), *African systems of kinship and marriage.* London: Oxford University Press.

—— 1953. The structure of unilineal descent groups. *American Anthropologist* 55: 17–41.

—— 1958. Introduction. In J. R. Goody (ed.), *The developmental cycle in domestic groups.* Cambridge: Cambridge University Press.

—— 1959. Descent, filiation and affinity: a rejoinder to Dr Leach. *Man* 59: 193–7, 206–12.

—— 1969. *Kinship and the social order: the legacy of Lewis Henry Morgan.* London: Routledge and Kegan Paul.

—— 1978. An anthropologist's apprenticeship. *Annual Review of Anthropology* 7: 1–30.

Fortes, M. and E. E. Evans-Pritchard (eds) 1940. *African political systems.* London: Oxford University Press.

Fox, J. 1987. The house as a type of social organisation on the island of Roti. In C. Macdonald (ed.), *De la hutte au palais.* Paris: CNRS.

Fox, R. 1967. *Kinship and marriage: an anthropological perspective.* Harmondsworth: Penguin Books.

—— 1973. *Encounter with anthropology.* New York: Harcourt, Brace, Jovanovich.

—— 1993. *Reproduction and succession: studies in anthropology, law, and society.* New Brunswick, NJ: Transaction Publishers.

Frake, C. O. 1960. The Eastern Subanun of Mindanao. In G. P. Murdock (ed.), *Social structure in Southeast Asia.* Viking Fund Publications in Anthropology 29. New York: Wenner Gren.

Freeman, J. D. 1955. *Iban agriculture*. Colonial Research Studies No. 18. London: Colonial Office.

—— 1958. The family system of the Iban of Borneo. In J. R. Goody (ed.), *The developmental cycle in domestic groups*. Cambridge: Cambridge University Press.

—— 1960. The Iban of Borneo. In G. P. Murdock (ed.), *Social structure in Southeast Asia*. Viking Fund Publications in Anthropology 29. New York: Wenner Gren.

—— 1961. On the concept of the kindred. *Journal of the Royal Anthropological Institute* 9: 192–220.

—— 1974. Kinship, attachment behaviour and the primary bond. In J. R. Goody (ed.), *The character of kinship*. Cambridge: Cambridge University Press.

Fried, M. H. 1957. The classification of corporate unilineal descent groups. *Journal of the Royal Anthropological Institute* 87: 1–30.

Friedman, J. 1974. Marxism, structuralism and vulgar materialism. *Man* (N.S.) 9: 444–69.

Fuller, C. J. 1976. *The Nayars today*. Cambridge: Cambridge University Press.

Geertz, C. 1966. Religion as a cultural system. In M. Banton (ed.), *Anthropological approaches to the study of religion*. ASA Monographs 3. London: Tavistock Publications.

Gellner, E. 1957. Ideal language and kinship terms. *Philosophy of Science* 24: 235–43.

—— 1969. *Saints of the Atlas*. London: Weidenfeld and Nicolson.

Gillison, G. 1980. Images of nature in Gimi thought. In C. MacCormack and M. Strathern (eds), *Nature, culture and gender*. Cambridge: Cambridge University Press.

Glasse, R. M. 1969. Marriage in South Fore. In R. M. Glasse and M. J. Meggitt (eds), *Pigs, pearlshells, and women: marriage in the New Guinea Highlands*. Englewood Cliffs, NJ: Prentice Hall.

Godelier, M. 1986 (1982). *The making of great men: male domination and power among the New Guinea Baruya*. Cambridge: Cambridge University Press.

Goldstein, M. C. 1971. Stratification, polyandry and family structure in central Tibet. *Southwestern Journal of Anthropology* 27: 64–74.

Goode, W. J. 1964. *The family*. Englewood Cliffs, NJ: Prentice Hall.

Goodenough, W. H. 1955. A problem in Malayo-Polynesian social organization. *American Anthropologist* 57: 71–83.

—— 1970. *Description and comparison in cultural anthropology*. Cambridge: Cambridge University Press.

Goody, E. N. 1982. *Parenthood and social reproduction: fostering and occupational roles in West Africa*. Cambridge: Cambridge University Press.

Goody, J. R. 1958. The fission of domestic groups among the LoDagaba. In J. R. Goody (ed.), *The developmental cycle in domestic groups*. Cambridge: Cambridge University Press.

—— 1959. The mother's brother and sister's son in West Africa. *Journal of the Royal Anthropological Institute* 89: 61–88.

—— 1962. *Death, property and the ancestors.* London: Tavistock Publications.

—— (ed.) 1971. *Kinship.* Harmondsworth: Penguin Books.

—— 1972. The evolution of the family. In P. Laslett and R. Wall (eds), *Household and family in past time.* Cambridge: Cambridge University Press.

—— 1973a. Bridewealth and dowry in Africa and Eurasia. In J. R. Goody and S. J. Tambiah (eds), *Bridewealth and dowry.* Cambridge: Cambridge University Press.

—— 1973b. Polygyny, economy and the role of women. In J. R. Goody (ed.), *The character of kinship.* Cambridge: Cambridge University Press.

—— 1976. *Production and reproduction: a comparative study of domestic domain.* Cambridge: Cambridge University Press.

—— 1990. *The Oriental, the ancient and the primitive: systems of marriage and the family in the pre-industrial societies of Eurasia.* Cambridge: Cambridge University Press.

Goody, J. R. and S. J. Tambiah (eds). 1973. *Bridewealth and dowry.* Cambridge: Cambridge University Press.

Gough, E. K. 1959. The Nayars and the definition of marriage. *Journal of the Royal Anthropological Institute* 89: 23–34.

—— 1961a. Variation in matrilineal systems. In D. M. Schneider and K. Gough (eds), *Matrilineal kinship.* Berkeley and Los Angeles: University of California Press.

—— 1961b. The modern disintegration of matrilineal descent groups. In D. M. Schneider and K. Gough (eds), *Matrilineal kinship.* Berkeley and Los Angeles: University of California Press.

—— 1971. The Nuer kinship: a re-examination. In T. O. Beidelman (ed.), *The translation of culture.* London: Tavistock.

Gudeman, S. 1972. The compadrazgo as the reflection of the natural and spiritual person. *Proceedings of the Royal Anthropological Institute of Great Britain and Ireland* for 1971: 45–71. London: Royal Anthropological Institute.

Hammel, E. A. and P. Laslett. 1974. Comparing household structure over time and between cultures. *Comparative Studies in Society and History* 16: 73–109.

Harris, C. C. 1990. *Kinship.* Milton Keynes: Open University Press.

Held, D. J. 1957. *The Papuans of Waropen.* The Hague: Nijhoff.

Hill, P. 1963. *Migrant cocoa-farmers of southern Ghana.* Cambridge: Cambridge University Press.

Hoebel, E. A. 1954. *The law of primitive man.* Cambridge, MA: Harvard University Press.

Holy, L. 1979a. The segmentary lineage structure and its existential status. In L. Holy (ed.), *Segmentary lineage systems reconsidered.* The Queen's University Papers in Social Anthropology 4. Belfast: The Queen's University.

—— 1979b. Nuer politics. In L. Holy (ed.), *Segmentary lineage systems reconsidered.* The Queen's University Papers in Social Anthropology 4. Belfast: The Queen's University.

—— 1986. *Strategies and norms in a changing matrilineal society: the Toka of Zambia.* Cambridge: Cambridge University Press.

—— 1989. *Kinship, honour and solidarity: cousin marriage in the Middle East.* Manchester: Manchester University Press.

Holy, L. and M. Stuchlik. 1983. *Actions, norms and representations: foundations of anthropological inquiry.* Cambridge: Cambridge University Press.

Howell, P. P. 1954. *A manual of Nuer law.* Oxford: Oxford University Press.

Howell, S. and M. Melhuus. 1993. The study of kinship; the study of person; a study of gender? In T. del Valle (ed.), *Constructing genders.* EASA Monograph 6. London: Routledge.

Ingold, T. 1990. An anthropologist looks at biology. Man (N.S.) 26: 208–29.

—— 1991. Becoming persons: consciousness and sociality in human evolution. *Cultural Dynamics* 4: 355–78.

Jolly, M. 1991. Soaring hawks and grounded persons: the politics of rank and gender in north Vanuatu. In M. Godelier and M. Strathern (eds), *Big men and great men: personifications of power in Melanesia.* Cambridge: Cambridge University Press.

Josselin de Jong, J. P. D. de. 1952. *Lévi-Strauss' theory on kinship and marriage.* Mededelingen van het Rijksmuseum voor Volkenkunde 10. Leiden: Rijksmuseum voor Volkenkunde.

Kaberry, P. M. 1967. The plasticity of New Guinea kinship. In M. Freedman (ed.), *Social organization: essays presented to Raymond Firth.* London: Cass.

Kato, T. 1982. *Matriliny and migration: evolving Minangkabau traditions in Indonesia.* Ithaca: Cornell University Press.

Keesing, F. M. 1958. *Cultural anthropology.* New York: Rinehart.

Keesing, R. M. 1970. Shrines, ancestors and cognatic descent: the Kwaio and Tallensi. *American Anthropologist* 72: 755–75.

—— 1971. Descent, residence and cultural codes. In L. R. Hiatt and C. Jaywardena (eds), *Anthropology in Oceania.* Sydney: Angus and Robertson.

—— 1975. *Kin groups and social structure.* New York: Holt, Rinehart and Winston, Inc.

Kelly, R. C. 1985. *The Nuer conquest: the structure and development of an expansionist system.* Ann Arbor: The University of Michigan Press.

—— 1993. *Constructing inequality: the fabrication of a hierarchy of virtue among the Etoro.* Ann Arbor: The University of Michigan Press.

Kopytoff, I. 1964. Family and lineage among the Suku of the Congo. In R. F. Gray and P. H. Gulliver (eds), *The family estate in Africa.* London: Routledge.

—— 1965. The Suku of southwestern Congo. In J. Gibbs, Jr (ed.), *Peoples of Africa.* New York: Holt, Rinehart and Winston.

—— 1977. Matrilineality, residence and residential zones. *American Ethnologist* 4: 539–58.

Krige, E. J. and J. D. Krige. 1943. *The realm of a Rain Queen.* London: Oxford University Press.

Kuper, A. 1982. Lineage theory: a critical retrospect. *Annual Review of Anthropology* 11: 71–95.

—— 1985. Social anthropology. In A. Kuper and J. Kuper (eds), *The social science encyclopedia*. London: Routledge and Kegan Paul.

LaFontaine, J. S. 1973. Descent in New Guinea: an Africanist view. In J. R. Goody (ed.), *The character of kinship*. Cambridge: Cambridge University Press.

—— 1981. The domestication of the savage male. *Man* (N.S.) 16: 333–49.

—— 1990. Power, authority and symbols in domestic life. *International Journal of Moral and Social Studies* 5: 187–205.

Langness, L. L. 1964. Some problems in the conceptualization of Highlands social structure. In J. B. Watson (ed.), *New Guinea: the Central Highlands*. *American Anthropologist* 66, No. 4, part 2, special publication: 162–82.

Laslett, P. and R. Wall (eds). 1972. *Household and family in past time: comparative studies in the size and structure of the domestic group over the last three centuries in England, France, Serbia, Japan and colonial North America, with further materials from Western Europe*. Cambridge: Cambridge University Press.

Leach, E. R. 1951. The structural implications of matrilateral cross-cousin marriage. *Journal of the Royal Anthropological Institute* 81: 23–55.

—— 1957. Aspects of bridewealth and marriage stability among the Kachin and Lakher. *Man* 57: 50–5.

—— 1961a. *Rethinking anthropology*. London: Athlone Press.

—— 1961b. *Pul Eliya, a village in Ceylon: a study of land tenure and kinship*. Cambridge: Cambridge University Press.

—— 1962. On certain unconsidered aspects of double descent systems. *Man* 62: 130–4.

—— 1963. Determinants of cross-cousin marriage. *Man* 63: 76–7.

—— 1966. Virgin birth. *Proceedings of the Royal Anthropological Institute* for 1966: 39–49.

—— 1970. *Lévi-Strauss*. Fontana Modern Masters. London: Wm. Collins and Co. Ltd.

—— 1982. *Social anthropology*. Fontana Paperbacks.

Leacock, E. 1978. Women's status in egalitarian society: implications for social evolution. *Current Anthropology* 19: 247–75.

Levine, N. E. 1987. Fathers and sons: kinship value and validation in Tibetan polyandry. *Man* (N.S.) 22: 267–86.

—— 1988. *The dynamics of polyandry: kinship, domesticity, and population on the Tibetan border*. Chicago: University of Chicago Press.

Lévi-Strauss, C. 1963. *Structural anthropology*. New York: Basic Books.

—— 1965. The future of kinship studies. *Proceedings of the Royal Anthropological Institute* for 1965.

—— 1969. *The elementary structures of kinship* (2nd edn). London: Eyre and Spottiswoode.

Levy, R. I. 1970. Tahitian adoption as a psychological message. In V. Caroll (ed.), *Adoption in Eastern Oceania*. ASAO Monograph No. 1. Honolulu: University of Hawaii Press.

Lewis, I. M. 1965. Problems in the comparative study of unilineal descent. In M. Banton (ed.), *The relevance of models for social anthropology*. ASA Monographs 1. London: Tavistock Publications.

Lewis, E. D. 1988. *People of the source: the social and ceremonial order of Tana Wai Brama of Flores*. Verhandlingen van het Koniklijk Instituut voor Taal-, Land-en Volkenkunde 135. Dordrecht: Foris Publications.

Lewis, W. A. 1955. *The theory of economic growth*. London: Allen and Unwin.

Leyton, E. (ed.) 1974. *The compact: selected dimensions of friendship*. Newfoundland Social and Economic Papers No. 3. Memorial University of Newfoundland: Institute for Social and Economic Research.

Lingenfelter, S. 1985. Review of D. M. Schneider's *A critique of the study of kinship*. *American Ethnologist* 12: 372–4.

Lowie, R. H. 1920. *Primitive society*. New York: Horace Liveright.

—— 1950. *Social organization*. London: Routledge and Kegan Paul.

McLennan, J. F. 1865. *Primitive marriage*. Edinburgh: Adam and Charles Black.

Maine, H. 1861. *Ancient law*. London: Murray.

Mair, L. 1965. *An introduction to social anthropology*. Oxford: Oxford University Press.

—— 1971. *Marriage*. Harmondsworth: Penguin Books.

Malinowski, B. 1913. *The family among the Australian Aborigines*. London: Hodder.

—— 1929. *The sexual life of savages in north-western Melanesia*. London: Routledge and Kegan Paul.

—— 1962. *Sex, culture, and myth*. New York: Harcourt, Brace and World.

Marcus, G. and M. Fisher 1986. *Anthropology as cultural critique: an experimental moment in the human sciences*. Chicago: University of Chicago Press.

Marriott, McK. 1976. Hindu transactions: diversity without dualism. In B. Kapferer (ed.), *Transaction and meaning*. ASA Essays in Anthropology 1. Philadelphia. ISHI Publications.

Marshall, M. 1977. The nature of nurture. *American Ethnologist* 4: 643–62.

Marvick, E. W. 1974. Nature versus nurture: patterns and trends in seventeenth-century French childrearing. In L. de Mause (ed.), *The history of childhood*. London: Souvenir Press.

Mauss, M. 1954. *The gift: forms and functions of exchange in archaic societies* (trans. I. Cunnison). London: Routledge and Kegan Paul.

Maybury-Lewis, D. H. P. 1960. Parallel descent and the Apinayé anomaly. *Southwestern Journal of Anthropology* 16: 191–216.

Mayer, P. 1949. *The lineage principle in Gusii society*. International African Institute Memorandum No. 24. London: International African Institute.

Mead, M. 1939. Sex and temperament in three primitive societies. In M. Mead, *From the South Seas: studies of adolescence and sex in primitive societies*. New York: William Morrow.

—— 1969 (orig. 1930). *Social organization of Manu'a*. Bernice P. Bishop Museum Bulletin 76. Honolulu: Bernice P. Bishop Museum.

Meek, C. K. 1957. *Land tenure and land administration in Nigeria and the Cameroons*. Colonial Research Sudies 22. London: HMSO.

Meggitt, M. J. 1965. *The lineage system of the Mae-Enga of New Guinea*. London: Oliver and Boyd.

Meigs, A. 1989. The cultural construction of reproduction and its relationship to kinship and gender (New Guineas Highlands). In Mac Marshall and J. L. Caughey (eds), *Culture, kin and cognition in Oceania: essays in honor of Ward H. Goodenough*. Special Publication of the American Anthropological Association No. 25. Washington, DC: American Anthropological Association.

Meillassoux, C. 1981. *Maidens, meal and money: capitalism and the domestic community*. Cambridge: Cambridge University Press.

Middleton, J. and D. Tait (eds). 1958. *Tribes without rulers*. London: Routledge and Kegan Paul.

Mitchell, J. C. 1956. *The Yao village: a study in the social structure of a Nyasaland tribe*. Manchester: Manchester University Press.

Mitchell, W. E. 1963. Theoretical problems in the concept of kindred. *American Anthropologist* 65: 343–54.

Montagu, M. F. A. 1937. *Coming into being among the Australian Aborigines*. London: Routledge.

Moore, H. 1988. *Feminism and anthropology*. Cambridge: Polity Press.

Morgan, L. H. 1871. *Systems of consanguinity and affinity of the human family*. Washington, DC: Smithsonian Institution.

—— 1877. *Ancient society: researches in the lines of human progress from savagery, through barbarism to civilization*. New York: Henry Holt.

Murdock, G. P. 1949. *Social structure*. New York: Macmillan.

Nakane, C. 1967. *Garo and Khasi: a comparative study in matrilineal systems*. Paris: Mouton.

Needham, R. 1958. A structural analysis of Purum society. *American Anthropologist* 60: 75–101.

—— 1960a. A structural analysis of Aimol society. *Bijdragen tot de Taal-, Land-, en Volkenkunde* 116: 81–108.

—— 1960b. Descent systems and ideal language. *Philosophy of Science* 27: 96–101.

—— 1962. *Structure and sentiment: a test case in social anthropology*. Chicago: University of Chicago Press.

—— 1971. Remarks on the analysis of kinship and marriage. In R. Needham (ed.), *Rethinking kinship and marriage*. ASA Monographs 11. London: Tavistock Publications.

—— 1973. Prescription. *Oceania* 42: 166–81.

—— 1974. *Remarks and inventions: skeptical essays about kinship*. London: Tavistock Publications.

Netting, R. M., R. Wilk and E. Arnould (eds). 1984. *Households: comparative and historical studies of the domestic group*. Berkeley: University of California Press.

Notes and Queries in Anthropology. 1951. 6th edn. London: Routledge and Kegan Paul.

Ortner, S. B. 1984. Theory in anthropology since the sixties. *Comparative Studies in Society and History* 26: 126–66.

Ortner, S. B. and H. Whitehead. 1981. Introduction. In S. B. Ortner and H. Whitehead (eds), *Sexual meanings: the cultural construction of gender and sexuality*. Cambridge: Cambridge University Press.

Parsons, T. and R. F. Bales. 1955. *Family, socialization and interaction process*. Glencoe, IL: Free Press.

Pasternak, B. 1976. *Introduction to kinship and social organization*. Englewood Cliffs, NJ: Prentice Hall.

Pehrson, R. N. 1954. Bilateral kin groupings as a structural type. *Journal of East Asiatic Studies* 3: 199–202.

—— 1957. *The bilateral network of social relations in Könkämä Lapp District*. Bloomington: Indiana University Research Center in Anthropology, Folklore and Linguistics.

Peletz, M. G. 1994. Neither reasonable nor responsible: contrasting representations of masculinity in a Malay society. *Cultural Anthropology* 9: 135–78.

—— 1995. Kinship studies in late twentieth-century anthropology. *Annual Review of Anthropology* 24: 343–72.

Peranio, R. D. 1961. Descent, descent line and descent group in cognatic social systems. *Proceedings of the 1961 Annual Spring Meeting of the American Ethnological Society*: 93–113.

Peters, L. 1967. Some structural aspects of feud among the camel-herding Bedouin of Cyrenaica. *Africa* 37: 261–82.

Pitt-Rivers, J. 1968. Kinship: III. Pseudo-kinship. *International Encyclopedia of the Social Sciences*, Vol. 8: 408–13. New York: Macmillan.

—— 1973. The kith and the kin. In J. R. Goody (ed.), *The character of kinship*. Cambridge: Cambridge University Press.

Poewe, K. O. 1981. *Matrilineal ideology: male–female dynamics in Luapula, Zambia*. London: Academic Press.

Pouwer, J. 1960. Loosely structured societies in Netherlands New Guinea. *Bijdragen tot de Taal-, Land-, en Volkenkunde* 116: 109–18.

Radcliffe-Brown, A. R. 1935. Patrilineal and matrilineal succession. *Iowa Law Review* 20: 286–303.

—— 1941. The study of kinship systems. *Journal of the Royal Anthropological Institute* 71: 1–18.

—— 1950. Introduction. In A. R. Radcliffe-Brown and D. Forde (eds), *African systems of kinship and marriage*. London: Oxford University Press.

—— 1952. *Structure and function in primitive society*. London: Cohen and West.

Raheja, G. 1988. *The poison in the gift: ritual, prestation and the dominant caste in a north Indian village*. Chicago: University of Chicago Press.

Randle, M. C. 1951. Iroquois women: then and now. In W. N. Fenton (ed.), *Symposium on local diversity in Iroquois culture*. Bureau of American Ethnology Bulletin No. 149. Washington, DC: US Government Printing Office.

Rapp, R. 1979. Anthropology: a review essay. *Signs* 4: 497–513.

Read, K. E. 1951. The Gahuku-Gama of the Central Highlands. *South Pacific* 5: 154–64.

—— 1954. Cultures of the Central Highlands of New Guinea. *Southwestern Journal of Anthropology* 10: 1–43.

Reay, M. O. 1971. Structural covariants of land shortage among patrilineal peoples. In P. Lawrence and R. M. Berndt (eds), *Politics in New Guinea*. Nedlands: University of Western Australia Press.

Richards, A. I. 1950. Some types of family structure amongst the Central Bantu. In A. R. Radcliffe-Brown and D. Forde (eds), *African systems of kinship and marriage*. London: Oxford University Press.

Rivers, W. H. R. 1906. *The Todas*. New York: Macmillan.

—— 1910. The genealogical method of anthropological inquiry. *Sociological Review* 3: 1–12.

—— 1915. Mother right. In J. Hastings (ed.), *Encyclopedia of religion and ethics*, Vol. 8: 851–9. Edinburgh: T. and T. Clark.

—— 1924. *Social organization*. London: Kegan Paul.

Rivière, P. G. 1971. Marriage: a reassessment. In R. Needham (ed.), *Rethinking kinship and marriage*. ASA Monographs 11. London: Tavistock Publications.

—— 1985. Unscrambling parenthood: the Warnock Report. *Anthropology Today* 1, No. 4: 2–7.

—— 1993. The Amerindianization of descent and affinity. *L'Homme* 33: 507–16.

Roberston, A. F. 1991. *Beyond the family: the social organization of human reproduction*. Cambridge: Polity Press.

Rogers, S. C. 1978. Women's place: a critical review of anthropological theory. *Comparative Studies in Society and History* 20: 123–62.

Rosaldo, M. 1980. The use and abuse of anthropology: reflections on feminism and cross-cultural understanding. *Signs* 5: 389–417.

Rosaldo, M. Z. and J. M. Atkinson. 1975. Man the hunter and woman. In R. Willis (ed.), *The interpretation of symbolism*. London: Malaby.

Rosaldo, M. Z. and J. F. Collier. 1981. Politics and gender in simple societies. In S. B. Ortner and H. Whitehead (eds), *Sexual meanings: the cultural construction of gender and sexuality*. Cambridge: Cambridge University Press.

Ross, J. B. 1974. The middle class in urban Italy, fourteenth to early sixteenth century. In L. de Mause (ed.), *The history of childhood*. London: Souvenir Press.

Rubin, G. 1975. The traffic in women: notes on the 'political economy' of sex. In R. Reiter (ed.), *Toward an anthropology of women*. New York: Monthly Review Press.

Ryan, D. 1958–9. Clan foundation in the Mendi valley. *Oceania* 29: 257–89.

Sacks, K. 1976. State bias and women's status. *American Anthropologist* 78: 565–9.

—— 1979. *Sisters and wives*. Westport, CT: Greenwood Press.

Sahlins, M. 1961. The segmentary lineage: an organization of predatory expansion. *American Anthropologist* 80: 53–70.

—— 1965. On the ideology and composition of descent groups. *Man* 65: 104–7.

Salisbury, R. F. 1956. Unilineal descent groups in the New Guinea Highlands. *Man* 56: 2–7.

—— 1962. *From stone to steel*. Melbourne: Melbourne University Press.

Salzman, P. C. 1978. Does complementary opposition exist? *American Anthropologist* 80: 53–70.

Scheffler, H. W. 1964. Descent concepts and descent groups: the Maori case. *Journal of the Polynesian Society* 73: 126–33.

—— 1965. *Choiseul Island social structure*. Berkeley: University of California Press.

—— 1966. Ancestor worship in anthropology: or, observations on descent and descent groups. *Current Anthropology* 7: 541–51.

—— 1970a. *The elementary structures of kinship* by C. Lévi-Strauss: a review article. *American Anthropologist* 72: 251–68.

—— 1970b. Review of Fortes, *Kinship and the social Order*. *American Anthropologist* 72: 1464–6.

—— 1973. Kinship, descent and alliance. In J. J. Honigman (ed.), *Handbook of social and cultural anthropology*. Chicago: Rand McNally and Co.

—— 1985. Filiation and affiliation. *Man* (N.S.) 20: 1–21.

—— 1991. Sexism and naturalism in the study of kinship. In M. di Leonardo (ed.), *Gender at the crossroads of knowledge: feminist anthropology in the postmodern era*. Berkeley: University of California Press.

Scheffler, H. W. and F. G. Lounsbury. 1971. *A study in structural semantics: the Siriono kinship system*. Englewood Cliffs, NJ: Prentice Hall.

Schieffelin, E. 1976. *The sorrow of the lonely and the burning of the dancers*. New York: St Martin's Press.

Schlegel, A. 1977. Toward a theory of sexual stratification. In A. Schlegel (ed.), *Sexual stratification*. New York: Columbia University Press.

Schneider, D. M. 1961. Introduction. In D. M. Schneider and K. Gough (eds), *Matrilineal kinship*. Berkeley and Los Angeles: University of California Press.

—— 1964. The nature of kinship. *Man* 64: 180–1.

—— 1965. Some muddles in the models: or how the system really works. In M. Banton (ed.), *The relevance of models for social anthropology.* ASA Monographs 1. London: Tavistock Publications.

—— 1969. Kinship, nationality and religion in American culture: toward a definition of kinship. In R. F. Spencer (ed.), *Forms of symbolic action.* Proceedings of the 1969 Annual Spring Meeting of the American Ethnological Society. Seattle: University of Washington Press.

—— 1972. What is kinship all about? In P. Reining (ed.), *Kinship studies in the Morgan centennial year.* Washington, DC: Anthropological Society of Washington.

—— 1980. *American kinship: a cultural account.* 2nd edn. Chicago: University of Chicago Press.

—— 1984. *A critique of the study of kinship.* Ann Arbor: University of Michigan Press.

Schneider, D. M. and R. T. Smith. 1973. *Class differences and sex roles in American kinship and family structure.* Englewood Cliffs, NJ: Prentice Hall.

Schuler, S. R. 1987. *The other side of polyandry: property, stratification and nonmarriage in the Nepal Himalayas.* Boulder, CO: Westview Press.

Seddon, D. 1979. Political ideologies and political forms in the eastern Rif of Morocco, 1890–1910. In L. Holy (ed.), *Segmentary lineage systems reconsidered.* The Queen's University Papers in Social Anthropology 4. Belfast: The Queen's University.

Sharma, U. 1980. *Women, work and property in north-west India.* London: Tavistock.

Sider, K. I. 1967. Kinship and culture: affinity and the role of the father in the Trobriands. *Journal of Anthropological Research* 23: 90–109.

Silverman, M. G. 1970. Banaban adoption. In V. Caroll (ed.), *Adoption in Eastern Oceania.* Honolulu: University Press of Hawaii.

Smelser, N. J. 1963. Mechanisms of change and adjustments to change. In B. F. Hoselitz and W. E. Moore (eds), *Industrialisation and society.* Paris: Mouton.

Smith, M. G. 1956. On segmentary lineage systems. *Journal of the Royal Anthropological Institute* 86: 39–79.

Smith, R. T. 1956. *The Negro family in British Guiana.* London: Routledge and Kegan Paul.

—— 1973. The matrifocal family. In J. R. Goody (ed.), *The character of kinship.* Cambridge: Cambridge University Press.

Southall, A. 1952. *Lineage formation among the Luo.* International African Institute Memorandum No. 26. London: International African Institute.

Strathern, A. 1969. Descent and alliance in the New Guinea Highlands: some problems of comparison. *Proceedings of the Royal Anthropological Institute* for 1968: 37–52. London: Royal Anthropological Institute.

—— 1973. Kinship, descent and locality: some New Guinea examples. In J. R. Goody (ed.), *The character of kinship*. Cambridge: Cambridge University Press.

Strathern, M. 1981. Self-interest and the social good: some implications of the Hagen gender imagery. In S. B. Ortner and H. Whitehead (eds), *Sexual meanings: the cultural construction of gender and sexuality*. Cambridge: Cambridge University Press.

—— 1984. Domesticity and the denigration of women. In D. O'Brien and S. Tiffany (eds), *Rethinking women's roles: perspectives from the Pacific*. Berkeley: University of California Press.

—— 1985. Kinship and economy: constitutive orders of a provisional kind. *American Ethnologist* 12: 191–209.

—— 1988. *The gender of the gift: problems with women and problems with society in Melanesia*. Berkeley: University of California Press.

—— 1992a. *After nature: English kinship in the late twentieth century*. Cambridge: University of Cambridge Press.

—— 1992b. *Reproducing the future: essays on anthropology, kinship and the new reproductive technologies*. Manchester: Manchester University Press.

—— 1994. New knowledge for old? Reflections following Fox's *Reproduction and succession*. *Social Anthropology* 2: 263–79.

Terray, E. 1972. *Marxism and 'primitive' societies*. New York: Monthly Review Press.

Thomas, E. M. 1959. *The harmless people*. New York: Knopf.

Tilly, L. and J. Scott. 1978. *Women, work and family*. New York: Holt, Rinehart and Winston.

Turner, V. 1957. *Schism and continuity in an African society: a study of Ndembu village life*. Manchester: Manchester University Press.

Turton, D. 1979. A journey made them: territorial segmentation and ethnic identity among the Mursi. In L. Holy (ed.), *Segmentary lineage systems reconsidered*. The Queen's University Papers in Social Anthropology 4. Belfast: The Queen's University.

Tylor, E. B. 1889. On a method of investigating the development of institutions applied to laws of marriage and descent. *Journal of the Royal Anthropological Institute* 18: 245–72.

Van Baal, J. 1975. *Reciprocity and the position of women*. Amsterdam: van Gorcum.

Van Gennep, A. 1906. *Mythes et legendes d'Australie*. Paris: Guilmoto.

Van Velsen, J. 1964. *The politics of kinship*. Manchester: Manchester University Press.

Wagner, R. 1972. Incest and identity: a critique and theory on the subject of exogamy and incest prohibition. *Man* (N.S.) 7: 601–13.

—— 1974. Are there social groups in the New Guinea Highlands? In M. J. Leaf (ed.), *Frontiers of anthropology*. New York: D. van Nostrand Company.

Warnock, M. 1985. *A question of life: the Warnock Report on human fertilisation and embryology*. Oxford: Basil Blackwell.

Watson, J. B. 1964. Anthropology in the New Guinea Highlands. In J. B. Watson (ed.), *New Guinea: the Central Highlands. American Anthropologist* 66, No. 4, part 2, special publication: 1–19.

—— 1983. *Tairora culture: contingency and pragmatism*. Seattle: University of Washington Press.

Weiner, A. 1976. *Women of value, men of renown: new perspectives in Trobriand exchange*. Austin: University of Texas Press.

—— 1992. *Inalienable possessions: the paradox of keeping while giving*. Berkeley: University of California Press.

Weiner, J. F. 1982. Substance, siblingship and exchange: aspects of social structure in New Guinea. *Social Analysis* 11: 3–34.

Weismantel, M. 1995. Making kin: kinship theory and Zumbagua adoptions. *American Ethnologist* 22: 685–709.

Whatmore, S. 1991. *Farming women: gender, work and family enterprise*. London: Macmillan.

Witherspoon, G. 1975. *Navajo kinship and marriage*. Chicago: University of Chicago Press.

Yanagisako, S. J. 1978. Variance in American kinship: implications for cultural analysis. *American Ethnologist* 5: 15–29.

——1979. Family and household: the analysis of domestic groups. *Annual Review of Anthropology* 8: 161–205.

—— 1985. *Transforming the past: tradition and kinship among Japanese Americans*. Stanford, CA: Stanford University Press.

Yanagisako, S. J. and J. F. Collier. 1987. Toward a unified analysis of gender and kinship. In J. F. Collier and S. J. Yanagiskao (eds), *Gender and kinship: essays toward a unified analysis*. Stanford, CA.: Stanford University Press.

Yeatman, A. 1983. The procreative model: the social ontological bases of the gender-kinship system. *Social Analysis* 14: 3–30.

INDEX